Climate Change Law, Technology Transfer and Sustainable Development

This book explores the possibilities and scope o[illegible]ating innovation and transfer of environmentally sound technologies in the post-Paris climate era. The book will first focus on the role of the climate finance and technological cooperation mechanisms in innovation and transfer of environmentally sound technologies. Secondly, the book will focus on role of the 'flexible mechanism' (i.e. indirect financial mechanisms), which has been re-introduced by the Paris Agreement as the 'voluntary cooperation' or 'sustainable development' mechanism in innovation and transfer of environmentally sound technologies. Thirdly, the book will contain a comparative analysis of the efficiency of the technology transfer mechanism under the global climate regime in comparison with the technology transfer mechanism that exists under other multilateral environmental agreements (MEAs).

In addition to the above, since the issue of trans-boundary technology transfer is also a matter of concern for international trade, the book will discuss to what extent the international trade related laws, e.g. intellectual property laws, investment related laws governed by the World Trade Organization (WTO), can play a role in facilitating transfer of environmentally sound technologies.

Another important aspect that this book will cover is the potential roles that private sectors can play in innovating and transferring environmentally sound technologies under the above-mentioned instruments of international law.

In short, this book will be based on the argument that if the global climate regime and the international trade regime collaborate with each other in creating an enabling environment and attracting private sector investment in the field of environmentally sound technologies, the global challenges of innovation and the transfer of environmentally sound technologies to the developing and least developed countries can be fulfilled in a more efficient manner. From a conceptual perspective, discussions and analyses in the book will be made in the light of the principles of equity and common but differentiated responsibilities and respective capabilities (CBDR-RC) – two of the guiding principles of the international laws on climate change.

This book will be of great interest to scholars of climate change, technology transfer, intellectual property and sustainable development. In addition, national and international level policy-makers dealing with climate change and sustainable development will benefit greatly from this book.

Mahatab Uddin, PhD (Aarhus) is an expert in International Environmental Law, Climate Change Law, Intellectual Property Law, Technology Transfer and Sustainable Development. He is a Postdoctoral Fellow, University of Southern Denmark and Adjunct Professor, University of Guelph.

Routledge Research in International Environmental Law

Environmental Governance in Europe and Asia
A Comparative Study of Institutional and Legislative Frameworks
Jona Razzaque

Climate Change, Forests and REDD
Lessons for Institutional Design
Edited by Joyeeta Gupta, Nicolien van der Grijp and Onno Kuik

International Environmental Law and the Conservation of Coral Reefs
Edward J. Goodwin

International Environmental Law and the International Court of Justice
Aleksandra Cavoski

Enforcement of International Environmental Law
Challenges and Responses at the International Level
Martin Hedemann-Robinson

Marine Pollution, Shipping Waste and International Law
Gabriela Argüello

Compensation for Environmental Damage Under International Law
Jason Rudall

International Environmental Law Compliance in Context
Mechanisms and Case Studies
Belen Olmos Giupponi

https://www.routledge.com/Routledge-Research-in-International-Environmental-Law/book-series/INTENVLAW

Climate Change Law, Technology Transfer and Sustainable Development

Mahatab Uddin

Routledge
Taylor & Francis Group
LONDON AND NEW YORK

First published 2021
by Routledge
2 Park Square, Milton Park, Abingdon, Oxon OX14 4RN

and by Routledge
605 Third Avenue, New York, NY 10158

Routledge is an imprint of the Taylor & Francis Group, an informa business

British Library Cataloguing-in-Publication Data
A catalogue record for this book is available from the British Library

Library of Congress Cataloging-in-Publication Data
A catalog record has been requested for this book

ISBN: 978-0-367-46836-1 (hbk)
ISBN: 978-1-032-02289-5 (pbk)
ISBN: 978-1-003-05641-6 (ebk)

DOI: 10.4324/9781003056416

Typeset in Bembo
by Taylor & Francis Books

Dedicated to scientists who are working for the innovation of environmentally sound technologies

Contents

Illustrations

Figures

Table

Acknowledgements

This book has been developed from my PhD thesis entitled 'Transfer of Environmentally Sound Technologies and Promotion of Sustainable Development in the Least Developed Countries'. In that connection, I express my gratitude to the Ministry of Higher Education and Science, Denmark for granting an 'International Mobility Scholarship' in my favour.

I express my deep acknowledgement to my thesis supervisor Prof. Dr. Ellen Margethe Basse for her guidance in developing my thesis. My acknowledgement also goes to Prof. Dr. Tine Sommer for her guidance and supervision during the first phase of my PhD study. Similarly, I acknowledge the help of Associate Prof. Dr. Matthew James Elsmore for sharing his knowledge and views and making suggestions as co-supervisor of my project.

I must acknowledge the help of Prof. Dr. Christina Voigt, who has enriched my research with her expert opinions during my research stay at the Department of Law, Oslo University, Norway. Likewise, I am also grateful to Prof. Dr. Hans Christian Bugge of Oslo University for his valuable suggestions and comments on the content of my research. My thanks also go to Prof. Dr. Charlotta Zetterberg, of Uppsala University who supervised my master's thesis on technology transfer issues.

I am grateful to Prof. Dr. Atiq Rahman for allowing me to utilize the resources of his organization – Bangladesh Centre for Advanced Studies (BCAS) – at the initial stage of my research. I am also grateful to Prof. Dr. Ainun Nishat for enriching my research thoughts through sharing his practical knowledge and views concerning my research issues. Thanks also go to Prof. Dr. Saleemul Huq who allowed me to be part of his organization – International Centre for Climate Change & Development (ICCCAD) – and helped me to continue my research on climate change issues.

My gratitude goes to Mr. Md. Ziaul Haque and Mr. Mirza Shawkat Ali of the Department of Environment of Bangladesh Government for their cooperation in conducting my empirical study. In connection with my empirical study, I am also grateful to Mr. Joergen Fenhann, a senior scientist of the United Nations Environment Programme (UNEP) Risø, for sharing his research relevant experiences and knowledge as well as making valuable suggestions.

I am grateful to Prof. Dr. Fakrul Alam of the University of Dhaka for his expert guidance in preparing my book proposal. At the same time, my gratitude goes to

Associate Prof. Dr. Saiful Karim of Queensland University of Technology for sharing his insights and views, which assisted me in accomplishing the whole process of writing this book.

My special thanks and gratitude will always go to Prof. Dr. Shah Alam (deceased) of the University of Chittagong and Prof. Dr. Marianne Levin of Stockholm University. Prof. Alam's outstanding classroom lectures blended with knowledge and wisdom first motivated my interest in the field of public international law. Prof. Levin's enormous knowledge and deep insight facilitated my interest in intellectual property law and international development/sustainable development related research issues.

In this short note, I would also like to thank my family members (that includes my parents, siblings and all my other relatives), friends, and colleagues who encouraged me in pursuing my academic research.

Finally, I am ever grateful and thankful to the Almighty for everything I belong to and I do not yet belong to.

National constitutions and laws

Charter for the Environment of France
Constitution of Argentina
Constitution of Bangladesh
Constitution of Brazil
Constitution of Czech Republic
Constitution of Estonia
Constitution of Finland
Constitution of Germany
Constitution of Greece
Constitution of Italy
Constitution of Latvia
Constitution of Lithuania
Constitution of Netherlands
Constitution of Poland
Constitution of Portugal
Constitution of Slovakia
Constitution of Slovenia
Constitution of South Africa
Constitution of Spain
Constitution of Sweden
Constitution of Switzerland (federal constitution)
Constitution of Ukraine
Environment Conservation Act of Bangladesh
Environment Conservation Rules of Bangladesh
Fundamental Law of Hungary

List of cases

International cases

Case Concerning Gabcikovo-Nagymaros Dam Project (Hungary vs. Slovakia)
Case Concerning Pulp Mills on the River Uruguay (Argentina vs. Uruguay)
Case Concerning the Barcelona Traction, Light and Power Company Limited (Belgium vs. Spain)
Case Concerning the Continental Shelf (Libyan Arab Jmahiriya vs. Malta)
Case Concerning the Continental Shelf (Libya vs. Tunisia)
Maritime Delimitation and Territorial Questions Between Qatar and Bahrain (Qatar vs. Bahrain)
Iron Rhine Arbitration (Belgium vs. Netherlands)
Tunisia/Libya Continental Shelf Case (Tunisia vs. Libya)

National cases

Farooque vs. Government of Bangladesh (Bangladesh)
Fuel Retailers Association of Southern Africa vs. Director-General: Environmental Management, Department of Agriculture, Conservation and Environment, Mpumalanga Province, and Others (South Africa)
Minors Oposa vs. Secretary of the Department of Environmental and Natural Resources (Philippines)
Narmada Bachao Andolan vs. Union of India (India)

List of abbreviations

AAU	Assigned Amount Unit
ADP	Ad Hoc Working Group on the Durban Platform for Enhanced Action
AF	Adaptation Fund
AFB	Adaptation Fund Board
AGF	Advisory Group on Climate Change Financing
ASEAN	Association of Southeast Asian Nations
AU	African Union
BECA	Bangladesh Environment Conservation Act
BECR	Bangladesh Environment Conservation Rules
BOCM	Bilateral Offset Credit Mechanism
BRAC	Bangladesh Rural Advancement Committee
CBD	Convention on Biological Diversity
CBDR-RC	Common but Differentiated Responsibilities-Respective Capabilities
CDM	Clean Development Mechanism
CDM PDD	Clean Development Mechanism Project Design Document
CDM PoA	Clean Development Mechanism Programme of Activities
CER	Certified Emission Reduction
CFL	Compact Fluorescent Lamp
CME	Coordinating/Managing Entity
CMP	Conference of the Parties serving as the Meeting of the Parties
CO_2	Carbon Dioxide
COP	Conference of the Parties
CPA-DD	CDM Programme Activity Design Document
CSD	Commission on Sustainable Development
CTCN	Climate Technology Centre and Network
DNA	Designated National Authority
DOE	Department of Environment
EBRD	European Bank for Reconstruction and Development
EC	European Commission
ECR	Environmental Conservation Rules
EEPRB	Energy Efficiency Programme in Rural Bangladesh

EGTT	Expert Group on Technology Transfer
EIA	Environmental Impact Assessment
EIT	Economies In Transition
ELIB	Efficient Lighting Initiative of Bangladesh
EPO	European Patent Office
ERU	Emission Reduction Units
EST	Environmentally Sound Technology
EU	European Union
FAO	Food and Agriculture Organization of the United Nations
FMO	Netherlands Development Finance Company
FSF	Fast Start Finance
FSP	Full-Size Project
GCF	Green Climate Fund
GDP	Gross Domestic Product
GEB	Global Environmental Benefit
GEF	Global Environmental Facility
GHG	Greenhouse Gas
GNP	Gross National Product
GOB	Government of Bangladesh
GS	Grameen Shakti
GTZ	Gesellschaft für Technische Zusammenarbeit/German Technical Cooperation
HHK	Hybrid Hoffman Kiln
ICJ	International Court of Justice
ICL	Incandescent Lamp
ICS	Improved Cooking Stove
IDCOL	Infrastructure Development Company Limited
IIDFC	Industrial and Infrastructural Development Finance Company Limited
ILA	International Law Association
INDC	Intended Nationally Determined Contribution
IPCC	Inter-governmental Panel on Climate Change
IPR	Intellectual Property Rights
IREA	International Renewable Energy Agency
IRENA	International Renewable Energy Agency
ITPGRFA	International Treaty on Plant Genetic Resources for Food and Agriculture
IUCN	International Union for Conservation of Nature
JI	Joint Implementation
JPMVEC	J.P. Morgan Ventures Energy Corporation
LCA	Long Term Cooperative Action
LDC	Least Developed Country
LDCF	Least Developed Countries Fund
MDGs	Millennium Development Goals
MEAs	Multilateral Environmental Agreements

MOEF	Ministry of Environment and Forest and Climate Change
MOU	Memorandum of Understanding
MSP	Medium-Sized Project
NAMA	Nationally Appropriate Mitigation Activity
NAP	National Agriculture Policy
NAPA	National Adaptation Programmes of Action
NDC	Nationally Determined Contribution
NGO	Non-Governmental Organization
ODA	Official Development Assistance
OECD	Organisation for Economic Cooperation and Development
PDD	Project Design Document
PIF	Project Identification Form
PO	Partner Organization
PoA	Programme of Activities
PoA-DD	Programme of Activities Design Document
POPs	Convention on Persistent Organic Pollutants
PSF	Private Sector Facility
R&D	Research and Development
SBE	Small Business Enterprise
SCCF	Special Climate Change Fund
SD	Sustainable Development
SDM	Sustainable Development Mechanism
SME	Small and Medium Enterprise
SSC-PoA	Small-Scale Programme of Activities
TAP	Technology Action Plan
TEC	Technology Executive Committee
TNA	Technology Needs Assessment
TRIMS	Agreement on Trade Related Investment Measures
TRIPS	Agreement on the Trade Related Aspects of Intellectual Property Rights
TT	Technology Transfer
TT:Clear	Technology Transfer Clearing House
UDHR	Universal Declaration of Human Rights
UN	United Nations
UNCCD	United Nations Convention to Combat Desertification in Those Countries Experiencing Serious Drought and/or Desertification, Particularly in Africa
UNCED	United Nations Conference on Environment and Development
UNCLOS	United Nations Convention on the Law of the Sea
UNCSD	United Nations Conference on Sustainable Development
UNDP	United Nations Development Programme
UNEP	United Nations Environment Programme
UNESCO	United Nations Educational, Scientific and Cultural Organization
UNFCCC	United Nations Framework Convention on Climate Change

UN-MDGs	United Nations Millennium Development Goals
UNSDGs	United Nations Sustainable Development Goals
US	United States
WCED	World Commission on Environment and Development
WGTTT	Working Group on Trade and Technology Transfer
WHO	World Health Organization
WHO FCTC	World Health Organization Framework Convention on Tobacco Control
Wp	Watt-Peak
WSSD	World Summit on Sustainable Development
WTO	World Trade Organization
WWF	World Water Forum
WWF	Worldwide Fund for Nature
WWR	Worldwide Recycling

List of agreements, treaties, conventions, protocols, directives and declarations

1 Statute of the International Court of Justice
2 Universal Declaration of Human Rights
3 Convention for the Establishment of an Inter-American Tropical Tuna Commission
4 Treaty on Principles Governing the Activities of States in the Exploration and Use of Outer Space, Including the Moon and Other Celestial Bodies
5 African Convention on the Conservation of Nature and Natural Resources (Algiers) (1968 African Nature Convention)
6 UNESCO Conference on the Biosphere
7 Vienna Convention on the Law of Treaties
8 Convention Concerning the Protection of the World Cultural and Natural Heritage
9 Convention on the Prevention of Marine Pollution by Dumping of Wastes and Other Matter
10 Declaration of the United Nations Conference on the Human Environment (Stockholm Declaration)
11 Convention on the Conservation of Migratory Species of Wild Animals (Bonn Convention)
12 African Charter on Human and Peoples' Rights ('Banjul Charter')
13 ASEAN Agreement on the Conservation of Nature and Natural Resources
14 Vienna Convention for the Protection of the Ozone Layer
15 Montreal Protocol on Substances that Deplete the Ozone Layer
16 Convention on the Control of Transboundary Movement of Hazardous Wastes and Their Disposal (Basel Convention)
17 Convention on Biological Diversity (1992 Biodiversity Convention)
18 Rio Declaration on Environment and Development
19 United Nations Conference on Environment and Development (Earth Summit)
20 United Nations Convention on the Law of the Sea
21 United Nations Framework Convention on Climate Change
22 Vienna Declaration and Programme of Action
23 Agreement on Trade-Related Aspects of Intellectual Property Rights
24 Agreement on Trade-Related Investment Measures

Foreword

Since the innovation and transfer of environmentally sound technologies is critically important to battle against climate change and promote sustainable development globally, this book is a timely contribution by Mahatab Uddin to the academic discourses and policy level discussion surrounding the implementation of the Paris Agreement 2015 and the promotion of global sustainable development. This scholarly work is a unique effort in the sense that it not only covers the diverse fields of law that are concerned with the innovation and transfer of environmentally sound technologies, but also explores the potential opportunities for the enhanced involvement of the private sector in the innovation of environmentally sound technologies as well as the promotion of sustainable development. Moreover, this book includes a comparison between the technology transfer provisions and mechanisms introduced by various multilateral environmental agreements. Since the issue of innovation and transfer of environmentally sound technologies concerns different fields of international law, Uddin investigates the issue and explores the possibilities from the perspectives of both international law on climate change and international trade law that necessarily includes intellectual property law and international investment related laws. In addition to the above issues, while the Paris Agreement 2015 introduces a kind of 'voluntary cooperation' or 'sustainable development' mechanism that shares common features with previously introduced clean development mechanisms (CDMs), Uddin's investigative study on the technology transfer impact of the CDM projects hosted by Bangladesh could motivate future similar mechanisms in countries with similar conditions. In the book Uddin discusses and analyses core issues in the light of the principles of equity and common but differentiated responsibilities and respective capabilities (CBDR-RC), which are two of the main guiding principles of both the UNFCCC and the Paris Agreement. Finally, Uddin has successfully addressed and elaborated his main argument that the collaboration of both the international legal regime on climate change and international trade law can effectively facilitate the innovation and transfer of environmentally sound technologies as well as promote sustainable development, particularly by expediting the enhanced involvement of private sector investment in environmentally sound technology. Given the issues covered by this book, this book will be of interest to academics as well as national and international level policy-makers, particularly those working in the field of climate change, technology transfer and sustainable development.

Prof. Saleemul Huq, PhD
Director
International Centre for Climate Change and Development (ICCCAD) &
Professor of Environmental Science and Management
Independent University, Bangladesh
Dhaka, Bangladesh

1 Introduction

This book will look at how global sustainable development can be promoted through the transfer of environmentally sound technologies. Accordingly, this book will contain a comprehensive account of the role of international laws on climate change (e.g. United Nations Framework Convention on Climate Change (UNFCCC),[1] Kyoto Protocol,[2] Paris Agreement[3]) in innovating and transferring environmentally sound technologies as well as promoting sustainable development. The discussion and analysis will also contain a comparison between technology mechanisms established under the current global climate regime and similar provisions adopted by other multilateral environmental agreements (MEAs) (e.g. International Treaty on Plant Genetic Resources for Food and Agriculture (ITPGRFA),[4] United Nations Convention to Combat Desertification (UNCCD),[5] Basel Convention on the Control of Transboundary Movements of Hazardous Wastes and their Disposal (Basel Convention),[6] and Convention on Biological Diversity (CBD),[7] etc.). At the same time, this book will critically examine the application of the principle of equity and the principle of common but differentiated responsibilities (CBDR) in promoting the innovation and transfer of environmentally sound technologies. In addition, this study will contain an analysis of how international trade related laws (e.g. intellectual property rights (IPRs), transboundary investment related

1 United Nations Framework Convention on Climate Change, May 9, 1992, 1771 U.N.T.S. 107, 1992.
2 Kyoto, 10 December 1997, 16 February 2005; reprinted at 37 ILM 22, 1998.
3 Conference of the Parties' Twenty-first Session, U.N. Framework Convention on Climate Change, Paris Agreement, U.N. Doc. FCCC/CP/2015/L.9/Rev.1, 2015.
4 FAO Conference Res. 3/2001, Rome, November 3, 2001, in force June 29, 2004. See www.planttreaty.org.
5 Convention to Combat Desertification in Those Countries Experiencing Serious Drought and/or Desertification, Particularly in Africa (Paris) June 17, 1994, in force December 26, 1996, 33 ILM 1328, 1994 (1994 Desertification Convention).
6 Convention on the Control of Transboundary Movement of Hazardous Wastes and Their Disposal (Basel), March 22, 1989, in force 1992, 28 ILM 657,1989 (1989 Basel Convention).
7 Convention on Biological Diversity (Rio de Janeiro) June 5, 1992, in force December 29, 1993, 31 ILM 822,1992 (1992 Biodiversity Convention).

DOI: 10.4324/9781003056416-1

laws) can facilitate the innovation and transfer of environmentally sound technologies. Moreover, it will also address the potential to increase the engagement of the private sector in the innovation and transfer of environmentally sound technologies. The discussions and analyses will be carried out in the light of the current legal fora of global climate change. In other words, this study will analyse the application of the principle of equity, along with the principle of CBDR, within the post-Paris international legal framework in promoting sustainable development through transferring environmentally sound technologies from developed countries to developing countries, as well as from advanced developing countries to other developing countries. A special focus will be given to the need for the transfer of environmentally sound technologies to the least developed countries (LDCs). In this connection, this book will contain a case study regarding the transfer of environmentally sound technologies to Bangladesh.

In view of the above, this introductory chapter glimpses at international laws on climate change, and ideas about environmentally sound technologies, sustainable development, technology transfer, international trade related laws that concern the innovation and transfer of environmentally sound technologies and the necessity for the increased involvement of the private sector in innovating environmentally sound technologies. Thereafter, this chapter will indicate the scope and limitations of the present study which will be followed by a short overview of the whole book.

1.1 International laws on climate change

In order to hold 'the increase in the global average temperature to well below 2 °C above pre-industrial levels and pursuing efforts to limit the temperature increase to 1.5 °C above pre-industrial levels',[8] in 2015 all nations agreed to sign the Paris Agreement (hereinafter also referred to as the Agreement). The Agreement shows nation states' earnest promise to combat climate change. However, the process of global consensus to deal with climate change can be traced back to the last decade of the twentieth century. In 1992, with a view to overcoming the challenges derived from climate change, all nations signed the United Nations Framework Convention on Climate Change (UNFCCC) (hereinafter also referred to as the Convention). The Convention aims to 'stabilize greenhouse gas concentrations in the atmosphere at a level that would prevent dangerous anthropogenic interference with the climate system'.[9] Accordingly, the Parties to the Convention agreed to fulfil their commitment on the basis of the principle of common but differentiated responsibilities. In 1997, the Convention was supplemented by the Kyoto Protocol (hereinafter also referred to as the Protocol) whose tenure was scheduled to end in 2020, as such the Paris Agreement (concluded in 2015) has become the most relevant globally agreed legal instrument on climate change issues. The aim of the Paris Agreement explicitly includes 'enhancing the implementation of the

8 Art. 2(a) of the Paris Agreement 2015.
9 Art. 2 of the UNFCCC 1992.

Convention' which includes the Convention's objectives and aims 'to strengthen the global response to the threat of climate change, in the context of sustainable development and efforts to eradicate poverty'.[10] Hence, while the Agreement expresses its aim to hold 'the increase in the global average temperature to well below' a certain degree above pre-industrial levels,[11] the measures to be taken to fulfil this goal also require fulfilling one of the main objectives of the Convention (i.e. promotion of global sustainable development).[12]

The uniqueness of the Paris Agreement 2015 lies in bringing all Parties to the Agreement under an obligation to reduce greenhouse gas emissions as per their own nationally determined contributions (NDCs).[13] This is a major shift from the provisions of the Kyoto Protocol, which only imposed legally binding obligations on developed countries (Annex I Parties to the Convention) to reduce greenhouse gas emissions into the global atmosphere.[14] Besides, as will be explained in the later stages of this book, several important plans and decisions have been made under the umbrella of the UNFCCC. Amongst these, most importantly, in 2007, the Conference of the Parties (hereinafter also referred to as the COP) to the UNFCCC agreed to work on common future commitments under the Bali Action Plan. This plan introduced four basic pillars to combat climate change: enhanced national/international action on mitigation of climate change; enhanced action on adaptation; enhanced action on technology development and technology-transfer supporting actions on mitigation and adaptation; and enhanced actions on the provision of financial resources and investment supporting mitigation, adaptation and technology cooperation.[15] In December 2013, these pillars were further supported by the inclusion of an 'international mechanism for loss and damage associated with climate change impacts' introduced by COP 19 which took place in Warsaw, Poland.[16]

Considering the third pillar of the Bali Action Plan (i.e. enhanced action on technology development and technology-transfer supporting actions on mitigation and adaptation), this book considers environmentally sound technologies to be those technologies that are essential for climate change mitigation and adaptation. Adaptation to climate change refers to 'adjustments in ecological, social, or economic systems in response to actual or expected climatic stimuli and their effects or impacts'.[17] Mitigation to climate change refers to 'efforts to

10 Art. 2(1) of the Paris Agreement 2015.
11 Art. 2(1)(a) of the Paris Agreement 2015.
12 Preamble to Paris Agreement 2015, Para 8; Art. 2 of the Paris Agreement 2015.
13 Art. 3 of the Paris Agreement 2015.
14 Art. 2 and Art. 3 of the Kyoto Protocol 1997.
15 Decision 1/CP.13, FCCC/CP/2007/6/Add.1, 14 March 2008.
16 Decision 2/CP.19, FCCC/CP/2013/10/Add.1, 31 January 2014.
17 UNFCCC, 'What Do Adaptation to Climate Change and Climate Resilience Mean?', available at https://unfccc.int/topics/adaptation-and-resilience/the-big-picture/what-do-adaptation-to-climate-change-and-climate-resilience-mean (last accessed on August 10, 2020).

reduce emissions and enhance sinks'.[18] Institutionally, the range of the term 'adaptation and mitigation related technologies' or environmentally sound technologies includes 'the total systems, which include know-how, procedures, goods and services, and equipment as well as organizational and managerial procedures'.[19] While for the purpose of combating climate change it is important to ensure that all nations have reasonable access to the technologies that are essential for climate change adaptation and mitigation, this book focuses on the transfer of environmentally sound technologies from the most economically developed countries (i.e. Annex II Parties to the Convention) to the developing countries (i.e. non-Annex I Parties to the Convention) as well as from the advanced developing countries to the less advanced developing countries as an important instrument in the international policy of sustainable development under the post-Paris climate regime.

Like the UNFCCC, the Paris Agreement acknowledges the principle of equity and the CBDR as guiding principles that all Parties to the Convention need to follow at the time of taking measures to 'protect the climate system for the benefit of present and future generations of humankind'.[20] Besides, as mentioned above, one of the important objectives of the UNFCCC is to ensure that the measures taken as a response to the adverse impact of climate change must also take in to account the sustainable development goals of the country concerned.[21] In this regard, the principle of equity and CBDR, which receives a broader and wider interpretation in the Paris Agreement,[22] are two important legal principles of the concept of sustainable development.[23]

1.2 Sustainable development and climate change

Since no unitary definition of sustainable development exists,[24] the concept has been defined and interpreted from various perspectives. Consequently, it is not unlikely that one may get confused by the different kinds of definition and interpretations of the concept.[25] However, one thing is arguably 'common' among all the different definitions and interpretations of sustainable development – all of them lead to a kind of balanced scenario amongst the diverse

18 UNFCCC, 'Introduction to Mitigation', available at https://unfccc.int/topics/mitigation/the-big-picture/introduction-to-mitigation (last accessed on August 10, 2020).

19 Chapter 34(3) of Agenda 21.

20 Art. 3(1) of the UNFCCC 1992.

21 Art. 3(4) of the UNFCCC 1992.

22 See generally Christina Voigt and Felipe Ferreira, 'Dynamic Differentiation': The Principles of CBDR-RC, Progression and Highest Possible Ambition in the Paris Agreement, *Transnational Environmental Law* 5(2):285–303, October 2016.

23 Luis A. Aviles, 'Sustainable Development and Environmental Legal Protection in the European Union: A Model for Mexican Courts to follow?', *Mexican Law Review,* Vol. VI(2), June 2014, 251–272, 266.

24 Peter P. Rogers, *An Introduction to Sustainable Development,* Routledge, 2008, 92.

25 Ibid.

'competing claims'.[26] Of all the definitions and interpretations there are, arguably the most accepted definition of sustainable development was stated in the 1987 Brundtland Report, which refers to meeting the 'needs of the present generation without compromising the ability of future generations to meet their own needs'.[27]

Though different scholars have different views on and justifications and explanations for the sustainable development concept, it is widely accepted now that sustainable development is based on three basic pillars: social responsibility, environmental protection and economic viability – popularly known as the 'Triple Bottom Line'.[28] The World Summit on Sustainable Development (WSSD) 2002 has also acknowledged the 'Triple Bottom Line' interpretation of sustainable development through assuming 'a collective responsibility to advance and strengthen the interdependent and mutually reinforcing pillars of sustainable development – economic development, social development and environmental protection – at local, national, regional and global levels'.[29] The Inter-Governmental Panel on Climate Change (IPCC) has also accepted economic, social and environmental dimensions as standard for the evaluation of sustainable development.[30] This was later also acknowledged by a decision of the Thirteenth Conference of the Parties (COP-13) of the UNFCCC.[31]

Hence, sustainable development needs to follow a holistic approach that takes into account economic sustainability, social sustainability and environmental sustainability. Taking such simultaneous accounting of all environmental, social and economic sustainability is known as the 'integration' approach of sustainable development.[32] The economic sustainability of the sustainable development

26 M. Stillwell, 'Trade and Environment in the Context of Sustainable Development', in Marcus W. Gehring and Marie-Claire Cordonier Segger, *Sustainable Development in World Trade Law,* Kluwer Law International, 2005, 45.

27 United Nations World Commission on Environment and Development (WCED) (ed.), *Report of the World Commission on Environment and Development: Our Common Future*, Oxford University Press, 1987, Chapter 2, Para 1. The definition is further elaborated in the following section of this chapter.

28 The 'three pillars' concept was first introduced by John Elkington in his book *Cannibal with Forks*, Capstone, 1997. They are also known as the 3Ps of sustainability – people, planet, profit. See https://sustainabilitydefinition.org/the-3-ps-of-sustainability (last accessed on September 30, 2019).

29 Johannesburg Declaration on Sustainable Development and Plan of Implementation of the World Summit on Sustainable Development: The final text of agreements negotiated by governments at the World Summit on Sustainable Development, August 26–September 4, 2002, Johannesburg, South Africa, New York: United Nations Department of Public Information, 2003, Para 5.

30 IPCC, Climate Change 2007: Synthesis Report. Contribution of Working Groups I, II and III to the Fourth Assessment Report of the Intergovernmental Panel on Climate Change [Core Writing Team, Pachauri, R. K. and Reisinger, A. (eds.)], IPCC, Geneva, Switzerland, 2007, 87.

31 Decision 3/CP.13, FCCC/CP/2007/6/Add.1. 14 March 2008.

32 Ramon Pichs et al. (eds), *Development, Sustainability, and Equity*, IPCC and WMO, 2000, 67.

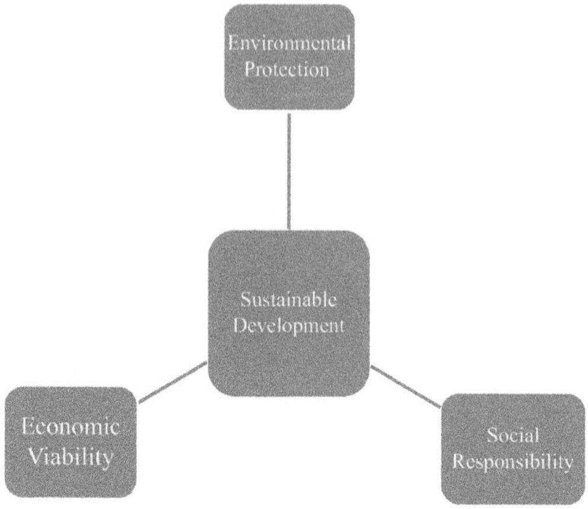

Figure 1.1 The triple bottom line of sustainable development

concept means that the realization of the social and environmental pillars of sustainable development must be attained in the light of economic efficiency in resource allocation.[33] Social sustainability means that the realization of the economic and environmental pillars of sustainable development must be carried out in the light of social considerations of intra-generational and inter-generational equity.[34] The environmental sustainability of the sustainable development concept means that the economic and social pillars of sustainable development needs to be explained in the light of the necessity of protecting and promoting the environment. It also involves making decisions and acting on economic or social development issues in a manner that does not distress the interests of the natural world and impede the environment from supporting human life.[35]

One of the early pioneers of ecological sustainability, Harman Daly (1990), proposed three principles for achieving environmental sustainability. The first principle is 'sustainable yielding for renewable resources', which means the rate of harvest should not exceed the rate of regeneration. The second is 'sustainable waste disposal', which suggests that the rate of waste disposal from a project should not exceed the assimilative capacity of the environment. The third principle is 'sustainable yielding for non-renewable resources', which is to say the rate of depletion of non-renewable resources should be accompanied by a comparable development of renewable resources, which can be considered to be a substitute for the depleted non-renewable resources.[36]

33 Ibid.
34 Ibid. For more about inter-generational equity and intra-generational equity, see *infra* Chapter 2.6.
35 Ibid.
36 H. E. Daly, 'Boundless Bull', *Gannett Center Journal*, Vol. 4(3), 1990, 113–118.

However, a close inter-relationship certainly exists between the discourses of climate change and sustainable development.[37] For instance, if greenhouse gas emissions are reduced as part of the mitigation strategies, this also results in a decreased rate of death and illness caused by air pollution.[38] Similarly, if we establish projects to generate renewable energy, like solar plants, windmills or biogas plants, this will also create jobs in the locality in which they operate. Hence, it is important that the steps taken to deal with climate change issues consider the sustainable development issues of any specific locality and vice versa.[39]

The relationship between climate change and sustainable development has already been discussed in academia from diverse points of view. A report of the International Law Association (ILA) published in 2008 states: '[s]ustainable development is a deeply integrated concept, affecting a diverse array of issues ranging from climate change to international investment, and the links between such issues are becoming ever more complex and nuanced'.[40]

In order to understand the connection between sustainable development and climate change, it is essential to understand how climate change interacts with all three elements of sustainable development – economic sustainability, social sustainability and environmental sustainability both individually and collectively.

Economic sustainability is closely related to climate change. This is because the adoption of policies for the economic growth of a country may cause increased greenhouse gas emissions in the atmosphere and increased greenhouse gas emissions in the atmosphere leads to global warming, as such global climate change. To avoid such negative consequences of economic growth policies, it is essential that national economic growth policies are adopted in line with the economic sustainability approach, which considers the environmental and social impact of the relevant strategies of economic growth.

In this regard, it is the inclusion and application of the environmentally sound technologies in economic growth policy that can reduce the negative impact of climate change through reducing the rate of greenhouse gas emissions significantly.[41] The introduction of environmentally sound technologies also has a positive impact on social sustainability. This is because the inclusion and application of new environmentally sound technologies create new job opportunities.[42]

37 IPCC 2007 pointed out the iterative relationship between climate change and sustainable development, and that the two can be mutually reinforcing, see IPCC, 2007, *supra* note 30.

38 Beg et al., 'Linkages between Climate Change and Sustainable Development', *Climate Policy*, 2(2–3), 2002, 129–144.

39 Ibid.

40 The ILA's International Law on Sustainable Development Committee, *International Law on Sustainable Development*, Third Report, Rio de Janeiro Conference, 2008, 25.

41 Ramon Pichs et al. (eds), *Development, Sustainability, and Equity*, IPCC and WMO, 2000, 68.

42 United Nations Development Programme (UNDP), *Human Development Report*, UNDP, 1998, 96.

A relationship also exists between social sustainability and climate change. If social development takes place without following the approach of equity, it can have a negative effect on social unity. Such a lack of social unity may lead to conflict over resources and climate change. If social growth takes place without considering the impact on the environment, the social development results in a disparity in wealth and living standards between different groups of people in society. This is because rich people contribute more to pollution and waste generation causing global warming, whereas poor people are stuck in a vicious circle of poverty that also leads to environmental degradation and global warming. The vicious circle of poverty also implies a vicious circle of poverty – environmental resource degradation – poverty. Consequently, it leads to the process of global warming resulting in climate change.[43]

Climate change also has a negative impact on social sustainability. It may cause social inequalities due to the disparate distribution of the costs associated with damage, adaptation and mitigation initiatives. The adverse impact of climate change are most likely to affect those groups of countries which are financially poor and which in fact contributed a very nominal role, or no role at all, to global warming and climate change.[44] As a result, it is acknowledged that the degree and level of poverty of those countries will worsen as a consequence of climate change. Moreover, the adverse effects are most likely to affect the poorest members of the population of those countries who depend on harvesting for their livelihoods.[45] For instance, Bangladesh is one of those financially poor countries that are most affected by the adverse impact of climate change (although it played a nominal role in causing global warming). If the adverse effects posed by climate change are not dealt with properly, it is obvious that Bangladesh will suffer from increased poverty.

However, even if it is not possible to address all the social inequality issues under the international legal regime of climate change, one could argue that the legal regime of climate change should ensure that the current scenario of inequity is not worsened by the adverse impact of climate change. Facilitating social sustainability is arguably possible by implementing the principle of equity in association with both the principle of CBDR and the 'polluter pays' principle of international environmental law.[46] Consequently, equity and the principle of CBDR have already been accepted as the guiding principles of the international climate regime governing treaty – the UNFCCC.[47]

According to the 'polluter pays' principle, the entities that cause pollution are liable to compensate the entities affected by pollution.[48] This principle is not

43 Ibid.
44 See generally M. Munasinghe, 'Development, Equity and Sustainability (DES) in the Context of Climate Change', paper prepared for the IPCC Expert Meeting on Development, Equity and Sustainability, Colombo, Sri Lanka, April 27–29, 1999.
45 UNDP, 1998, 4.
46 Cf. Ramon Pichs et al. (eds), 2000, 21.
47 Art. 3 of the UNFCCC 1992.
48 See generally M. Munasinghe, 1999.

solely based on economic efficiency but also on equity and fairness. An extended idea of the principle is recompensing victims by collecting revenues from polluters.[49] A similar approach is found under the principle of CBDR, whereby the entities liable for causing any 'harm' are held responsible for addressing and resolving the 'harm'.[50]

Environmental sustainability relates to climate change through an interaction between the adverse impacts of climate change and other environmental problems. For instance, climate change interacts with national, regional and global-level environmental problems like urban pollution, loss of biodiversity, land use changes, changes in land or river ecosystems, acid rain and stratospheric ozone depletion, etc. For this reason, when taking responsive measures to climate change it is important to make sure that they do not impede or degrade national, regional or global environmental sustainability.

The literature suggests that taking all environmental, social and economic sustainability into account also leads to a scenario of a realization of 'strong sustainability', whereas the lack of consideration of any of these criteria leads to a realization of 'weak sustainability'.[51] Moreover, sustainable development can be seen both as a goal to be attained and as a process to be followed.[52]

1.3 Technology transfer and international laws on climate change

Transfer of technology, also viewed as an instrument of attaining sustainable development, has received international attentions for decades.[53] Transfer of technology is linked with this scholarly work in two different ways. First, it is known to be a tool for attaining sustainable development. Second, it is a way of realizing the principles of equity and CBDR.[54]

The concept of technology has given rise to much discussion. Some scholars view technology as a commodity, knowledge or socio-economic process, which can easily be reproduced/copied and transferred from one place to another.[55] Others argue that technology is knowledge that, through research

49 Ramon Pichs et al. (eds), 2000, 21.
50 Cf. *infra* Chapter 2.7.
51 S. Dovers, and J. Handmer, 'Contradictions in Sustainability', *Environmental Conservation*, Vol. 20(3), 1993, 217–222; D. Mebratu, 'Sustainability and Sustainable Development: Historical and Conceptual Review', *Environmental Impact Assessment Review*, Vol. 18, 1998, 493–520.
52 M. Lehtonen, 'The Environmental-Social Interface of Sustainable Development: Capabilities, Social Capital, Institutions', *Ecological Economics*, Vol. 49(2), 2004, 199–214; J. Robinson, 'Squaring the Circle? Some Thoughts on the Idea of Sustainable Development', *Ecological Economics*, 48(4), 369–384.
53 Philippe Cullet, *Differential Treatment in International Environmental Law*, Ashgate, 2003, 96.
54 See *infra* Chapter 2.7.2.
55 N. Rosenberg, *Inside the Black Box: Technology and Economics,* Cambridge University Press, 1982, 245 ff.

and invention, can bring new products/processes/services to a particular place or market.[56] The latter group of scholars argue that technology transfer is a complete process of learning,[57] and for as long as the technology receiver does not understand the complete process of use of a particular technology, one cannot claim that any technology transfer has taken place.[58]

Thus a fundamental criterion for ensuring technology transfer is enabling the receiving entity to employ or adapt technology to its own socio-economic circumstances.[59] One may argue that the lack of proper understanding and the lack of capacity of the receiving entities may result in choosing inappropriate technologies or the kind of technologies that have a negative social, economic or environmental impact.[60] The necessity of taking into account the capacity building issue as an element of technology transfer has also been addressed under Chapter 34 of Agenda 21: 'when discussing transfer of technologies, the human resource development and local capacity-building aspects of technology choices, including gender-relevant aspects, should also be addressed'.[61] Relating capacity building, technological cooperation and the transfer of know-how to the transfer of environmentally sound technologies, Chapter 34(4) of Agenda 21 stated:

> [t]here is a need for favourable access to and transfer of environmentally sound technologies, in particular to developing countries, through supportive measures that promote technology cooperation and that should enable transfer of necessary technological know-how as well as building up of economic, technical, and managerial capabilities for the efficient use and further development of transferred technology ....

Chapter 34(4) of Agenda 21 further elaborates 'technology cooperation' as follows:

> [t]echnology cooperation involves joint efforts by enterprises and Governments, both suppliers of technology and its recipients. Therefore, such cooperation entails an iterative process involving government, the private sector, and research and development facilities to ensure the best possible

56 M. Kranzberg, 'The Technical Elements in International Technology Transfer: Historical Perspectives', in J. R. McIntyre and D. S. Papp (eds.), *The Political Economy of International Technology Transfer*, Quorum Books, 1986, cited in M.R Amin, *Technology Transfer for Sustainable Development through Clean Development Mechanism (CDM): The Bangladesh Perspectives*, Doctoral thesis, Murdoch University, Australia, 2005, 33.

57 M. R. Amin, 'Technology Transfer for Sustainable Development through Clean Development Mechanism (CDM): The Bangladesh Perspectives', Doctoral thesis, Murdoch University, Australia, 2005, 33.

58 Ibid.

59 Ibid.

60 Ibid.

61 Chapter 34.3 of Agenda 21.

> results from transfer of technology. Successful long-term partnerships in technology cooperation necessarily require continuing systematic training and capacity-building at all levels over an extended period of time.

The Special Report of the IPCC (2000) defined technology transfer in relation to climate change as follows:

> Technology Transfer encompasses the broad set of processes that cover the flows of knowledge, experience, and equipment for mitigating and adapting to climate change among different stakeholders. These include governments, international organizations, private sector entities, financial institutions, NGOs, and research and/or education institutions. It comprises the process of learning to understand, utilize, and replicate the technology, including the capacity to choose it, adapt it to local conditions, and integrate it with indigenous technologies.[62]

Hence, in a broader sense, technology transfer includes the transfer of a set of knowledge through any transaction. This may include the grant or assignment of industrial property rights; communication of technical know-how in a documentary form; communication of technical or other know-how in the supply of services; assistance in the commissioning of an industrial plant; the sale or lease of machinery; and providing services to assist in the recruitment and training of staff and the institution of managerial and accounting procedures; and providing services in relation to the marketing and distribution of the product of the plant.[63] In addition to big infrastructural projects, services concerning environmental know-how can also be treated as technology transfer under the international climate change regime.

Under the Paris Agreement 2015, the transfer of environmentally sound technologies, as an important tool in combating climate change, will probably take place through financial and technology mechanisms established by the concerned parties.[64] These also include a new kind of 'flexible mechanisms' in the form of a 'voluntary cooperation mechanism' or 'sustainable development mechanism'.[65] Art. 6(1) of the Paris Agreement 2015 has acknowledged that some parties to the Convention 'choose to pursue voluntary cooperation in the implementation of their nationally determined contributions'. Such 'voluntary cooperation' amongst the Parties is aimed to ensure that the Parties can set higher mitigation and adaptation targets and

62 B. Metz et al. (eds.), *Methodological and Technological Issues in Technology Transfer,* Special Report of the Intergovernmental Panel on Climate Change (IPCC), Cambridge University Press, 2000, 3.
63 M. Blakeney, *Legal Aspects of the Transfer of Technology to Developing Countries,* ESC Publishing Ltd., 1989, 3.
64 Art. 10 of the Paris Agreement 2015.
65 Art. 6 of the Paris Agreement 2015.

fulfil the same.[66] More to the point, such voluntary cooperation of the Parties is also intended to promote environmental integrity and sustainable development.[67]

While Art. 6(1) does not explicitly mention anything about a 'carbon trading mechanism', Art. 6(2) of the Agreement refers to the fact that the 'voluntary cooperation' of the Parties in terms of mitigation may involve 'the use of internationally transferred mitigation outcomes towards nationally determined contributions'.[68] Subsequently, Art. 6(3) expressly establishes a 'mechanism to contribute to the mitigation of greenhouse gas emissions and support sustainable development, which is possible to be denoted as 'sustainable development mechanism'.[69]

In addition to promoting greenhouse gas mitigation and fostering sustainable development, the three other aims of the proposed mechanism have been listed under Art. 6(4) of the Agreement as: a) facilitating participation of both public and private parties authorized by a Party to the Agreement; b) contributing emission reduction in both the host country and the country that wishes to fulfil its intended nationally determined contribution; and c) delivering an overall reduction in global greenhouse gas emissions. Importantly, the mechanism needs to avoid the 'double counting' of the emission reductions unit.[70] However, a share of the profit that might be generated from selling a carbon reduction unit will be used to cover the administrative costs and assist developing country Parties to the Agreement in meeting their adaptation costs.[71] This provision of the Paris Agreement is very similar to the Clean Development Mechanism (CDM) that was established under the Carbon Trading Mechanism of the Kyoto Protocol where a share of profit was allotted to the Adaptation Fund of the UNFCCC.[72] Apart from this specific feature, the other features of this newly established mechanism, such as promoting greenhouse gas mitigation in the atmosphere and simultaneously fostering sustainable development, are also similar to the features of the CDM.[73]

While the 'voluntary cooperation' of Art. 6 might result in three separate mechanisms of which two will be based on 'market' and one will be based on 'non-market' approaches,[74] arguably the newly established 'sustainable development mechanism' will be an advanced version of CDM (established under the Kyoto Protocol). Although the Paris Agreement did not refer to the CDM or Joint Implementation (JI) (established under the Kyoto Protocol), it noted that 'the new mechanism should draw on the experience gained from existing

66 Art. 6(1) of the Paris Agreement 2015.
67 Art. 6(2) of the Paris Agreement 2015.
68 Ibid.
69 Art. 6(3) of the Paris Agreement 2015.
70 Art. 6(2) of the Paris Agreement 2015.
71 Art. 6(6) of the Paris Agreement 2015.
72 Art. 12(1) of the Kyoto Protocol 1997.
73 Cf. Art. 12(2) of the Kyoto Protocol 1997.
74 Carbon Brief, 'In-depth Q&A: How "Article 6" Carbon Markets Could "Make or Break" the Paris Agreement', September 29, 2019, available at https://www.carbonbrief.org/in-depth-q-and-a-how-article-6-carbon-markets-could-make-or-break-the-paris-agreement (last accessed on July 29, 2020).

mechanisms'.[75] However, as with the CDM, the 'voluntary cooperation mechanism' or 'sustainable development mechanism' of the Paris Agreement should also be considered as a means of transferring environmentally sound technologies.

It is important to note that technology transfer and financial assistance as tools in intra-generational resource distribution are also considered to be tools in the realization of the principle of CBDR.[76] Moreover, the transfer of environmentally sound technologies to the developing and least developed countries is considered a tool in bringing intra-generational equity and attaining sustainable development through combating climate change and facilitating the eradication of poverty. For this reason, it is arguable that the principles of equity and CBDR, the concept of sustainable development and the issue of transfer of environmentally sound technologies are all interconnected.[77] The principles of equity and CBDR have special importance in connection with the issues of the transfer of environmentally sound technologies and the promotion of sustainable development in the least developed countries.[78]

1.4 Technology transfer and international trade related laws

In relation to facilitating innovation and the transfer of environmentally sound technologies, the importance of different trade related agreements or Doha negotiation is undeniable. In this regard, the most important factor is IPRs. Although the Agreement on the Trade Related Aspects of Intellectual Property Rights (TRIPS) 1994,[79] a global agreement governing IPRs under the auspices of the World Trade Organization (WTO)[80] does not explicitly mention the necessity of transferring environmentally sound technologies, the preamble to TRIPS only refers to the necessity of technology transfer in general.[81] The preamble acknowledges 'the underlying public policy objectives of national systems for the protection of intellectual property, including developmental and technological objectives'.[82] It further acknowledges 'the special needs of the least developed country Members in respect of maximum flexibility in the domestic implementation of laws and regulations in order to enable them to create a sound and viable technological base'.[83]

75 Centre for Climate and Energy Solutions, 'What's Ahead for Carbon Markets after COP 21?', available at https://www.c2es.org/document/whats-ahead-for-carbon-markets-after-cop-21 (last accessed on August 6, 2020).
76 See *infra* Chapter 2.7, see also *infra* in-text refs to Figure 2.3.
77 See *infra* Chapter 2, see also *infra* in-text refs to Figure 3.1.
78 See *infra* in-text refs to Figures 2.2, 2.3 and 3.1.
79 Agreement on Trade-Related Aspects of Intellectual Property Rights, April 15, 1994, Marrakesh Agreement Establishing the World Trade Organization, Annex 1C, 1869 U.N.T.S. 299, 33 I.L.M. 1197,1994 (hereinafter TRIPS Agreement).
80 Marrakesh Agreement Establishing the World Trade Organization, April 15, 1994, 1867 U.N.T.S. 154, 33 I.L.M. 1144, 1994.
81 Preamble to the TRIPS Agreement 1994.
82 Ibid.
83 Ibid.

The objective clause of the TRIPS explicitly mentions that 'the protection and enforcement of intellectual property rights should contribute to the promotion of technological innovation and to the transfer and dissemination of technology'.[84] As is the case with the preamble, the notions of the objective clause regarding the positive role of IPRs in innovation and transfer of technologies are arguably too general to relate them to the issue of the transfer of environmentally sound technologies. Yet, the importance of these notions for ensuring flexible interpretation of other provisions of the IPRs regime for the purpose of promoting the innovations of particular sectors is undeniable.[85] For instance, the Doha Declaration on TRIPS and Public Health 2000 exclusively refers to the importance of this clause (Art. 7 of the TRIPS) as a guiding principle for the global intellectual property regime.[86] In connection with promotion of technology transfer under the TRIPS, the Doha Declaration also creates the Working Group on Trade and Technology Transfer (WGTTT) conferring responsibility for technology transfer negotiations.[87]

In addition to IPRs factors, the possibility of the transfer of environmentally sound technologies through foreign direct investment has also fallen within the international trade regime. International investment issues are dealt with under the Agreement on Trade Related Investment Measures (TRIMS)[88] of the WTO.

1.5 Private sector involvement

The Paris Agreement requires all parties to 'incentivize and facilitate participation' of both public and private entities in the mitigation of greenhouse gas emissions and 'in the implementation of nationally determined contributions'.[89] However, the current financial mechanism of the UNFCCC has not yet been evident as a sufficient source of finance to meet global needs.[90] The issue will be seen as crucial in the near future. In a study conducted by the UNFCCC, it

84 Art. 7 of the TRIPS Agreement 1994.

85 United Nations, Vienna Convention on the Law of Treaties, 23 May 1969, United Nations, Treaty Series, vol. 1155, 331, available at https://www.refworld.org/docid/3ae6b3a10.html (last accessed on May 31, 2020), Art. 31(2).

86 WTO, 'Doha WTO Ministerial 2001: TRIPS', WT/MIN(01)/DEC/2, 20 November 2001.

87 WTO, Working Group on Trade and Transfer of Technology, available at https://www.wto.org/english/tratop_e/devel_e/dev_wkgp_trade_transfer_technology_e.htm (last accessed on May 31, 2020).

88 Agreement on Trade-Related Investment Measures, April 15, 1994, Marrakesh Agreement Establishing the World Trade Organization, Annex 1A, 1868 U.N.T.S. 186 (hereinafter TRIMs Agreement).

89 Art.6(4)(b) and Art. 8(4)(b) of the Paris Agreement 2015.

90 See generally UNFCCC, *Investment and Financial Flows to Address Climate Change*, 2008, available at http://unfccc.int/resource/docs/publications/financial_flows.pdf (last accessed on August 10, 2020).

has been shown that in 2030 the amount of additional investment and financial flows to combat climate change will be 0.3–0.5 per cent of global domestic product and 1.1– 1.7 per cent of global investment. Though this represents a very small amount in comparison to global figures, it is still large in comparison to the public and private climate finances currently available.[91]

Investments in many sectors such as the power sector are expected to triple between 2000 and 2020. Of the total investment needed in 2030, it is estimated that 46 per cent will flow to developing countries (including least developed countries) which might result in a reduction of 68 per cent in global emissions in 2030. Though no precise figure is currently available, an investment of several billion US$ has been predicted as also being necessary for global climate change adaptation.[92]

However, as the UNFCCC climate funding mechanisms do not currently possess adequate funds and the future funding of these mechanisms are also dependent on the contribution of the Parties, specially developed countries, different suggestions have been made as to how the huge need for funding for climate change adaptation and mitigation should be met. The suggestions include the expansion of existing financial mechanisms, the existing carbon market, current official development assistance (ODA) and providing the private sector with incentives to invest in climate change adaptation and mitigation.[93]

In addition to managing its own climate exposure, the private sector has immense potential to finance climate change adaptation in several ways, such as generating new finances in order to help to fill the massive deficit in current funds, creating and distributing goods and services that might reduce the vulnerability of individuals and communities to climate change and providing risk management tools like insurance.[94]

The potential of the private sector in innovating and transferring environmentally sound technologies can be calculated on the basis of the fact that currently 86 per cent of the total global investment and financial flows come from the private sector.[95] Scholars predict that the role of the private sector in the supply of future environmentally sound technologies will be vital, even if

91 Ibid.

92 UNFCCC, *Guidelines for Completing the Project Design Document (CDM-PDD), and the Proposed New Baseline and Monitoring Methodologies (CDM-NM),* Bonn, UNFCCC, version 07, 2008, 92.

93 UNFCCC, *Fact sheet: Financing Climate Change Action- Investment and Financial Flows for a Strengthened Response to Climate Change,* June, 2009, 3–4, available at https://unfccc.int/files/press/backgrounders/application/pdf/fact_sheet_financing_climate_change.pdf (last accessed on August 12, 2020).

94 Aaron Atteridge, *Private Sector Finance and Climate Change Adaptation, How Can Voluntary Private Finance Support Adaptation in Developing Countries?* Stockholm Environment Institute, 2009, 1.

95 UNFCCC, *Financing Climate Change Action – Investment and Financial Flows for a Strengthened Response to Climate Change,* June 2009, 3.

the flow of public finances increases in the expected manner.[96] This prediction has also been reflected in the Paris Agreement.[97]

According to the jointly published Report (2017) of the European Patent Office (EPO) and International Renewable Energy Agency (IRENA), although the effort of the private sector to invent technologies for climate change mitigation has increased globally over the past decade, the challenge remains: how can those inventions be integrated in reliable power systems and how can we deal with the uncertainty in terms of return on investment? In both cases, it is the climate laws and policies that will play a vital role in integrating environmentally sound technology innovation into local systems and in creating stable markets for the same.[98]

1.6 Scope and limitation of the study

The study and analysis of the innovation and transfer of environmentally sound technologies covered by this book will merely focus on the potential ways of transferring environmentally sound technologies in developing countries – with a special focus on the least developed countries. Specific definitions of developed, developing and least developed countries have yet to be formed under the post-Paris climate regime. However, under the UNFCCC, all Parties can be divided into three groups – Annex II Parties, Annex I Parties and non-Annex I Parties. The divisions were made based on the then interpretation of the principle of CBDR which considered countries' historical responsibilities for and contributions to global emissions as well as countries' respective capabilities in combating climate change.

The Annex II Parties are those countries that were members of the Organisation for Economic Co-operation and Development (OECD)[99] at the time of concluding the UNFCCC (i.e. in 1994). The Annex I Parties consist of those countries that were members of the OECD in 1992 plus those countries whose

96 J. Brown and M. Jacobs, *Leveraging Private Investment: The Role of Public Sector Climate Finance,* Background Note, Overseas Development Institute (ODI), 2011, 1.

97 Cf. Art.6(4)(b) and Art. 8(4)(b) of the Paris Agreement 2015.

98 Ilja Rudyk et al., *Development and Deployment of Climate Change Mitigation Technologies: Evidence to Support Policy Making*, European Patent Office (EPO) and International Renewable Energy Agency (IREA), 2017, 6, available at http://documents.epo.org/projects/ babylon/eponet.nsf/0/ C6AD54B736F9B9E5C125814E0040E951 /$FILE/ Development_and_deployment_of_climate_change_mitigation_technologies-Policy_Brief_en.pdf (last accessed on August 12, 2020).

99 The Organisation for Economic Co-operation and Development (OECD) is '[a]n intergovernmental organization (based in Paris, France) which provides a forum for discussion and cooperation among the governments of industrialized countries committed to democracy and the market economy. The primary goal of the OECD and its member countries is to support sustainable economic growth, boost employment, raise living standards, maintain financial stability, assist other countries' economic development, and contribute to growth in world trade.' See https://www.nrc.gov/reading-rm/basic-ref/glossary/organisation-for-economic-co-operation-and-development-oecd.html (last accessed on August 25, 2020).

economies were in transition in 1994 (i.e. countries that were members of the former Soviet Union).[100] While under the Paris Agreement all Parties have an obligation to reduce their annual greenhouse gas emissions as per their nationally determined contribution, under the UNFCCC, it is only the Annex I Parties that are obliged to reduce annual greenhouse gas emissions.[101] Furthermore, under the UNFCCC only Annex II Parties are responsible for financial and technological cooperation with the developing and least developed countries (i.e. non-Annex I Parties).[102] The UNFCCC also requires special attention be given to the small island and least developed country Parties in the Convention.[103]

Since the principle of CBDR receives a new interpretation and meaning under the Paris Agreement, the previous method of dividing countries and the pre-defined differentiated obligations of countries' emission reduction (as enumerated under the UNFCCC) do not exist under the Paris regime. However, this book will consider developing countries as those countries which were considered as non-Annex I Parties under the UNFCCC. In this regard, this book will also consider the fact that some non-Annex I Party developing countries have made significant economic progress in the last three decades. For instance, for the purpose of this book emerging economies like China and South Korea will not be considered as developing countries where the transfer of environmentally sound technologies is a dire necessity. For the purposes of this book least developed countries will be those countries that are identified as a least developed country by the Committee for Development Policy of the United Nations.[104]

1.7 Short overview of the book

In addition to the 'Introduction' chapter, this book contains five other chapters. Chapter 2, entitled 'Sustainable development and global climate regime', will provide a comprehensive understanding of the concept of sustainable development and highlight two relevant aspects of the concept – sustainable development as a legal principle and sustainable development as a global goal. Thereafter, the chapter will include discussions about how international laws are framed to include sustainable development as a part of their objective. After that, the chapter will include a short discussion on the important concepts and principles of international laws, which are accepted as essential principles to attain global sustainable development. Among the concepts and principles, the chapter will illuminate two important principles – equity and CBDR because these two principles are also the

100 Annex I of the UNFCCCC 1992.
101 Art. 4(2) of the UNFCCC 1992.
102 Art. 4(3). Art. 4(4), and Art. 4(5) of the UNFCCC 1992.
103 Art. 4(8), Art. 4(9) of the UNFCCC 1992.
104 United Nations, *LDC Identification Criteria & Indicators,* available at https://www.un.org/development/ desa/dpad/least-developed-country-category/ldc-criteria.htm l (last accessed on June 14, 2020).

main guiding principles of the international laws on climate change. General discussions on the principle of CBDR will entail how this principle is interpreted and adopted by both UNFCCC and the Paris Agreement. The chapter will also demonstrate how these two principles are realized in the international climate regime – through financial and technological cooperation. In this manner, Chapter 2 will establish a clear connection between the transfer of environmentally sound technologies and its impact on promoting sustainable development.

Chapter 3, entitled 'Technology transfer under the global climate regime', will address three main mechanisms introduced by international laws on climate change, which are directly or indirectly delegated to promote the innovation and transfer of environmentally sound technologies. These mechanisms are: financial mechanisms, technology mechanisms and indirect financial mechanisms or flexible mechanisms (reintroduced by the Paris Agreement as 'voluntary cooperation mechanisms'). These mechanisms are not only known as practical methods of transferring environmentally sound technologies, but also considered to be methods of realizing the principle of CBDR and the promotion of sustainable development. Discussions about financial mechanisms will include both Global Environment Facilities (GEFs)[105] and the Green Climate Fund (GCF).[106] In addition, the discussion will also cover the Adaptation Fund (AF),[107] the Least Developed Countries Fund (LDCF)[108] and the Special Climate Change Fund (SCCF)[109] and their role in facilitating the innovation and transfer of the environmentally sound technologies. The Technology Mechanisms part of the chapter will address the role of the technology mechanism and the technology framework of the international climate regime in facilitating the innovation and transfer of environmentally sound technologies.

The 'flexible mechanism' part of Chapter 3 will cover the flexible mechanisms established under the Kyoto Protocol and the Paris Agreement. As part of the Kyoto Protocol's flexible mechanism, the discussion will mainly cover the CDM.[110]

After discussion and analysis of the diverse financial and technology transfer mechanisms established under the climate regime, the chapter will contain a critical comparative analysis section. This section will critically analyse and compare the efficiency of the technology transfer mechanisms established under the climate regime with similar provisions adopted by some other multilateral environmental agreements.

In addition to the above-stated mechanisms, Chapter 3 will also include discussion about the possibilities and scope for the involvement of the private sector in the innovation and transfer of environmentally sound technologies. Since the Paris Agreement acknowledges the urgency of involving the private

105 See *infra* Chapter 3.2.1.
106 See *infra* Chapter 3.2.3.
107 See *infra* Chapter 3.2.2.1.
108 See *infra* Chapter 3.2.2.2.
109 See *infra* Chapter 3.2.2.3.
110 See *infra* Chapter 3.4.1.

sector in climate finance and technology innovation, the discussion will reflect the post-Paris international laws on climate change.

Chapter 4, entitled 'Technology transfer under the global trade regime', will provide an inclusive understanding as to the role of international trade related laws (e.g. intellectual property laws, international investment laws) in facilitating the innovation and transfer of technologies. In order to do so, first, the chapter will address the overall role of IPRs in the innovation and transfer of environmentally sound technologies. Thereafter, the chapter will critically analyse the relevant provisions and flexibilities of the TRIPS[111] that can widen the scope and opportunities to facilitate the innovation and transfer of environmentally sound technologies. After this discussion, the chapter will demonstrate what role TRIMs[112] can play in facilitating transboundary foreign direct investment in the field of environmentally sound technology.

Chapter 5, entitled 'Case study', will contain empirical studies on the role of the flexible mechanisms in transferring environmentally sound technologies and promoting sustainable development. For the purpose of the empirical study on the 'flexible mechanism', this chapter will consider the CDM projects and program of activities hosted by Bangladesh and their role in facilitating the transfer of environmentally sound technologies and promoting sustainable development in the country. Since the Paris Agreement's 'voluntary cooperation mechanism' or 'sustainable development mechanism' contains the same features as CDM, Chapter 5 aims to assist the new mechanism by recounting the experiences of the similar old mechanism.

Chapter 6, the concluding chapter, is entitled 'Concluding remarks'. This chapter will include the author's observations and remarks on direct financial mechanisms as well as indirect financial mechanisms (e.g. 'flexible mechanisms', 'voluntary cooperation mechanisms') in connection with their role in the innovation and transfer of environmentally sound technologies. This chapter will also include the author's comments on the involvement of the private sector in the innovation and transfer of environmentally sound technologies.

111 See *supra* note 79.
112 See *supra* note 88.

2 Sustainable development and the global climate regime

2.1 Introduction

Since sustainable development is the guiding principle in achieving the commitments of the UNFCCC[1] as well as the Paris Agreement,[2] arguably it is also a guiding principle for the transfer of environmentally sound technologies under the international legal regime on climate change. In view of this, the concept of sustainable development is a very important one in this book, but the two major principles of sustainable development – equity and CBDR – are of equal importance. This is because the transfer of environmentally sound technologies to developing and least developed countries is not only a way of promoting sustainable development but also a method of promoting equity based on the realization of the principle of CBDR.

2.2 Development of the concept of sustainable development

The concept of sustainable development has been developed over a long period of time. The International Court of Justice (ICJ) has acknowledged the ancient root of the concept in the *Case Concerning the Gabcikovo-Nagymaros Dam Project.* In this case the ICJ denotes sustainable development as 'one of the most ancient ideas in the human heritage'.[3]

Looking back in history, it is not easy to determine exactly when the notion 'sustainability' was first mooted, and where the concept was first practised.[4] It has been argued that the concept existed in different ancient civilizations, for example in ancient irrigation practices in Sri Lanka, sub-Saharan cultures and in similar practices in China, South America and Europe.[5] It has also been claimed

1 Art. 3(4) of the UNFCCC 1992.
2 Art. 2 of the Paris Agreement 2015.
3 *Case Concerning the Gabcikovo-Nagymaros Dam Project*, ICJ Reports 7, 1997, 12.
4 W. L. Filho, 'Dealing with Misconceptions on the Concept of Sustainability', *International Journal of Sustainability in Higher Education*, Vol. 1(1), 2000, 9–19.
5 Christina Voigt, *Sustainable Development as a Principle of International Law: Resolving Conflicts between Climate Measure and WTO Law*, Martinus Nijhoff Publishers, 2009, 11; see also the ICJ Reports 7,1997,12.

DOI: 10.4324/9781003056416-2

that the concept of sustainability was in use in the household economics of Aristotle in ancient Greece (in 400 BCE).[6]

Between the twelfth and sixteenth centuries, the sustainability concept was applied in the forestry sector of Europe. The application of the concept was intended to ensure a balance between resource depletion and reproduction.[7] Forest management is a historical model of sustainable management in France. The old French term 'soustenir' was used to describe the sustainable conditions in *L'ordonnance de Brunoy*, the first known forest regulation in French, enacted on May 29, 1346 by Philippe VI of France. The regulation required the owners of forests to investigate and visit all the woods and forests and to conduct sales of timber that would enable the forests to be kept in good condition.[8]

From the eighteenth century onwards the concept spread to other sectors such as the fishing industries in Europe and North America.[9] In legal texts in those sectors, the term 'sustainable development', referring to a balance between resource depletion and reproduction, was first found in laws governing forest management practices (*Forstordnungen*) during the latter part of the eighteenth century.[10]

In 1962, based on an earlier 1961 United Nations Educational, Scientific and Cultural Organization (UNESCO) statement,[11] the UN General Assembly passed a resolution[12] urging the Parties to take immediate protective measures for the protection of natural resources, flora and fauna in parallel with continuous development. While the resolution emphasized the necessity of development, at the same time it urged 'rational use' of the natural resources.[13] In 1972 the Club of

6 In the Greek 'household concept' the household had to be self-sustaining at least to a certain extent and could not just be consumption oriented, see Ina Ehnert, *Sustainable Human Resource Management: A Conceptual and Exploratory Analysis from a Paradox Perspective*, Physica-Verlag, 2009, 35–36.

7 W. L. Filho, 2000, 9–19..

8 Art. 4 of *L'ordonnance de Brunoy, see Vincent* Clément, *Sustainable Development: A Geographical Concept?, 2004,* available at http://geoconfluences.ens-lyon.fr/doc/transv/DevDur/DevdurScient.htm.

9 M. Hu¨lsmann, *Management im Orientierungsdilemma: Unternehmen zwischen Effizienzund Nachhaltigkeit*, Germany, German Universitats-Verlag, 2003; see also Ina Ehnert, 2009, 35–36.

10 Marie-Claire Cordonier Segger, 'Sustainable Development in International Law', in Hans Christian Bugge and Christina Voigt (eds.), Sustainable Development in International and National Law, Europa Law Publishing, 2008, 92.

11 UN Resolution 1831 (XVII) refers to this UNESCO statement as: '*Noting with satisfaction* the initiative taken by the United Nations Educational, Scientific, and Cultural Organization in the field of the conservation of nature, in the resolution adopted by its General Conference in 1962, and in particular the opinion expressed by that Organization that, to be effective, measures to preserve natural resources, flora and fauna should be taken at the earliest possible moment simultaneously with economic development, including industrialization and urbanization'. See *chapeau* of the UNGA Res 1831 (XVII),18 December 1962, UN Doc A/Res/XVII/1831.

12 UNGA Res 1831 (XVII), 18 December 1962, UN Doc A/Res/XVII/1831.

13 Marie-Claire Cordonier Segger, in Hans Christian Bugge and Christina Voigt (eds.), 2008, 92.

Rome published a seminal report entitled *The Limits to Growth*. Donella Meadows et al., the authors of *The Limits to Growth*, apprehended a widespread environmental, social and economic collapse that was possibly the result of an 'irrational' and 'unlimited' development race between the nations of the world.[14] This is acknowledged to be the first publication that connected sustainability with economic, social and environmental issues, while it expected a 'state of global equilibrium' to be maintained.[15] It achieved consensus among the stakeholders with respect to the need to renew the traditional concept of development.[16]

The Declaration of the United Nations Conference on the Human Environment (hereinafter referred to as Stockholm Declaration)[17] that was adopted on June 16, 1972 by the United Nations Conference on the Human Environment is the first document in international environmental law that recognized the right to a healthy environment. This Declaration is widely known as the landmark international legal instrument that started a new era in the development of soft law by looking at the concept of sustainability in the light of environmental as well as socio-economic aspects.[18] Principle 8 of the Stockholm Declaration states:

> [e]conomic and social development is essential for ensuring a favourable living and working environment for man and for creating conditions on earth that are necessary for the improvement of the quality of life.

The notions of Principle 8 arguably lead to a new concept of development where the scale of economic growth calculated on the basis of gross national product (GNP) or gross domestic product (GDP) should not solely measure the concept of development. It argues that the development should be measured on the basis of the 'improvement of the quality of life'. It presses for a reconciliation of conflicts between two of the world's major challenges: the 'needs of development' and 'need to protect and improve the environment'.[19] The Declaration in its *chapeau* refers to the fact that environmental protection is required for the sake of economic development – 'the protection and improvement of the

14 Ibid.

15 It is highlighted that 'We are searching for a model output that represents a world system that is: 1. sustainable without sudden and uncontrolled collapse; and 2. capable of satisfying the basic material requirements of all of its people', see D. Meadows et al., *The Limits to Growth*, Universe Books, 1972, 205.

16 Christina Voigt, 2009, 13.

17 UN General Assembly, United Nations Conference on the Human Environment, December 15, 1972, A/RES/2994, available at: https://www.refworld.org/docid/3b00f1c840.html (last accessed on August 12, 2020)

18 Christina Voigt, 2009, 13.

19 Principle 14 of the Stockholm Declaration 1972; see also Principle 13 of the Stockholm Declaration which states: 'States should adopt an integrated and coordinated approach to their development planning so as to ensure that development is compatible with the need to protect and improve the environment for the benefit of their population'.

human environment is a major issue which affects the well-being of peoples and economic development throughout the world'.[20]

Despite introducing the above texts in its *chapeau*, the Stockholm Declaration still referred to the need for economic growth: "[t]he environmental policies of all states should enhance and not adversely affect the present or future development potential of developing countries, nor should they hamper the attainment of better living conditions for all".[21] However, the process of redefining the concept of development by linking the 'necessity of environmental protection' with the 'necessity of development' gradually became widely recognized.[22] Eventually, in 1980, the concept became generally known and documented, and the World Conservation Strategy defined sustainable development as 'the modification of the biosphere and the application of human, financial, living, and non-living resources to satisfy human needs and improve the quality of human life'.[23] Though this definition of sustainable development was well defined, it failed to receive acceptance as a standard universal definition.

The most accepted definition of sustainable development can be found in the 1987 Report of the World Commission on Environment and Development (WCED)[24] (also known as the Brundtland Report) – 'Our Common Future'. The Brundtland Report defines sustainable development as the kind of development that 'meets the needs of the present without compromising the ability of future generations to meet their own needs'.[25] Though, this brief definition does not specifically include the words 'environment' and 'development', the obscurity is clarified by the following paragraphs of the Report. The Report not only provides a definition of the concept of sustainable development concept, it also provides an explanation of the concept.

Through the notion 'needs of the present', the first element of the definition admits that at present many of the world's populations are living below the poverty line and as such it is essential to meet their needs. This element is central in the analysis of the conditions for technology transfer from the developed countries to the developing and least developed countries. The word 'need' refers to the basic needs of food, water, housing, education and

20 *Chapeau* of Para 2 of the Stockholm Declaration 1972.
21 Principle 11 of the Stockholm Declaration 1972.
22 Christina Voigt, 2009, 13.
23 International Union for Conservation of Nature and Natural Resources (IUCN), *World Conservation Strategy: Living Resource Conservation for Sustainable Development*, IUCN, 1980, Chapter 1, Para 3.
24 'The World Commission on Environment and Development (WCED), also called the Brundtland Commission after its Chairman Gro Harlem Brundtland (a Norwegian physician), was an international commission that discussed and devised strategies for protecting the environment and promoting sustainable development.' See https://www.encyclopedia.com/environment/energy-government-and-defense-magazines/united-nations-world-commission-environment-and-development-wced-our-common-future-report-1987 (last accessed on August 30, 2020).
25 WCED, 1987, Chapter 2, Para 1.

health.[26] Thus, this element of sustainable development seeks to address the gap between financially rich and poor people/communities/nations and advocates for the necessity of 'economic growth' in the poor nations.[27] Phrased differently, the 'first element' of the definition of sustainable development refers to the need to achieve intra-generational equity by ensuring access to the resources that are needed to fulfil the basic conditions of human life of the present generation.[28] This scholastic study emphasizes the critical need of this element of sustainable development in developing and least developed countries. This is because the disparity in access to resources between rich and poor groups is increasing in most of these countries.[29] This increasing disparity has an enormously negative impact on the social sustainability of these countries.

However, the other element of the sustainable development definition of the Brundtland Report is related to 'inter-generational equity' which admits the necessity to meet the 'own needs' of future generations.[30] The phrase 'own needs' refers to the reality that the needs of future generations may be different from those of present generations, and it cannot presently be fully anticipated what the needs of future generations will be. Taking into account the latter meaning, it is the duty of the present generation not to deplete the environmental capital so imprudently that future generations do not have any choice in meeting their 'own needs'.[31] This aspect of sustainability actually requires that the environmental impact of the steps to be taken to ensure 'the needs of the present' does not result in the 'environmental capital' becoming exhausted in a manner that might result in failure to meet the needs of future generations. The Brundtland Report states:

> [w]e borrow environmental capital from future generations with no intention or prospect of repaying. They may damn us for our spendthrift ways, but they can never collect on our debt to them. We act as we do because we can get away with it: future generations do not vote; they have no political or financial power; they cannot challenge our decisions.[32]

As far as development issues are concerned, the Brundtland Report admits that 'human needs' are 'basic and essential'. The Report also admits that it is essential to ensure economic growth to fulfil human needs. In ensuring

26 Hans Christian Bugge, '1987–2007: "Our Common Future" Revised', in Hans Christian Bugge and Christina Voigt (eds.), 2008, 7.

27 It is stated that: 'A world in which poverty and inequity are endemic will always be prone to ecological and other crises. Sustainable development requires meeting the basic needs of all and extending to all the opportunity to satisfy their aspirations for a better life'. See WCED, 1987, 43–44.

28 For details about intra-generational equity see *infra* Chapter 2.6.

29 Brian Keeley, *Income Inequality: The Gap between Rich and Poor*, OECD Publishing, 2015, 11.

30 For details about inter-generational equity see *infra* Chapter 2.6.

31 Hans Christian Bugge in Hans Christian Bugge and Christina Voigt (eds.), 2008, 7.

32 WCED, 1987, Chapter 1, Para 25.

economic growth and fulfilling human needs, the Report states that the resources resulting from the economic growth should be distributed among poor people on the basis of 'equity' encouraged by the effective participation of the masses.[33] One could argue that the Brundtland Report requirement to achieve 'equity' has established a correlation between the international climate regime and sustainable development. This is because the principle of equity has been adopted as one of the main guiding principles of the UNFCCC.[34]

With regard to the impact of development on the environment, the Brundtland Report states that economic growth and development should be limited in order to protect and promote the environment: 'limitations imposed by the present state of technology and social organization on environmental resources and by the ability of the biosphere to absorb the effects of human activities – which should be related to environmental issues'.[35] One could say that the imposition of limitations is based on the fact that the unlimited development will create such an adverse impact on 'environmental resources', that they cannot be recovered by the natural ecosystem. Because of the failure of the natural ecosystem, the environmental and natural resources will be depleted soon and consequently future generations will be deprived of enjoying those resources to fulfil their 'own' needs.

However, for many years the two major challenges of the world – 'the necessity of development for the large portion of population of the world' and 'the environmental crisis threatening the survival of life on the planet' – were treated differently.[36] Bugge (2008) assumes that such different treatments were based on the impression that the first problem is only a problem of the poor nations and the second is only a matter of concern for the rich nations.[37] The Brundtland Report changed this way of thinking and for the first time bound these two concepts together by stating that 'the environment is where we all live and development is what we all do in attempting to improve our lot within that abode. The two are inseparable.'[38] Hence, by bundling 'environment' with 'development' the 1987 Brundtland Report came up with a goal on sustainable development to be attained by both developing and developed nations.[39]

33 Robert W. Kates et al., 'What is Sustainable Development? Goals, Indicators, Values, and Practices', *Environment, Science, and Policy for Sustainable Development,* Vol. 47(3), 8–21,2005, 11.

34 Cf. *infra* Chapter 2.6.2.

35 WCED, 1987, Chapter 1, Para 27.

36 Though the objective of the Stockholm Declaration was to combine these two discourses, more emphasis was given to the development agenda, see Principle 11 of Stockholm Declaration 1972. See also Christina Voigt, 2009, 13.

37 Hans Christian Bugge, in Hans Christian Bugge and Christina Voigt (eds.), *Sustainable Development in International and National Law: What Did the Brundtland Report Do to Legal Thinking and Legal Development, and Where Can We Go from Here?,* Europa Law Publishing, 2008, 5.

38 WCED, 1987, xi.

39 Hans Christian Bugge, in Hans Christian Bugge and Christina Voigt (eds.), 2008, 6.

By 1992 when the United Nations Conference on Environment and Development (UNCED)[40] was held in Rio de Janeiro (also known as the Earth Summit), the sustainability concept had already been recognized as an important goal of global policies through being adopted by some non-binding international documents.[41] The Parties at the UNCED added more value to the concept by laying down the foundations for the global institutionalization of sustainable development. The central focus of the Rio Declaration on Environment and Development (hereinafter referred to as Rio Declaration)[42] reflects the concept of sustainable development of the Brundtland Report. Principle 1 of the Rio Declaration denotes the purpose of sustainable development as ensuring the 'healthy and productive life' of human beings as well as ensuring 'harmony with nature'.[43]

However, in 2002, the discussions at the World Summit on Sustainable Development (WSSD)[44] brought a change in perception of sustainable development placing less emphasis on the environmental objective and more emphasis on the social and economic objectives. The 2002 World Summit integrated the Millennium Development Goals (MDGs) with sustainable development principles and practices.[45]

The realization of the UN Millennium Development Goals[46] was dependent on economic growth in various ways. Hence, one may argue that while the

40 'The United Nations Conference on Environment and Development (UNCED), also known as the "Earth Summit," was held at Rio de Janeiro, Brazil, from 3–14 June 1992. This global conference, held on the 20th anniversary of the first international Conference on the Human Environment, (Stockholm, 1972), brought together policy makers, diplomats, scientists, media personnel and non-governmental organization (NGO) representatives from 179 countries in a massive effort to reconcile the impact of human socio-economic activities on the environment and vice versa.' See https://www.unsystem.org/content/united-nations-conference-environment-and-development-unced-1992 (last accessed on August 22, 2020).

41 There are several other declarations that include sustainable development as one of the main guiding principles. Amongst them are the 1989 Declaration of the G7 Paris Summit, the 1989 Hague Declaration on the Environment, the 1990 Bergen Declaration of the UN Economic Commission for Europe and the 1990 Agreement establishing the European Bank for Reconstruction and Development (EBRD). See more in Christina Voigt, 2009, 17.

42 1992 Rio Declaration on Environment and Development.

43 Principle 1 of the Rio Declaration states: 'Human beings are at the centre of concern for sustainable development. They are entitled to a healthy and productive life in harmony with nature.'

44 UN General Assembly, World Summit on Sustainable Development: Resolution adopted by the General Assembly, 21 February 2003, A/RES/57/253, available at: https://www.refworld.org/docid/3f49ff934.html (last accessed on 12 August 2020)

45 John Drexhage and Deborah Murphy, *Sustainable Development: From Brundtland to Rio 2012,* UN, 2010, 8.

46 The UN Millennium Development Goals 2015 include: eradicating extreme poverty and hunger, achieving universal primary education, promoting gender equality and empowering women, reducing child mortality, improving mental health,

2002 World Summit on Sustainable Development integrates the sustainable development principles and practices with UN MDGs, the process of realization of the MDGs put an automatic emphasis on the 'social' and 'economic' pillars rather than the 'environmental' pillar of sustainable development.

However, the environmental objective regained its importance at the last UN Conference on Sustainable Development held in 2012 (popularly known as the Rio+20 Summit). At the Rio+20 Summit (and in pre-conference discussions) the developed nations (Annex I Parties to the UNFCCC) argued for a 'green economy roadmap' with environmental goals, targets and deadlines for meeting the targets. The developed countries group also supported new 'sustainable development goals' to attain environmental protection that would guarantee 'food and power to the poorest' nations and alleviate the poverty of poor nations.[47] In the document 'The Future We Want',[48] the Parties agreed on the importance of a future 'green economy' as an important tool for achieving sustainable development and eradicating poverty in the context of sustainable development. The notion of 'green economy' has been defined as a low carbon, resource efficient and socially inclusive economy that aims to improve 'human well-being and social equity, while significantly reducing environmental risks and ecological scarcities'.[49]

Though the Parties did not agree on any single global standard of 'green economy', they agreed on the substance of the concept as a path to attain global sustainable development. It was left to the Parties to lay down green economic policies taking into account their national circumstances, objectives and policies.[50] One could argue that the Parties' acknowledgement of a 'green economic' path as a tool to attain sustainable development is a sign of a shift in focus from a development objective (that includes social and economic development) towards an environment objective (that concerns protection of environmental degradation and promotion of environment) for sustainable development. If not, at least the concept of a green economy will ensure a more sensible international approach towards attaining sustainable development goals.

However, while in 2002 the World Summit integrated the MDGs with sustainable development principles and practices; by 2015 sustainable development

combating HIV/AIDS, malaria, and other diseases, ensuring environmental sustainability and developing a global partnership for development, etc.

47 J. Vidal, 'Rio+20: Earth Summit Dawns with Stormier Clouds than in 1992', *The Guardian*, June 19, 2012.

48 'The Future We Want' is a 49-page work paper that is the primary outcome of the United Nations Conference on Sustainable Development (UNCSD), 2012. See UN Doc. A/RES/66/288, available at https://undocs.org/A/RES/66/288 (last accessed on March 11, 2021).

49 United Nations Environment Programme (UNEP), available at www. unep.org/ greeneconomy /Default. aspx?tabid=29784 (last accessed on September 30, 2015).

50 M. Kettunen and P. T. Brink, 'Nature, Green Economy and Sustainable Development: The Outcomes of UN Rio+20 Conference on Sustainable Development', *Nature Conservation*, Vol. 2, 2012, 1–6.

had become the central character of the international development discourse. This is evident given that the UN decided to replace UN-MDGs with UN-SDGs (United Nations Sustainable Development Goals).[51]

2.3 Sustainable development and international laws on climate change

The international legal regime dealing with climate change and the international legal regime dealing with sustainable development have already admitted the close interrelationship between the discourses. At the 1992 Earth Summit the UNFCCC was signed as a legally binding treaty to govern climate change issues,[52] whereas the Rio Declaration and Agenda 21 were released as institutional frameworks of sustainable development. Since both kinds of instruments were released in parallel, one could argue that the concept of sustainable development has *de facto* been coupled with climate change issues since the birth of the UNFCCC.

However, to relate the sustainable development concept with the international legal regime for climate change – the UNFCCC, it was not easy to reach an agreement to recognize the 'right to promote sustainable development' as a principle of the Convention.[53] Since the Convention put the sustainable development concept under 'principle' clauses of the Convention, there were disagreements among different groups of Parties as to whether the principles of the Convention should be given legally binding status or not.[54]

Eventually, setting the disagreements aside, Art. 3, which contains the principles of the Convention, was finally placed under the operative part of the Convention. For this reason, sustainable development has now become one of the important guiding principles of the UNFCCC. In view of this, the concept should at least be considered to be a 'guiding policy' for all prospective actions derived from the UNFCCC regime.[55]

Later on, during the negotiation period of the Kyoto Protocol, Parties were able to reach 'sufficient consensus to recognize sustainable development as an

51 Secretary-General remarks to the 'Moving to Implementation: Findings from the UNDG Dialogues on post-2015 Implementation', New York, September 25, 2014.

52 *United Nations Conference on Environment and Development,* available at https://www.britannica.com/event/United-Nations-Conference-on-Environment-and-Development (last accessed on August 25, 2020).

53 Marie-Claire Cordonier-Seggerin in Hans Christian Bugge and Christina Voigt (eds.), 2008, 150. See also Art. 3(4) of the UNFCCC 1992.

54 Farhana Yamin and Joanne Depledge, *The International Climate Change Regime: A Guide to Rules, Institutions and Procedures,* Cambridge University Press, 2004, 67, cited in Christina Voigt, 2009, 62.

55 A principle 'expresses a general truth, which guidelines our action, serves as a theoretical basis for the various acts of life, and the application of which to reality produces a given consequence', see R. Dworkin, *Taking Rights Seriously*, Harvard University Press, 1977, 22–31.

object and purpose of the treaty'.[56] Consequently, sustainable development can be found as a guiding principle of instruments produced under the UNFCCC such as the Bali Action Plan, the Copenhagen Accord, the Cancun Agreement and the Durban Platform for Enhanced Action, etc.[57] The Paris Agreement has also acknowledged the same.[58]

Under the above circumstances, in addition to the application of the ordinary meaning of the text of the aforementioned legal instruments, interpretation of the texts should also be made in the light of the concept of sustainable development. This is because, Art. 31 of the Vienna Convention states, 'a treaty shall be interpreted in good faith in accordance with the ordinary meaning to be given to the terms of the treaty in their context and in the light of its object and purpose'.[59]

Though the specific notion of 'sustainable development' can only be found under the principle clause of the UNFCCC,[60] the Convention contains several similar notions such as 'sustainable economic growth and development',[61] 'sustainable management',[62] 'economic development to proceed in a sustainable manner'[63] and 'sustainable social and economic development'.[64]

Though it is mostly believed that the notion 'sustainable development' and the notion 'sustainable economic growth' do not imply any difference in meaning, a difference is perceptible if the wordings of Art. 3(4) and Art. 3(5) are examined closely. Art. 3(4) states that 'the Parties have a right to, and should, promote sustainable development'. Such a right of the Parties to promote sustainable development also needs to be in line with the principle of CBDR. This is because Art. 3(4) requires that the 'policies and measures to protect the climate system against human-induced change' should be 'appropriate for the specific conditions of each Party'.

Art. 3(4) further reflects the concept of sustainable development in the light of the principle of CBDR where it requires the Parties to take into account the necessity of economic development of the Parties at the time of integrating the 'policies and measures to protect the climate system against human-induced change' with their national development programmes. If these notions are read in conjunction with other texts of Art. 3(4), one may observe that the said flexibility is especially aimed at the non-Annex I Parties to the Convention.

56 Marie-Claire Cordonier Segger in Hans Christian Bugge and Christina Voigt (eds.), 2008, 150. See also Art. 2 of the Kyoto Protocol 1997.
57 Preamble to Decision 1/CP.13, Preamble to Decision 2/CP.15, Preamble to Decision 1/CP.16 and Preamble to Decision 1/CP.17.
58 Cf. Art. 2(1) of The Paris Agreement 2015.
59 Art. 31 of the Vienna Convention on the Law of Treaties 1961.
60 Art. 3(4) of the UNFCCC 1992.
61 Art. 3(5) of the UNFCCC 1992.
62 Art. 4(1)(d) of the UNFCCC 1992.
63 Art. 2 of the UNFCCC 1992.
64 Preamble to the UNFCCC 1992, Para 22.

This is also evident from the requirement to consider the 'specific conditions of each Party'.[65]

However, the right to promote sustainable development of the Parties to the Convention defined under Art. 3(4) of the Convention can be better understood if it is read in conjunction with Paragraph 8 of the Preamble to the Convention. Paragraph 8 of the Preamble to the Convention acknowledges the 'sovereign right' of the Parties 'to exploit their own resources pursuant to their own environmental and developmental policies'. The exploitation is also subject to the responsibility of the Parties 'to ensure that activities within their jurisdiction or control do not cause damage to the environment of other States or of areas beyond the limits of national jurisdiction'.[66]

Hence, the right of the Parties to promote sustainable development under the Convention first reflects the 'differentiated responsibility' part of the CBDR principle by requiring the Parties to consider the 'specific conditions of each Party' and to exploit the resources pursuant to their 'own environmental and developmental policies'.[67] Secondly, it reflects the 'common responsibility' part of the CBDR principle by requiring the Parties to protect the global climate by not causing 'damage to the environment of other States or of areas beyond the limits of national jurisdiction'.[68]

Thus, one could argue that the 'right' status of 'sustainable development' under the Convention has a different meaning from the ordinary meaning of the right to 'sustainable economic growth'. One could also argue that although each of the notions 'sustainable economic growth and development',[69] 'sustainable management',[70] 'economic development to proceed in a sustainable manner'[71] and 'sustainable social and economic development'[72] leads to a distinctive meaning, those meanings together ultimately lead to a broader concept of sustainable development.[73]

As far as promotion of sustainable development is concerned, an important implication of the UNFCCC is that it does not just confer 'rights' and 'duties' on the Parties to promote sustainable development, it also specifies the way in which greenhouse gases are to be stabilized in the atmosphere. Art. 2 of the UNFCCC specifies that the stabilization of greenhouse gases 'should be achieved in a time frame sufficient to allow the ecosystems to adapt naturally to climate change, to ensure that food production is not threatened and to enable economic development to proceed in a sustainable manner'.

65 Art. 3(4) of the UNFCCC 1992.
66 Preamble to the UNFCCC 1992, Para 8.
67 Cf. *infra* Chapter 2.6.
68 Preamble to the UNFCCC 1992, Para 8, See also Christina Voigt, 2009, 94.
69 Art. 3(5) of the UNFCCC 1992.
70 Art. 4(1)(d) of the UNFCCC 1992.
71 Art. 2 of the UNFCCC 1992.
72 Preamble to the UNFCCC 1992, Para 22.
73 Cf. Christina Voigt, 2009, 94.

Furthermore, Arts. 2, 10 and 12 of the Kyoto Protocol also directly refer to the concept of sustainable development. Art. 2 of the Kyoto Protocol gives a list of obligations on the Parties compliance with which will also promote sustainable development.

The *chapeau* of Art. 10 of the Kyoto Protocol requires the Parties to take into account the different national and regional 'development priorities, objectives, and circumstances' of other Parties at the time of complying with their commitments and obligations.[74] As different countries and regions have different national or regional development goals and policies, which are adopted on the basis of their own circumstances and necessities, the Parties to the Kyoto Protocol are required to consider those country-specific or region-specific development objectives when fulfilling their own objectives. In view of this, one can see that the substantive obligations derived from Art. 10 of the Protocol reflect the sustainable development objective of the Convention in the light of the principle of equity and CBDR. The *chapeau* of Art. 10 explicitly acknowledges that the purpose of 'continuing to advance the implementation' of the commitments of the Parties is 'to achieve sustainable development'.

Similarly, at the time of providing guidelines for the Annex I Parties, the *chapeau* of Art. 2(1) of the Kyoto Protocol states that the purpose of complying with those guidelines is to achieve 'quantified emission limitation and reduction commitments under Art.3' and 'to promote sustainable development'. In line with the aim of promotion of sustainable development, the target of the 'quantified emission limitation and reduction commitments under Art.3' needs to be accomplished on the basis of the principles of equity and CBDR. Since equity and the principle of CBDR are two important principles of sustainable development,[75] one could argue that the texts of Art. 2(1) of the Kyoto Protocol have twofold references to the promotion of sustainable development.

Though the term 'sustainable development' was not directly mentioned in the text of Art. 3(14) of the Kyoto Protocol, it urges the Annex I Parties to comply with their greenhouse gas emission reduction obligation in such a way that it minimizes 'adverse social, environmental and economic impacts on developing country Parties'. It especially requires the Parties to consider the special circumstances of the least developed countries, and other non-Annex I Parties that are enlisted under Arts. 4(8), and 4(9) of the UNFCCC. Arguably, the aforementioned reference to the 'adverse social, environmental, and economic impact' refers to the adverse impact on the sustainable development of these countries.[76]

74 Art. 10(c) of the UNFCCC 1992.

75 See *infra* Chapter 2.5.

76 Since the environment, economics and society are the three main pillars of sustainable development. See *supra* Chapter 1.2., see also *supra* in-text refs to Figure 1.1.

However, although the UNFCCC and the Kyoto Protocol refer to the notion of sustainable development in several places, from the viewpoint of practical application, climate change and sustainable development issues are actually dealt with by separate international legal instruments.[77] These two concepts first converge in Art. 12 of the Kyoto Protocol where it explicitly acknowledges sustainable development as one of the main objectives of the CDM.[78]

Art. 12 of the Kyoto Protocol does not indicate the process by which the CDM projects can help to attain sustainable development. In 2001, at the time of adoption of the Marrakesh Accords,[79] the Parties agreed on the rules and modalities to be followed by the CDM projects. The Preamble to the Marrakech Accords states: '[i]t is the host party's prerogative to confirm whether a clean development mechanism project activity assists in achieving sustainable development'.[80]

The CDM has not only established a link between climate change responsive measures and sustainable development, it has also established a link between the Annex I Parties and the non-Annex I Parties in climate change mitigation measures. Consequently, although the country in the case study used in this book – Bangladesh – is a non-Annex I Party to the Convention, it can take part in climate change mitigation by hosting CDM projects. Since Bangladesh is in need of huge economic growth, its participation in climate change mitigation activities by hosting CDM projects not only facilitates global climate change mitigation activities but also plays an important role in boosting much needed national economic growth and attaining local sustainable development.

Like the UNFCCC and the Kyoto Protocol, the Paris Agreement refers to sustainable development on several occasions. The preamble to the Agreement emphasizes 'the intrinsic relationship that climate change actions, responses and impacts have with equitable access to sustainable development and eradication of poverty'.[81]

While the aim of the Agreement is denoted as 'enhancing the implementation of the Convention, including its objective', it also includes strengthening 'the global response to the threat of climate change, in the context of sustainable development and efforts to eradicate poverty'.[82] This means the Agreement's provisions for responding to climate change not only require the Parties

77 The concept of sustainable development first came under policy framework through Agenda 21 (UNCED, 1992) and Rio Declaration 1992, whereas the UNFCCC (1992) is responsible for governing climate change issues.

78 Ibid, 530.

79 The Marrakesh (or Marrakech) Accords is the name of the agreements made at the Seventh Conference of the Parties (COP 7) at the UNFCCC held in October/November 2001 in Marrakesh, Morocco.

80 Decision 17/CP.7, FCCC/CP/2001/13/Add.2, 21 January 2002.

81 Preamble to the Paris Agreement 2015.

82 Art. 2(1) of the Paris Agreement 2015.

to consider the promotion of sustainable development but also to make an effort to eradicate poverty, which upholds observation of the principle of intra-generational equity.[83] Art. 4 of the Agreement reconfirms that Parties' actions 'in order to achieve the long-term temperature goal set out in Article 2' should necessarily be based on equity 'and in the context of sustainable development and efforts to eradicate poverty'.[84]

However, from the perspective of implementation, the Agreement considers sustainable development as the objective of the newly established 'voluntary cooperation' mechanism.[85] Art. 6(2) of the Agreement states that at the time of 'engaging on a voluntary basis in cooperative approaches that involve the use of internationally transferred mitigation outcomes towards nationally determined contributions' Parties shall 'promote sustainable development and ensure environmental integrity and transparency'.[86] Moreover, the Paris Agreement establishes a 'sustainable development mechanism', which aims 'to promote the mitigation of greenhouse gas emissions while fostering sustainable development'.[87] Besides, the Agreement's reference to non-market approaches to assist Parties 'in the implementation of their nationally determined contributions' also requires promotion of sustainable development.[88]

In addition to the above references to the concept of sustainable development, the Paris Agreement recognizes sustainable development as a goal of adaptation activities,[89] and recognizes 'the role of sustainable development in reducing the risk of loss and damage'.[90]

2.4 Sustainable development as a legal principle

Due to the diverse nature and scope of the interpretation of the concept, it is hard to find the legal relevance of sustainable development in the traditional sense of customary international law.[91] Instead, it is arguable that the best way of determining the status and legal relevance of the concept is to observe it in a non-traditional way. The non-traditional way could be by observing the role of the concept in 'soft-law' making policy documents,[92] in international

83 Cf. *infra* Chapter 2.6.
84 Art. 4(1) of the Paris Agreement 2015.
85 Art. 6(1) of the Paris Agreement 2015.
86 Art. 6(2) of the Paris Agreement 2015.
87 Art. 4(a) of the Paris Agreement 2015.
88 Arts. 6(8) and 6(9) of the Paris Agreement 2015.
89 Art. 7(1) of the Paris Agreement 2015.
90 Art. 8(1) of the Paris Agreement 2015.
91 Art. 38(1)(b) of the Statute of the International Court of Justice (adopted 26 June 1945, entered into force 24 October 1945) 33 UNTS 993 (ICJ Statute). See also D. Bodansky, 'Customary (and not so Customary) International Environmental Law', *Indiana Journal of Global Legal Studies*, Vol. 3, 1995, 105.
92 Art. 38(1)(c) of the ICJ Statute 1945, available at https://www.icj-cij.org/en/statute.

treaties,[93] in Decisions of the international courts and tribunals,[94] and in the views of different scholars in explaining the concept.[95]

The above discussion concerning the history of the development of the concept has already described how the concept of sustainable development has been addressed by global policy making 'soft laws' over the last four decades.[96] Direct or indirect inclusion and interpretation of the concept in the 1961 UNESCO Declaration, the 1962 UN General Assembly Resolutions, the 1972 Stockholm Declaration, the 1987 Brundtland Report, the 1992 Rio Summits, the 2002 Johannesburg Summit on Sustainable Development and the 2012 Rio+20 Summit appeared as 'soft law' in the form of declarations, guidelines and resolutions related to sustainable development. It has to be admitted that these 'soft laws' do not have direct legally binding force, but at the same time one could also argue that these 'soft laws' are not 'without legal relevance'.[97] The IPCC (2013) remarks, 'Through these global "soft-law"' policy-making processes, "sustainable development" has been brought to the forefront of international law in the context of integrating environmental and socio-economic interests''[98]

However, since the adoption of the most accepted modern definition of sustainable development given in the Brundtland Report (1987), the impact of the concept has gained a new dimension. The legal impact of the concept spread globally after being legally endorsed at the Rio Summit 1992.[99] In between the Rio Summit 1992 and the Rio Summit 2012, many international organizations were established to promote the idea of sustainable development. The United Nations established the Commission on Sustainable Development (CSD) and the United Nations Environment Programme (UNEP). Other institutions that have incorporated the concept in their policy, some with a legal basis in which the concept is mentioned include: the World Bank, the WTO, the GEF, the OECD, the Arctic Council, the World Water Forum and the African Union.[100]

Many states and even supra-national organizations, including the European Union (EU), have adopted 'sustainable development' either as an objective or a principle part of their legal framework. The European Council has also confirmed sustainable development as a 'fundamental objective' of the EU under the Lisbon Treaty.[101]

93 Art. 38(1)(a) of the ICJ Statute 1945, available at https://www.icj-cij.org/en/statute.
94 Art. 38(1)(d) of the ICJ Statute 1945, available at https://www.icj-cij.org/en/statute.
95 Onita Das, 2013, 48.
96 See *supra* Chapter 2.2.
97 Onita Das, 2013, 49.
98 Onita Das, 2013, 50.
99 See *supra* Chapter 2.2.
100 Christina Voigt, 2009, 19.
101 European Commission, 'Environment', available at http://ec.europa.eu/environment/eussd (last accessed on August 12, 2020).

The Association of Southeast Asian Nations (ASEAN) is one of the earliest international/regional cooperation treaties that referred to the concept of sustainable development. The 'fundamental principle clause' of the 1985 ASEAN Agreement on the Conservation of Nature and Natural Resources states its aim as:

> [t]o maintain essential ecological processes and life support systems, to preserve genetic diversity, and to ensure the sustainable utilization of harvested natural resources under their jurisdiction in accordance with scientific principles that and with a view *to attaining the goal of sustainable development.*[102]
>
> (Emphasis added)

The concept has also been codified in several conventions and legal instruments, such as: the UNFCCC (1992), the CBD (1992),[103] the Convention to Combat Desertification in those Countries Experiencing Serious Drought and/or Desertification, Particularly in Africa (Desertification Convention) (1994),[104] the Convention on the Prior Informed Consent Procedure Chemicals and Pesticides in International Trade (Rotterdam Convention) (1998),[105] the Convention on Access to Information, Public Participation in Decision-Making, and Access to Justice in Environmental Matters (Aarhus Convention) (1998),[106] the Cartagena Protocol on Bio-safety to the Convention on Biological Diversity (2000),[107] the Convention on Persistent Organic Pollutants (POPs) (2001),[108] the WHO Framework Convention on Tobacco Control (WHO FCTC) (2003),[109] the International Tropical Timber Agreement (2006) [110] and the Nagoya Protocol on Access to Genetic Resources and the Fair and Equitable Sharing of Benefits Arising from their Utilization to the Convention on Biological Diversity (Nagoya Protocol) (2010).[111]

The Rotterdam Convention, the Aarhus Convention, the Cartagena Protocol, the WHO FCTC, the International Tropical Timber Agreement and the Nagoya Protocol have acknowledged the necessity of promotion of sustainable development in Preambles to these documents. The Desertification Convention and the International Tropical Timber Agreement have also accepted sustainable development as part of their 'objective'.[112] The UNFCCC and the

102 Art. 1(1) of the ASEAN Agreement on the Conservation of Nature and Natural Resources, 1985.
103 Art. 8 of the CBD 1992.
104 Art. 9(1) of the Desertification Convention 1994.
105 Preamble to the Rotterdam Convention 1998.
106 Preamble to the Aarhus Convention 1998.
107 Preamble to the Cartagena Protocol 2000.
108 Art. 7(3) and Annex F(c) of the POPs 2001.
109 Art. 26 of the WHO FCTC 2003.
110 Preamble to the International Tropical Timber Agreement 2010.
111 Preamble to the Nagoya Protocol 2010.
112 Art.1 of the International Tropical Timber Agreement 2006; Art. 2 of the Desertification Convention 1994.

WHO FCTC have also accepted sustainable development as a principle of the conventions.[113]

However, in terms of legally binding force, comparatively more legal force of sustainable development is found in the CBD, the Desertification Convention and the POPs. The CBD and the Desertification Convention have included sustainable development as a legally binding obligation or commitment of the Parties.[114] The POPs included sustainable development under its implementation plan.[115]

Although the 'Preambles' or 'Objectives' of these legal documents do not have any direct legally binding effect, they do have 'certain legal implications'. French (2005) states, 'By including sustainable development as an objective, State Parties can seek to rely upon it to justify their actions or question the actions of others before parties or in formal adjudication'.[116]

With the codification of the concept of sustainability in constitutions and conventions, etc. the discussion concerning the legal status of the sustainable development concept has become part of the discussion among legal scholars. Several scholars have described the concept of sustainable development as a political or legal principle for states. Some have stated it as a 'general principle that states should ensure the development and use of their natural resources in a manner which is sustainable'.[117] However, it is still not clear whether 'sustainable development' has become a customary international law, or a general principle of international law, or if it is still a political goal guiding the implementation of the international agreements.

Concerning normative status, while some scholars consider the concept below the level of law,[118] others denote it as a 'pure aspiration'[119] or as a 'legitimate expectation'.[120] While some scholars are willing at best to confer sustainable development the status of 'soft law principles', a small but emerging number of scholars are agreed that the sustainable development concept has 'normative value'. Among those who agree on the 'normative value' status of sustainable development, some scholars did not agree to consider it as a 'customary' norm of international law: '(n)ormative uncertainty, coupled with the

113 Art. 3 of the UNFCCC 1992, and Art. 4 of the WHO FCTC 2003.

114 Art. 8 (e) of the CBD 1992; Arts.4, 9, 10, 17, and 18 of the Desertification Convention 1994.

115 Art. 7(3), and Annex F(c) of the POPs 2001.

116 D. French, *International Law and Policy of Sustainable Development,* Manchester University Press, 2005, 44, cited in Onita Das, 2013, 57.

117 Philippe Sands, *Principles of International Environmental Law,* 2nd ed., Cambridge University Press, 2003, 252–266.

118 P. Birnie et al., *International Law and the Environment*, 3rd ed., Oxford University Press, 2009, 81.

119 Christina Voigt, 2006, 219.

120 A. B. M. Christina Marong, 'From Rio to Johannesburg: Reflections on the Role of International Legal Norms in Sustainable Development', *Georgetown International Environmental Law Review,* XVI(1), 2003, 21–76, 45.

absence of justifiable standards for review strongly suggests that there is yet no international legal obligation that development must be sustainable'.[121]

However, in the *Case Concerning the Gabcikovo-Nagymaros Dam Project,* Judge Weeramantry, in his separate opinion, observed that sustainable development is evolving into a binding principle of customary law.[122] Although the judgment of the *Gabcikovo-Nagymaros* refers to the concept of sustainable development without denoting its legal status, in his separate opinion Vice-President Weeramantry states: "[t]he principle of sustainable development is thus a part of modern international law by reason not only of its inescapable logical necessity but also by reason of its wide and general acceptance by the global community". In line with the opinion of Judge Weeramantry, it has been observed that the Decisions of different national courts also recognized sustainable development as a principle of law. For instance, in the *Narmada River* case which concerns the construction of a dam on the Narmada River, the Supreme Court of India observes that 'when the effect of the project is known then the principle of sustainable development would come into play'. Hence, the Indian Supreme Court in its observation has explicitly acknowledged sustainable development as a principle.[123]

In the *Fuel Retailers* case, the South African Constitutional Court observes that the Constitution of South Africa recognizes the balance of socio-economic and environmental aspects 'through the ideal of sustainable development'.[124] The Court adds that the Constitution of South Africa also acknowledges the role of the judiciary 'in the context of the protection of environment and giving effect to sustainable development'.[125] Hence, one could argue that the Court's reference to sustainable development and the role of the judiciary in 'giving effect to sustainable development' as a constitutional requirement implies that the concept of sustainable development has been accepted as a 'legal principle' by the South African Constitutional Court.

However, the understanding of the legal characteristic of sustainable development in international law can be perceived by following two complementary approaches. First, sustainable development should be perceived as a real substantive area of law.[126] Second, sustainable development should be perceived as an individual type of norm having its own characteristic.[127] The first approach

121 Christina Voigt, *Sustainable Development as a Principle of Integration in International Law: Resolving conflicts between WTO Law and Climate Change Mitigation Measures,* Doctoral thesis, University of Oslo, 2006, 219.

122 Separate Opinion of Judge Weeramantry, see Philipe Sands, 2003, 254.

123 *Narmada Bachao Andolan v. Union of India,* AIR 2000, SC 3751, 32.

124 *Fuel Retailers Association of Southern Africa V. Director-General: Environmental Management, Department of Agriculture, Conservation and Environment, Mpumalanga Province, and Others,* 2007 (10) BCLR 1059 (CC) 24–40, 26, Para 45.

125 Ibid, 26, Para 102.

126 V. Lowe, 'Sustainable Development and Unsustainable Arguments', in A. Boyle and D. Freestone (eds.), *International Law and Sustainable Development: Past Achievements and Future Challenges,* Oxford University Press, 1999, 32.

127 V. Lowe, 'The Politics of Law-Making: Are the Method and Charter of Norm Creating Changing?' in M. Byers (ed.), *The Role of Law in International Politics:*

considers sustainable development to be a *corpus* of international law addressing the intersection among international laws concerning social, economic and environmental issues to come up with a lasting development.[128] The second approach admits the normative potential of sustainable development in promoting and arriving at a balance between the conflicting norms of different international law regimes concerning economic development, environmental protection and social justice. The second approach may be deemed to be based on the 'principle of reconciliation' or the 'principle of integration'.[129] The integration approach of sustainable development is shown in Figure 2.1.

The 'integration' approach or the 'principle of integration' in the context of sustainable development refers to considering the social, economic and environmental aspects (i.e. the three pillars of sustainable development) simultaneously at the time of taking any decision.[130] In considering these three basic elements simultaneously, the 'integration' approach suggests giving priority (in terms of both theory and practice) to the protection and promotion of the environmental resources (i.e. the natural life supporting system).[131]

Arguably inspired by the 'principle of integration' of sustainable development, the Rio Declaration explicitly states the need to integrate the environmental aspects in all development polices. Principle 4 of the Rio Declaration

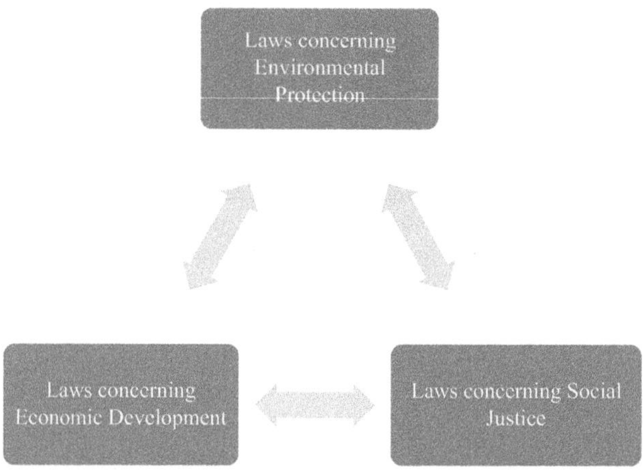

Figure 2.1 In the integration approach to the legal characteristics of sustainable development, higher priority is given to 'environmental protection' than to 'economic development' and 'social justice'

Essays in International Relations and International Law, Oxford University Press, 2000, 214–215.

128 M. C. Cordonier-Seggerand and A. Khalfan (eds.), *Sustainable Development Law: Principles, Practices, and Prospects,* Oxford University Press, 2004, 46.

129 Ibid.

130 See *supra* Chapter 1.2.

131 Christina Voigt, 2006, 220.

states: '[i]n order to achieve sustainable development, environmental protection shall constitute an integral part of the development process and cannot be considered in isolation from it'. Similarly, Agenda 21 establishes a set of actions concerning the social and economic dimensions of sustainable development. The set of actions include the process of conservation and management of natural resources, the role of the main actors and process of implementation.[132] The Preamble to Agenda 21 states:

> integration of environment and development concerns and greater attention to them will lead to the fulfilment of basic needs, improved living standards for all, better protected and managed ecosystems and a safer, more prosperous future. No nation can achieve this on its own; but together we can – in a global partnership for sustainable development.

The EU acknowledged its acceptance of the 'integration' approach by including the 'integration principle' in the Treaty on the Functioning of the European Union (the EU Treaty). Art. 11 of the EU Treaty states: '[e]nvironmental protection requirements must be integrated into the definition and implementation of the Union policies and activities, in particular with a view to promoting sustainable development'.[133]

Art. 174(1) of the Treaty Establishing the European Community includes the preservation of the environment, protecting human health, the rational utilization of natural resources and promoting regional and worldwide measures as essential elements for dealing with environmental problems. In line with the integration of the 'environment' with 'development', Art. 174 (3) of the Treaty Establishing the European Community confirms that the environmental policies of the EU shall take into account 'the economic and social development of the Community as a whole and the balanced development of its regions'.

Similarly, the 1981 African Charter on Human and Peoples' Rights states: '[a]ll peoples shall have the right to a general satisfactory environment favourable to their development'.[134] As in the case of the African Charter on Human and Peoples' Rights, Chapter 24 of the Constitution of South Africa states: '[e] veryone has the right to an environment that is not harmful to their health or well-being; and to have the environment protected, for the benefit of present and future generations …'.

However, specific reference to environmental protection or the promotion of sustainable development has also been observed in the constitutions of:

132 J. Drexhage and D. Murphy, *Sustainable Development: From Brundtland to Rio 2012,* UN, 2010, 8.

133 European Union, *Consolidated version of the Treaty on the Functioning of the European Union,* October 26, 2012, OJ L. 326/47–326/390; Art. 11, available at: https://www.refworld.org/docid/52303e8d4.html (last accessed on September 3, 2020).

134 Art. 24 of the African Charter on Human and Peoples' Rights, 1981.

Argentina,[135] Brazil,[136] the Czech Republic,[137] Finland,[138] France,[139] Germany,[140] Greece,[141] Hungary,[142] Italy,[143] the Netherlands,[144], Latvia,[145] Lithuania,[146] Poland,[147] Portugal,[148] Slovakia,[149] Slovenia,[150] Spain,[151] Sweden,[152] Switzerland[153] and Uruguay.[154]

The need to integrate the environment with development has also been urged in several judgments of the ICJ. In *Gabcikovo-Nagymaros,* the ICJ refers to the necessity of integration when addressing sustainable development as follows: '[the] need to reconcile development with protection of the environment is aptly expressed in the concept of sustainable development'.[155]

In reconciling 'development' with 'protection of the environment', the ICJ states that the Parties of the case 'should look afresh at the effects of the environment'.[156] Such a statement by the ICJ arguably implies that at the time of integrating or reconciling development goals with environmental protection goals, it is the environmental protection goal that should be considered first.

Further, in the *Pulp Mills* case, the ICJ reaffirms the necessity of reconciling or integrating environmental protection goals with development goals as:

> [t]he present case highlights the importance of the need to ensure environmental protection of shared natural resources while allowing for sustainable economic development; whereas it is particularly necessary to bear in mind the relevance of the Parties on the quality of the water of the River Uruguay for their livelihood and economic development: whereas from this point of view account must be taken of the need to safeguard the

135 Art. 41(1) of the Constitution of Argentina.
136 Art. 225(1) of the Constitution of Brazil.
137 Art. 7 of the Constitution of Czech Republic.
138 Art. 20 of the Constitution of Finland.
139 Art. 6 of the Charter for the Environment of France.
140 Art 20(a) of the Constitution of Germany.
141 Art. 24(1) of the Constitution of Greece.
142 Art. XXI of the Fundamental Law of Hungary.
143 Art. 9 of the Constitution of Italy.
144 Art. 21 of the Constitution of Netherlands.
145 Art. 115 of the Constitution of Latvia.
146 Art. 54(1) of the Constitution of Lithuania.
147 Art. 74(1) of the Constitution of Poland.
148 Art. 66(1) and Art. 66(2) of the Constitution of Portugal.
149 Art. 44(2) and Art.44(4) of the Constitution of Slovakia.
150 Art. 72 of the Constitution of Slovenia.
151 Art. 45(2) of the Constitution of Spain.
152 Chapter 1, Art. 2 of the Constitution of Sweden.
153 Art. 73 of the Constitution of Switzerland.
154 Art. 47 of the Constitution of Uruguay.
155 *Case Concerning Gabcikovo-Nagymaros Dam Project (Hungary/Slovakia)* Summary of the Judgment of 25 September 1997, available at https://www.icj-cij.org/files/case-related/92/7377.pdf (last accessed on July 30, 2020).
156 Ibid.

> continued conservation of the river environment and the rights of economic development of the riparian States.[157]

Connecting the 'integration' approach with the normative force of the sustainable development principle, in her Doctoral thesis Christina Voigt observes that sustainable development has a 'normative pull', which is employed through the 'integrative' characteristic of the concept. Such normative force is expected to be applied in the integration of various norms, which are essentially required to ensure a balanced function of 'essential natural processes.[158] Arguing in favour of the 'normative force' of sustainable development, Voigt also remarks that the principle of sustainable development has already received the status of *opinion juris communis* or universal public opinion.[159]

However, translating the understandings and application of the concept of sustainable development into legal text and legal argumentation is a challenge. Due to the diverse and vast nature of the concept, Voigt (2006) argues that it is more rational to consider sustainable development as a 'principle' rather than as a 'rule' or 'set of rules'.[160]

The 'rule' of law is different from the 'principle' of law in terms of the scope of legal consequences and application.[161] The 'rule' or 'set of rules' of law refers to specific duties and obligations. The 'principle' of law refers to a 'legal proposal' providing an overall 'orientation and direction' to come up with a positive law.[162] Since a 'principle' is a 'flexible instrument of action', it can be 'adapted and manipulated to suit the specific situations to which [it is] being applied'.[163] Thus, in specifying the legal nature of sustainable development, one can observe that the concept of sustainable development is more likely to be a 'principle' ('soft law') than a 'rule' due to its flexible scope of explanation and guiding characteristic.

Since the concept of sustainable development still has huge scope for development, the process of development is expected to include both 'horizontal' and 'vertical' approaches. Under the 'horizontal' approach – in the technology transfer agreements between different countries – the application of the principle should be integrated and balanced taking into account the arena of laws (in this case international environmental laws concerning climate change) related to the basic elements of sustainable development. Such a horizontal integration approach will prevent the exclusivity of any arena of the law and

157 *Case Concerning Pulp Mills on the River Uruguay (Argentina vs. Uruguay)* (Request for Indication of Provisional Measures, Order of 13 July 2006), ICJ Report 1, 19, Para 80.
158 Ibid, 170.
159 Christina Voigt, 2006, 240.
160 Ibid, 222.
161 Ibid. For standard definition of legal rule see H. L. A. Hart, *The Concept of Law,* Clarendon Press, 1961, 8–12, 27–32, 97.
162 Christina Voigt, 2006, 222.
163 Ibid, 223.

prevent any sort of bias. Of course, horizontal integration approaches must also consider the basic or fundamental ideas behind the sustainable development concept, where equity is one of these fundamental ideas.

The 'vertical' integration approach is expected to enhance the specificity of the principle. For instance, the vertical integration of the sustainable development principle in the climate change law regime starts with the UNFCCC[164] and the specificity of the principle is transmitted to the subsequent legal documents[165] and continues down to the implementation of mitigation obligations in the EU (e.g. by use of the CDM agreements with the developing country Parties to the Convention). Such a top-down approach of incorporation of the principle of sustainable development can gradually translate the broader sense of 'principle' status of law in to specific 'rule' status of law.[166]

Legitimacy of a 'principle' of law can be tested through its application in national, international and regional legal systems (e.g. the EU's legal system). For sustainable development, it is not just one of the two first-mentioned legal systems, but a combination of both systems that should be considered as the basis of normative force.[167]

As discussed above, the concept of sustainable development has already been adopted as a general principle in many national and international organizations. Art. 3(3) of the Treaty Establishing the European Community (EC) states: '[t]he Union shall establish an internal market, and it shall work for the sustainable development of Europe based on balanced growth.

The strongest criticism of the 'legal principle' status of sustainable development is related to its indeterminacy and uncertainty as a result of its wide-ranging scope, though such 'indeterminacy' does not necessarily invalidate the 'principle' of law status of the concept. According to Hart (1961), 'a penumbra of uncertainty' should be treated as a characteristic of the general principle of law.[168] Based on Hart's argument, one could argue that the substantive 'indeterminacy' resulting from the wide scope of explanations of sustainable development is an essential 'characteristic' which helps the concept become a 'general principle of law'.

However, even though debate exists amongst scholars about the current legal status of sustainable development, the above-mentioned discussions imply that there is no barrier to adopting the concept as a 'legal principle' or including it in legal texts. In this regard, Lowe (1997) remarks:

> [d]ecision-makers need not wait on state practice and *opinion juris* to develop the concept of sustainable development in the way that a primary

164 Art. 2 and Art. 3(3) of the UNFCCC 1992.
165 Kyoto Protocol and Decisions of the COP.
166 Christina Voigt, 2006, 224.
167 Ibid, 236 ff.
168 H. L. A. Hart, 1961, 8–12, 27–32, 97.

> rule of international law would be developed. They may take the initiative and develop the concept themselves.[169]

The Permanent Court of Arbitration made a similar kind of recommendation. In 2005 in the *Iron Rhine* case, the Permanent Court observed as follows:

> [t]here is considerable debate as to what, within the field of environmental law, constitutes "rules" or "principles"; what is "soft law"; and which environmental treaty law or principles have contributed to the development of customary international law. Without entering further into those controversies, the Tribunal notes that in these entire categories environment is broadly referred to as including air, water, land, flora and fauna, natural ecosystems and sites, human health and safety, and climate. *The emerging principles, whatever their current status, make reference to conservation, management, notions of prevention and of sustainable development, and protection of future generations.*[170]
>
> (Emphasis added)

Hence, whether it is admitted as a legal principle or not, one can conclude that 'environmentally sustainable development is now part of the lexicon of international law'.[171]

2.5 Sustainable development and the principles of international law

The principles of international laws related to sustainable development are still 'emergent principles of law'.[172] Under the international legal framework, the need to develop proper international law on sustainable development was mentioned under Principle 27 of the Rio Declaration and Chapter 39 of Agenda 21. This has resulted in different initiatives. In 2002 the International Law Association (ILA)[173] through its 'Declaration of Principles of International Law' came up with several suggestive principles for sustainable development. The principles suggested by the ILA also include two principles of special

169 V. Lowe, in A. Boyle and D. Freestone (eds.), 1999, 37.

170 *Iron Rhine Arbitration (Belgium vs. Netherlands),* Award, ICGJ 373 (PCA 2005), 24th May 2005, Permanent Court of Arbitration [PCA], 28.

171 Richard L. Revesz et al., *Environmental Law, the Economy and Sustainable Development: The United States, the European Union and the International Community,* Cambridge University Press, 2008, 408.

172 Onita Das, 2013, 58.

173 'The International Law Association was founded in Brussels in 1873. Its objectives, under its Constitution, are "the study, clarification and development of international law, both public and private, and the furtherance of international understanding and respect for international law". The ILA has consultative status, as an international non-governmental organisation, with a number of the United Nations specialized agencies.' See https://www.ila-hq.org/index.php/about-us/aboutus2 (last accessed on August 25, 2020).

relevance for transfer of technology between the developed countries (Annex I Parties to the Convention) and the developing/least developed countries (non-Annex I Parties to the Convention) under the UNFCCC:[174] the principle of equity and eradication of poverty, and the principle of CBDR.

Marcrory (2006) also identifies the principle of CBDR,[175] and the principles of equity (both intra-generational equity, and inter-generational equity) along with the principle of integration, and the duty to co-operate over environmental development and the protection of the environment as principles of international law concerning sustainable development.[176]

Sands (2003) considers the principles of both intra-generational and inter-generational equity as principles of sustainable development. Four essential principles of international law that Sands (2003) considers to be principles of sustainable development are: the principle of inter-generational equity, the principle of equitable use or intra-generational equity, the principle of sustainable use and the principle of integration.[177]

2.6 The principle of equity

The principle of equity is derived from the concept of social justice. The concept of social justice refers to:

> a belief that there are some things which people should have, that there are basic needs that should be fulfilled, that burdens and rewards should not be spread too divergently across the community, and that policy should be directed with impartiality, fairness and justice towards these ends.[178]

Though not exactly synonymous with the term 'equality', the principle of equity refers to 'a need of fairness in the distribution of gains and losses, and the entitlement of everyone to an acceptable quality and standard of living'.[179] In other words, the principle of equity refers to the concept of 'fairness and justice'.[180]

174 It is noteworthy that the ILA is not an international organization comprised of sovereign states. It is an association of researchers and academic experts.
175 See also *infra* Chapter 2.6. and 2.7.
176 Richard Macrory, *Reflections on 30 Years of EU Environmental Law: A High Level of Protection,* Europa Law Publishing, 2006, 20–22.
177 Philippe Sands, 2003, 231. Regarding principle of inter and intra-generational equity see *infra* Chapter 2.6.
178 J. Falk, *Social Equity and the Urban Environment, Report to the Commonwealth Environment Protection Agency,* Commonwealth Environment Protection Authority, 1993, 2.
179 Sharon Beder, 'Costing the Earth: Equity, Sustainable Development and Environmental Economics', *New Zealand Journal of Environmental Law,* Vol. 4, 2000, 229.
180 Antoinette Heidering, *International Law, Sustainable Development and Water Management,* Eburon Publishers, 2004, 89.

Since the principle of equity is an ethical as well as a social concept that concerns society, the principle is aimed at ensuring fairness in both decision-making processes and the implementation of those decisions.[181] In this manner, it ensures a wide-ranging legitimacy and acceptance of decisions. Accordingly, the principle of equity arguably inspires Parties of international treaties and agreements to realize the mutually agreed decisions.[182] Hence, the basic fairness of equity refers to both procedural and consequential equity.[183]

An effective method of realizing equity is to strengthen and facilitate pluralisms and promote the participation of the disadvantaged group of people in the decision-making process. The determiner of the 'disadvantaged group of people' can be gender, ethnicity, religion or income, etc.[184]

The principle of equity in the discourse of sustainable development has two dimensions: the 'intra-generational equity' and the 'inter-generational equity'.[185] Intra-generational equity is concerned with equity between people of the same generation. This is separate from inter-generational equity, which is about equity between present and future generations. The implementation of intra and inter-generational equity is important to promote the social sustainability element of sustainable development. The role of intra-generational equity is important in addressing and solving the inequalities between countries, regions and social groups of the same generation. At the same time implementation of inter-generational equity is essential to address the inequalities between countries, regions and social groups of present and future generations.[186]

Inter-generational equity means 'the rights of future generations to enjoy a fair level of the common patrimony'.[187] Agius (1998) refers to inter-generational equity as the 'principle of ordering of the community of mankind, which will make it possible for every generation, by virtue of its own effort and responsibility, to secure a proportionate share in the common good of the human species'.[188] The relevance of inter-generational equity to this academic study lies in the role of modern technologies in resource protection. Such modern technologies include: technologies used for utilizing waste as a source of energy, technologies used for recycling products and, particularly, renewable energy technologies such as wind energy technologies, solar energy technologies, etc.

181 The three dimensions of sustainable development are the social, economic and environmental dimensions, see *supra* Chapter 1.2.
182 Christof Schwarte, and Emily Massawa, *Equity Issues in the Climate Change Negotiations,* European Capacity Building Initiative (ECBI) Policy Report, August 2009, 1.
183 Ramon Pichs et al. (eds), *Development, Sustainability, and Equity*, IPCC and WMO, 2000, 13.
184 Ibid, 14.
185 *Supra* Chapter 2.2.
186 Ramon Pichs et al. (eds.), 2000, 43.
187 ILA Resolution 3/2002, in ILA *Report of the Seventieth Conference*, 2002, Principle 2.
188 E. Agius, 'Obligations of Justice Towards Future Generations: A Revolution on Social and Legal Thought', in E. Agius and S. Busuttil (eds.), *Future Generations and International Law*, Routledge, 1998, 10.

However, the other element of the principle of equity – intra-generational equity – means 'the rights of all peoples within the current generation of fair access to the current generation's entitlement to the Earth's natural resources'.[189] It is closely related to the eradication of poverty, which is another pre-requirement of ensuring environmental protection. The 1987 Brundtland Report denotes poverty as 'a major cause and effect of global environmental problems'. The Report further states: 'It is therefore fruitless to attempt to deal with environmental problems without a broader perspective that encompasses the factors underlying world poverty and international inequality'.[190] This statement of the Brundtland Report is comparable with the scenario of least developed countries. Since these countries suffer from chronic poverty, the measures for the protection of their environment seem to be a 'luxury' that is pointless if parallel steps are not simultaneously taken to eradicate their mass poverty.

Consequently, as far as this book is concerned, the purpose of which is to deal with the issues of promoting technology transfer and sustainable development in developing and least developed countries, the principle of intra-generational equity has more relevance than inter-generational equity. This is because intra-generational equity along with the alleviation of poverty is one of the key features of economic policies that facilitate overall human welfare,[191] and technology transfer is a method of realizing intra-generational equity simultaneously with of the principle of CBDR.[192]

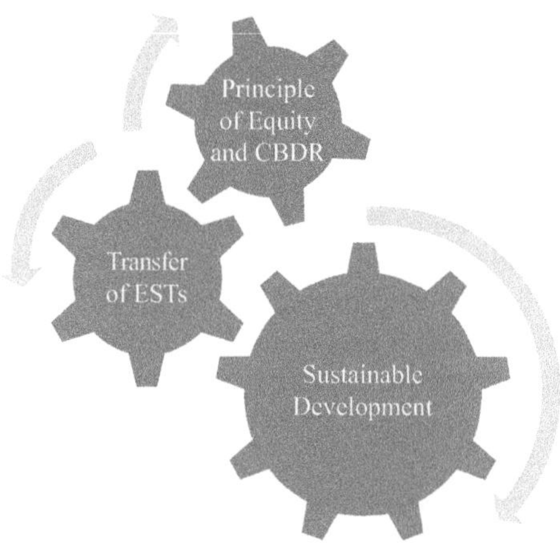

Figure 2.2 Relationship between principle of equity and CBDR, transfer of environmentally sound technologies (ESTs) and promotion of sustainable development

189 Principle 2 of the ILA Resolution 3/2002.
190 WCED, 1987, chapter 1, Para 8.
191 See generally Amartya Sen, *Poverty and Famines: An Essay on Entitlement and Deprivation*, Oxford University Press, 1981; see also Amartya Sen, *Resources, Values and Development*, Harvard University Press, 1984.
192 See *infra* Chapter 2.7.2.

Intra-generational equity requires the elimination of asymmetric socio-economic conditions of access to resources. This is because the asymmetric opportunity of access to resources causes poverty, and poverty may in turn facilitate unsound environmental degradation. The 1987 Brundtland Report addresses the problem as follows:

> [t]hose who are poor and hungry will often destroy their immediate environment in order to survive: They will cut down forests; their livestock will overgraze grasslands; they will overuse marginal land; and in growing numbers they will crowd into congested cities. The cumulative effect of these changes is so far-reaching as to make poverty itself a major global scourge.[193]

However, it is not only poverty that may have a negative impact on the environment. Sometimes access to excess wealth can arguably worsen the impact on the environment and climate system. Since abundance of wealth may lead to more consumption which may in turn lead to more waste, it can result in an increased average 'carbon footprint'.[194] Accordingly, the access to excess wealth may create a negative footprint on the environment and global climate system. Beder (2000) observes that global temperature increases and chemical contamination are caused not by poverty, but rather by an affluence of resources.[195]

Based on the above arguments, one may find that it is important to ensure implementation of the intra-generational equity principle in order to bring a balance between poverty and affluence of resources for the sake of attaining global sustainable development.[196] In this manner, intra-generational equity can play a role in facilitating 'social sustainability'.[197] Since economic and social disparity between rich and poor people is one of the issues that need to be addressed in developing and least developed countries, implementation of the principle of intra-generational equity at a national level is of vital importance.[198]

Another important aspect of intra-generational equity is the need to eliminate the inequalities in decision-making processes in relation to environmental impact or environmental policies.[199] Inequalities in power distribution affect the ability of the people to influence decisions, which may affect their own environment.[200] Failure to include any particular group/groups of people in a

193 WCED, 1987, 72.

194 For more about carbon footprint, see http://timeforchange.org/what-is-a-carbon-footprint-definition (last accessed on July 30, 2020).

195 Cf. Sharon Beder, 2000, 230.

196 J. Hepburn and A. Khalfan, *The Principle of Equity and the Eradication of Poverty*, Draft Working Paper, CISDL, March 2005, 5.

197 Cf. *supra* Chapter 1.2.

198 Ramon Pichs et al. (eds.), 2000, 14.

199 Sharon Beder, 2000, 230.

200 Ibid.

community (e.g. on the basis of gender or ethnicity) in the decision-making process on issues that may affect the local environment or local sustainability also prevents the realization of the intra-generational aspect of the principle of equity.[201]

2.6.1 Equity as an international and national norm

The first mark of international recognition of the principle of equity was found in the 1948 Universal Declaration of Human Rights (UDHR).[202] The Preamble to the UDHR states: 'recognition of the inherent dignity and of the equal and inalienable rights of all members of the human family is the foundation of freedom, justice and peace in the world'.[203] This statement expresses the principle of equity in the sense of the equality of each human being to enjoy inherent dignity and inalienable fundamental rights.

Subsequently, after being endorsed by the 1987 Brundtland Report, the principle of equity was included in many sustainable development strategies and policies. The 1992 Rio Earth Summit reaffirmed the central nature of the principle of equity in its policy documents (e.g. Agenda 21 and the Rio Declaration).[204]

The principle of equity as a general principle of international law was accepted as an important part of international sea law.[205] It was included as an important principle of international water law in the sense of 'equitable and reasonable utilization'.[206] In the *Continental Shelf* case (Libya vs. Tunisia) the equity was denoted as a legal concept, which 'is a direct emanation of the idea of justice'.[207] Furthermore, in the *Libya /Malta* case the ICJ remarked:

> [t]hus the Justice of which equity is an emanation, is not an abstract justice but justice according to the rule of law; which is to say that its application

201 Cf. Robert Bullard, 'The Politics of Race and Pollution: An Interview with Robert Bullard', *Multinational Monitor*, June, 1992, 21–25; cf. Valerie A. Brown and Margaret A. Switzer, *Engendering the Debate: A Discussion Paper for Consideration by the ESD Working Groups*, Office of the Status of Women, Canberra, June 1991.

202 UN General Assembly, Universal Declaration of Human Rights, 10 December 1948, 217 A (III), available at https://www.refworld.org/docid/3ae6b3712c.html (last accessed on August 31, 2020).

203 A principle 'expresses a general truth, which guidelines our action, serves as a theoretical basis for the various acts of life, and the application of which to reality produces a given consequence', see R. Dworkin, *Taking Rights Seriously*, Harvard University Press, 1977, 22–31.

204 Preamble to and Principle 3 of the Rio Declaration 1992; see also Chapter 3 of Agenda 21.

205 Arts. 79, 74 and 83 of the United Nations Convention on the Law of the Sea, Dec. 10, 1982, 1833 U.N.T.S. 397.

206 Antoinetter Heidering, *International Law, Sustainable Development and Water Management*, Edburon Publishers, 2004, 89.

207 *Continental Shelf* case, ICJ Reports 1982, 18, 60, cited in Antoinetter Heidering, 2004, 89.

> should display consistency and a degree of predictability; even though it looks with particularity to the peculiar circumstances of an instant case, it also looks beyond it to principles of more general application.[208]

Hence, one can observe that equity in the sense of equitable utilization has already become a known general principle of international law.[209] However, the normative role of inter and intra-generational equity in international law is still emerging.

Though it does not mention the term inter-generational equity, the Brundtland Report refers to the inter-generational approach of equity when it mentions the 'ability of future generations to meet its own needs' as part of the definition of sustainable development. A similar implication about the inter-generational aspect has been found in the 1972 Stockholm Declaration, as it specified man's responsibility to protect the environment and Earth's natural resources.[210]

The 1992 Rio Declaration explicitly refers to inter-generational equity by referring to the right to development that should be fulfilled in order to 'equitably meet developmental and environmental needs of present and future generations'.[211] The same approach can also be found in the 1993 Vienna Declaration on Human Rights.[212] The UNFCCC adopts the approach by requiring its Parties to 'protect the climate system for the benefit of present and future generations of humankind'.[213]

The intra-generational equity approach was adopted by Agenda 21 by addressing the disparity between rich and poor, and giving priority to the fulfilment of the needs of the poor as an important element of sustainable development and the Brundtland Commission Report followed its example.[214] Boyale and Freestone (2001) argue that the policies adopted by the Ozone Convention, the CBD and the UNFCCC prohibiting irreversible harm to environmental and natural resources are also instances of reflection on the principle of inter-generational equity in international law.[215] According to Boyale and Freestone (2001), the Fisheries Conservation treaties requiring cooperation in the management of stocks and ecosystems for the purpose of maintaining sustainable productivity, the prohibitions on dumping radioactive

208 *Case Concerning the Continental Shelf (Libyan Arab Jmahiriya vs. Malta),* The ICJ Judgment of 3 June 1985, Para 45.

209 Alan E. Boyle and David Freestone (eds.), *International Law and Sustainable Development: Past Achievements and Future Challenges*, Oxford University Press, 2001, 15.

210 Ibid, 13; Principles 1 and 2 of the Stockholm Declaration 1972. See also 1968 African Convention on the Conservation of Nature and Natural Resources, 1001, UNTS 4.

211 Principle 3 of the Rio Declaration 1992.

212 Vienna Declaration and Programme of Action, adopted by the World Conference on Human Rights in Vienna on 25 June 1993, Part I, Para 11.

213 Art. 3(1) of the UNFCCC 1992.

214 Chapter 3 of Agenda 21.

215 Alan E. Boyle and David Freestone (eds.), 2001, 13.

waste at sea, the expansion of a comprehensive regime of ecosystem protection for Antarctica, denoting the Antarctica as a World Park, and the expanded control on whaling through the Whaling Commissions are also instances of a concern for the well-being of future generations.[216]

Despite a delimitation in defining its scope, the inter-generational dimension of the principle of equity has received wider recognition and it is considered an 'integral feature' of several legal instruments dealing with the concept of sustainable development. As Judge Weeramnatry has already suggested by conferring the status of customary international law on the principle of inter-generational equity, now only a wider scale of judicial and political support can turn the suggestion into reality.[217]

At the national level, a Philippine Supreme Court Decision of 1993 considered both the 'intra' and 'inter'-generational aspects of equity. The case was about the state management of public forestland.[218] The petitioners of the case wanted to stop timber felling by government licensed authorities on the basis that the continuous felling of timber was a violation of their constitutional right to enjoy a healthy environment, and it would cause irreparable harm to the present and future generations in the Philippines. The Supreme Court considered the case from the perspective of inter-generational equity and decided that the petitioners had *locas standi* to sue on behalf of present and future generations. Considering the inter-generational aspect of equity, the court also decided in favour of the petitioners and interrupted timber felling in order to ensure that the forest would be preserved and would maintain a healthy environment for the present and future generations.

In a comparable proceeding before the Supreme Court of Bangladesh, the precedent of the Supreme Court of Philippines was not considered.[219] However, the Bangladesh Constitution has recently adopted the concept of protection of future generations as one of the fundamental principles of the state.[220]

The inclusion of 'present and future generations' in the South African Constitution,[221] and 'present and future citizens' in the Bangladesh Constitution are arguably implications of reference to the sustainable development definition of the 1987 Brundtland Report. These notions also imply a requirement to promote intra and inter-generational equity. The need to protect both present and future generations has also been found in the Constitutions of the Czech Republic, Estonia, Poland, Switzerland (federal constitution) and Ukraine.[222]

216 Ibid.
217 J. Hepburn and A. Khaflan, 2005, 20.
218 *Minors Oposa v. Secretary of the Department of Environmental and Natural Resources,* Supreme Court of the Philippines, 33 ILM 173,1994, the full judgment is available at www.elaw.org/node/1343 (last accessed on September 30, 2015).
219 *Farooque vs. Government of Bangladesh,* 1997, 49 DLR, (AD) 1.
220 Art. 18(A) of the Constitution of Bangladesh.
221 Chapter 24 of the Constitution of South Africa.
222 Preambles to the Constitutions of the Czech Republic, Estonia, Poland, Switzerland (federal constitution) and Ukraine.

At the regional level the African Convention on Conservation of Nature and Natural Resources is known as one of the earliest treaties that refer to the inter-generational equity approach.[223]

Although it has been acknowledged by several national and international legal documents, the normative status of the principle of inter-generational equity in international law is still emerging. The normative role of the principle of intra-generational equity is found mainly in the Rio instruments and their subsequent legal regimes.[224] Despite the fact that Weiss (1989) argued that inter-generational equity had already become a part of international law,[225] Heidering (2004) agreed to confer the inter-generational equity *de lege ferneda* status. However, Heidering (2004) was sceptical whether inter-generational equity had emerged as a general principle of international law.[226]

While the Rio Declaration does not mention the term intra-generational equity, it refers to the underlying meaning of the intra-generational equity in different substantive provisions. Referring to the underlying spirit of the principle of intra-generational equity, the Rio Declaration states:

> [a]ll people shall cooperate in the essential task of eradicating poverty as an indispensable requirement for sustainable development, in order to decrease the disparities in standards of living and better meet the needs of the majority of the people of the world.[227]

Moreover, Boyale and Freestone (2001) also argued that the reference to the 'special needs of developing countries' of the Rio Declaration was an implicit reference to intra-generational equity.[228]

The Convention on Biological Diversity observed the principle of the intra-generational equity in a more explicit manner. The Convention's establishment of the framework for a 'fair and equitable' share of developing countries' benefits generated from the utilization of genetic resources taken from their territories is a bold example of the realization of the principle of intra-generational equity in international environmental law.[229]

In several cases, the ICJ established the principle of equity's (in the sense of intra-generational equity) role in eradicating poverty. In the *Continental Shelf* case (Libya vs. Tunisia), the ICJ viewed poverty as a 'virtually extraneous'

223 Preamble to the African Convention on the Conservation of Nature and Natural Resources 1968.
224 Alan E. Boyle and David Freestone (eds.), 2001, 15.
225 Brown-Weiss, *In Fairness to Future Generations,* Dobbs Ferry, 1989, cited in Boyale and Freestone (eds), 2001, 13.
226 Antoinetter Heidering, 2004, 92.
227 Principle 5 of the Rio Declaration 1992.
228 Principles 6 and 11 of the Rio Declaration 1992; see also Boyale and Freestone (eds.), 2001, 15.
229 Art. 15(7) of the Convention on Biological Diversity.

factor, despite its opinion in favour of upholding an 'equitable result' (i.e. equitable delimitation):

> [t]he Court is, however, of the view that *these economic considerations cannot be taken into account for the delimitation of the continental shelf areas appertaining to each Party*. They are virtually extraneous factors since they are variables .... As to the presence of oil-wells in an area to be delimited, it may, depending on the facts, be an element to be taken into account in the process of weighing al1 relevant factors to achieve an equitable result.[230]
>
> (Emphasis added)

In *Maritime Delimitation and Territorial Questions Between Qatar and Bahrain (Qatar vs. Bahrain),*[231] a dissenting opinion of three judges of the ICJ was in favour of considering poverty as a relevant issue in finding more equitable solutions of international disputes.[232]

In the *Case Concerning the Barcelona Traction, Light and Power Company Limited (Second Phase) (Belgium vs. Spain),*[233] Judge Ammoun upheld the principle of eradication of poverty and intra-generational equity by stating that 'an equitable sharing of the profits is mandatory'. Judge Ammoun also suggested that these principles should guide the development of international law and dispute settlement decisions, as follows:

> [t]he development of international law cannot therefore have as its sole or principal object the protection of foreign nationals and of the international economic activities of the industrialized Powers. It must set itself an objective which is more comprehensive and more just, *and a more equitable and more humanitarian ideal, in which the material and intangible interests of the weaker and deprived peoples are factors to be taken into account.*[234]
>
> (Emphasis added)

One could argue that the suggestion of Judge Ammoun to follow the principle of intra-generational equity in the process of development of international law has accelerated the normative status of the principle in the regime of international law.

2.6.2 Equity under the global climate regime

Art. 3(1) of the UNFCCC that sets out the principle of the Convention refers to the principle of equity by requiring the Parties to protect 'the climate system

230 *Case Concerning the Continental Shelf (Libya vs. Tunisia)*, 1982, ICJ Report 18.
231 *Maritime Delimitation and Territorial Questions Between Qatar and Bahrain (Qatar vs. Bahrain),* 2001, I.C.J. Rep. 40.
232 Joint Dissenting Opinions of Judges Bedjaoui, Ranjeva and Koroma, ibid, 212–14.
233 *Case Concerning the Barcelona Traction, Light and Power Company Limited (Belgium vs. Spain)*, Second Phase, 1970, I.C.J. Rep. 3, Separate Opinion of Judge Ammoun, 290.
234 Ibid.

for the benefit of present and future generations of humankind, *on the basis of equity* and in accordance with their common but differentiated responsibilities and respective capabilities' (emphasis added). This reference to the principle of equity includes both the 'intra-generational equity' and 'inter-generational equity' elements of the sustainable development concept. Since Art. 3(1) of the Convention requires the Parties to take into account the 'climate system for the benefit of the present generation', it arguably refers to the need to realize 'intra-generational' equity.[235] 'Intra-generational' equity also leads to the eradication of poverty and equal distribution of resources between communities or people of the present generation.[236]

In obliging the Parties to protect the climate system for the benefit of the future generation, Art. 3 (1) arguably refers to 'inter-generational equity'.[237] One could argue that the texts of Art. 3(1) echoed the main spirit of the sustainable development definition of the 1987 Brundtland Report by securing 'intra-generational equity' without causing any harm to 'inter-generational equity'.[238]

However, by referring to the protection of the climate system, Art. 3(1) has also arguably considered other equity related principles of international law. These principles are: the principle of CBDR, the precautionary principle, the right to promote sustainable development, the need to consider the special circumstances of the Parties, and a pledge to promote a 'supportive and open international economic system'.[239]

The principle of equity and the relevant principles under the UNFCCC refer to the rights of the developing and least developed countries (the non-Annex I Parties to the Convention) to ensure their development through receiving support from the developed countries (the Annex II Parties to the Convention) on the basis of their acknowledgement of responsibilities for global environmental degradation and 'the technology and financial resources they command'.[240]

Art. 3(1) of the Convention required the Annex I Parties to 'take the lead in combating climate change and the adverse effects thereof'. Art. 4 laid down the differentiated commitments of the Parties to implement the principle of equity within the international climate change regime. In order to 'take the lead in combating climate change', Art. 4(2) of the Convention requires 'equitable and appropriate contributions' of the countries (the Annex I Parties). One could

235 Cf. *supra* Chapter 2.6.
236 Ibid.
237 Ibid.
238 Cf. *supra* Chapter 2.2. and Chapter 2.6.
239 Art. 3(1) –Art. 3(5) of the UNFCCC 1992. For more about the principle of common but differentiated responsibilities and respective capabilities, see also *infra* Chapter 2.7.
240 Christoph Schwarte and Emily Massawa, *Equity Issues in the Climate Change Negotiations,* European Capacity Building Initiative (ECBI) Policy Report, August 2009, 1; see also Principle 7 of the Rio Declaration 1992.

argue that the requirement of 'equitable and appropriate contributions' from the Annex I Parties to take a 'leading role' to combat climate change is a clear indication of the implementation of the 'equity' principle among the Annex I Parties to Convention.

In addition, the UNFCCC also requires the application of the principle of equity in its financial mechanism, while Art. 11(2) of the Convention states: 'the financial mechanism shall have an equitable and balanced representation of all Parties within a transparent system of governance'.

In addition to the aforementioned direct references to the principle of equity, the issue of eradication of poverty, which is closely connected to the principle of 'intra-generational equity', has also been recognized by the UNFCCC.[241] Art. 4(7) of the Convention states 'that economic and social development and poverty eradication are the first and overriding priorities of the developing country Parties'.

Though the Kyoto Protocol does not explicitly refer to the principle of equity, or eradication of poverty, the Protocol acknowledges the guiding role of the principle of equity by acknowledging the guiding role of Art. 3 of the Convention.[242]

The principle of equity in the Paris Agreement reflects the need to continue the 'burden sharing approach', as it was enumerated in the Convention.[243] During negotiation sessions although Parties agreed to continue to include this principle, disagreement took place over 'the practical implications of this on the obligation of parties'.[244] This is mainly because some countries that had been categorized as 'developing countries' under the Convention had become 'major economies' as well as 'significant emitters' at the time of adoption of the Paris Agreement.

Hence, two major concerns surrounded the debate. First, the capacity of some countries had increased, and this being the case their responsibilities under the regime should therefore also be increased. Secondly, many developing countries' contribution to global emissions had increased and, this being the case, their emission level should therefore be brought under emission reduction obligations.[245]

Taking all these factors into account while the Preamble to the Agreement accepts the Convention's guiding principles including the equity and CBDR principles, it adds a qualifier in Art. 2(2) – 'in the light of different national circumstances'.[246] The qualifier , 'in the light of different national circumstances', refers to a scenario that confers a 'dynamic approach' to the principle

241 Cf. *supra* Chapter 2.6.
242 Preamble to the Kyoto Protocol 1997.
243 E. O. Babatunde, 'In the Light of Different National Circumstances: Equity under the Paris Agreement', *Cambridge Law Review*, Vol. IV(II), 2019, 105–137, 130.
244 Ibid., 131.
245 Ibid., 131.
246 Preamble to the Paris Agreement 2015.

of equity especially in terms of the implementation of diverse commitments made under the Agreement.[247]

However, as with the reference to the Convention, the Paris Agreement's reference to the principle of equity is associated with the Parties' aim of attaining sustainable development. Art. 4 enumerates that Parties' action 'to achieve the long-term temperature goal' should necessarily be 'on the basis of equity, and in the context of sustainable development and efforts to eradicate poverty'.[248] Besides, the Preamble to the Agreement acknowledges that 'when taking action to address climate change' Parties should 'respect, promote and consider their respective obligations on "intergenerational equity", which is an essential element of attaining sustainable development.[249]

It is important to note that reference to the principle of equity is also found in the Paris Agreement's provision regarding 'global stock take'. According to Art. 14, the Conference of the Parties, serving as the meeting of the Parties to this Agreement, needs to assess Parties' implementation activities in the light of equity and the best available science.[250]

2.7 The principle of CBDR

Rooted in the idea of the 'common heritage of mankind', the principle of CBDR is a manifestation of the general principle of equity in international law.[251] It is made up of two fundamental elements: 1) common responsibilities; and 2) differentiated responsibilities.[252]

Taking into account 'the integral and interdependent nature of the Earth, our home',[253] the 'common responsibility' element of the principle of CBDR refers to the common responsibility of the nation states of the Earth for the protection of the whole environment or any part of it in a global, regional or local level.[254] Due to the fact that the global ecological system is interdependent, environmental problems are widely accepted as a global problem and the steps to protect environmental degradation are considered to be a

247 Sandrine Maljean-Dubois, 'The Paris Agreement: A New Step in the Gradual Evolution of Differential Treatment in the Climate Regime?', Review of European, Comparative & International Environmental Law, Vol. 25(2), 2016, 153, cited in E. O. Babatunde, 2019, 131.

248 Art. 4(1) of the Paris Agreement 2015.

249 Preamble to the Paris Agreement 2015.

250 Art. 14 of the Paris Agreement 2015.

251 Marie-Claire Cordonier Segger et al., 'Prospects for Principles of International Sustainable Development Law after the WSSD: Common but Differentiated Responsibilities, Precaution and Participation', Review of European Community & International Environmental Law, Vol. 12(1), 2003, 56; see also Philippe Sands, 2003, 285.

252 Philippe Sands et al., *Principles of International Environmental Law,* Vol. I, Manchester University Press, 1994, 217–218.

253 Preamble to the Rio Declaration 1992.

254 Marie-Claire Cordonier Segger et al., 2003, 56.

'common concern of human kind'.[255] For this reason, environmental degradation is not a mere domestic issue but an issue that requires global partnership.[256]

Thus, the concept of common responsibility through its obligation of international cooperation requires states to share equally the burden of environmental protection to uphold the 'common human concern'. By stating its aim – to set 'common principles to inspire and guide the peoples of the world in the preservation and enhancement of the human environment' – the Stockholm Declaration is accepted to be the first international document that implicitly admitted the 'common responsibility' of nation states to preserve the human environment.[257]

However, in the broader arena of international laws the example of 'common responsibility' was first observed in 1949. In its Preamble the 1949 Convention for the Establishment of an Inter-American Tropical Tuna Commission ascribed tuna and other sea fishes as 'of common concern' to those states that are continuously dependent on the consumption of those fishes.[258] Since then, the 'common responsibility' concept has taken its place in several international treaties and agreements on different subjects such as natural and cultural heritage (referred to as 'part of the world heritage of mankind as a whole'),[259] outer space and the moon (referred to as the 'province of all mankind'),[260] climate change (referred to as 'a common concern of human kind'),[261] biodiversity (referred to as 'a common concern of humankind')[262] and the conservation of wild animals (referred to as 'for the good of mankind'),[263] etc. The 'common responsibility' element of the principle of CBDR is relevant to this book in the context of climate change, because it focuses on

255 Report of the Expert Group Meeting on Identification of Principle of International Law for Sustainable Development, Department for Policy Coordination and Sustainable Development, Geneva, Switzerland, September 26–28, 1995, Paras 82–83; see also Philippe Sands, 'International Law in the Field of Sustainable Development', *British Yearbook of International Law*, Vol. 65, 1994, 343–344.

256 Ibid.

257 Preamble to the Stockholm Declaration, 1972, see e.g. A. C. Trinidade and D. J. Attard, 'The Implication of the "Common Concern of Mankind" Concept' in Toru Iwama (ed.), *Policies and Laws on Global Warming: International and Comparative Analysis*, Environmental Research Centre, 1991, 7 ff.; Kemal Baslar, *The Concept of the Common Heritage of Mankind in International Law*, Martinus Nijhoff Publishers, 1998,107.

258 Preamble to the Convention for the Establishment of an Inter-American Tropical Tuna Commission, 1949.

259 Preamble to the Convention Concerning Protection of World Cultural Property and Natural Heritage, 1972.

260 Art. 1 of the Treaty on Principles Governing the Activities of States in the Exploration and Use of Outer Space, Including the Moon and Other Celestial Bodies, 1966.

261 Art. 4(1) of the UNFCCC 1992.

262 Preamble to the CBD 1992.

263 Preamble to the Convention on the Conservation of Migratory Species of Wild Animals 1979.

the transfer of those technologies that are essential to combat the adverse effects of climate change and/or prevent greenhouse gas emissions in the atmosphere.

Though the aforementioned references to 'common responsibility' made by various international legal documents have different meanings and applications, which vary depending on the nature of the treaty and environmental resource, all those notions explicitly or implicitly refer to the idea of 'commonality'.[264]

The idea of 'differentiated responsibilities' is derived from two contexts – the 'differing contributions of states' to any specific matter and the 'different capacities of states to take remedial measures' to rectify that specific matter.[265] It has been aimed to promote substantive equality rather than formal equality between developing and developed communities within a particular regime.[266]

However, the concept of differentiation of responsibilities is not new in the arena of international law. The 1972 London Convention was the first international convention to require its member states to 'take effective measures individually, according to their scientific, technical and economic capabilities, and collectively'.[267] Art. 11(3) of the 1976 Barcelona Convention stated that one of the 'priorities' of the Parties should be to give particular attention 'to the special needs of developing countries in the Mediterranean region'. The Preamble to the 1982 United Nations Convention on the Law of the Sea (UNCLOS) also addressed the 'special interests and needs' of developing countries. In its Preamble the 1985 Vienna Convention for the Protection of the Ozone Layer requires the Parties to take into account 'the circumstances and particular requirements of developing countries',[268] as does Art. 4(4) of the Convention.

Like the 1985 Vienna Convention, in its Preamble the 1987 Montreal Protocol on Substances that Deplete the Ozone Layer acknowledged that 'special provision is required to meet the needs of developing countries'. The Protocol included an article that especially concerns the 'special situation of developing countries'.[269]

264 Philippe Sands, 2003, 287.

265 Cf. 'The notion of differentiated responsibilities derived from both the differing contributions of states to climate change and different capacities of states to take remedial measures', cited in Lavanya Rajamani, 'Principle of Common but Differentiated Responsibilities and the Balance of Commitments under the Climate Regime', *Review of European Community & International Environmental Law,* Vol. 9 (2), 2002, 121.

266 CISDL, 'The Principle of Common but Differentiated Responsibilities: Origins and Scope for the World Summit on Sustainable Development' (for the World Summit on Sustainable Development 2002), a CISDL Legal Brief, available at http://cisdl.org/public/docs/news/brief_common.pdf (last accessed on September 30, 2015).

267 Art. II of the London Convention on the Prevention of Marine Pollution by Dumping of Wastes and Other Matter (London Convention) 1972.

268 Preamble to the Vienna Convention for the Protection of the Ozone Layer 1985, Para 3.

269 Preamble and Art. 5 of the Montreal Protocol on Substances that Deplete the Ozone Layer 1987.

The differentiation between developing countries is specified in the UNFCCC by recognizing the 'specific needs and special circumstances of developing country Parties, especially those that are particularly vulnerable to the adverse effects of climate change'.[270] These statements of the UNFCCC are of particular importance to small island and least developed countries that are in need of specific technologies and suffer from special circumstances as a result of the adverse effects of climate change.

However, the CBDR principle – a juxtaposition of 'common responsibilities', and 'differentiated responsibilities' – involves two practical elements – participation and implementation followed by adoption. The first element requires all Parties of any international environmental treaty to participate in international response measures, which address the environmental issues. The second element requires all Parties to adopt and implement the different commitments set by the international agreement. This adoption and implementation must be subject to the individual situation of the Parties, the individual circumstances and capacities of the Parties, the historical contribution of the parties to a problem and the future development needs of the parties.[271] Since the adoption and implementation of the commitments are subject to the individual circumstances and capabilities of the concerned Party – the principle is also known as principle of common but differentiated responsibility and respective capabilities (CBDR-RC).

2.7.1 Development of the principle of CBDR

The common but differentiated responsibilities approach was implicitly first found in the 1972 Stockholm Declaration. Principle 23 of the Stockholm Declaration refers to the need to consider 'the extent of the applicability of standards which are valid for the most advanced countries but which may be inappropriate and of unwarranted social cost for the developing countries'.[272] Principle 11 of the Declaration refers to the approach more clearly by stating that 'the environmental policies of all States should enhance and not adversely affect the present or future development potential of developing countries, nor should they hamper the attainment of better living conditions for all'.[273]

The common but differentiated responsibilities approach was further echoed in the 1992 Rio Declaration. Principle 6 of the Declaration states:

> [t]he special situation and needs of developing countries, particularly the least developed and those most environmentally vulnerable, shall be given

270 Art. 3(2) of the UNFCCC 1992.

271 Tuula Kolari, 'The Principle of Common but Differentiated Responsibilities as Contributing to Sustainable Development through Multilateral Environmental Agreements' in Hans Christian Bugge and Christina Voigt (eds.), 2008, 252.

272 Principle 23 of the Stockholm Declaration 1972.

273 Principle 11 of the Stockholm Declaration 1972.

special priority. International actions in the field of environment and development should also address the interests and needs of all countries.

The text of Principle 6 implies that in addressing the 'common responsibility' of the need for international action in the field of the environment and development, states are required to observe their 'differentiated responsibility' by focusing on the 'special situation and needs' of developing countries. Principle 11 of the Rio Declaration supports the requirements of Principle 6:

> [e]nvironmental standards, management objectives and priorities should reflect the environmental and developmental context to which they apply. Standards applied by some countries may be inappropriate and of unwarranted economic and social cost to other countries, in particular developing countries.

The requirements of Principle 11 implicitly refer to the principle of CBDR by acknowledging the need to apply different standards taking into account the different socio-economic conditions of the countries. While the texts of Principles 6 and 11 imply the spirit of the differentiated responsibilities of the Parties, they do not provide a clear reference to CBDR. The first explicit mention of CBDR in international law can be found under Principle 7 of the Rio Declaration:

> [i]n view of the different contributions to global environmental degradation, States have common but differentiated responsibilities. The developed countries acknowledge the responsibility that they bear in the international pursuit of sustainable development in view of the pressures their societies place on the global environment and of the technologies and financial resources they command.

In line with the spirit of the principle of CBDR, while Principle 6 of the Rio Declaration acknowledges the special need of least developed countries and most climate change vulnerable countries, Principle 11 of the Rio Declaration reconfirms it by stating: 'environmental standards, management objectives and priorities should reflect the environmental and developmental context to which they apply'.

One could argue that Principle 6 of the Rio Declaration confers a positive obligation on its Parties on the basis of the spirit of the principle of CBDR by stating that the 'international actions in the field of environment and development should also address the interests and needs of all countries'. Principle 11 of the Rio Declaration makes it clear why the international actions should 'address the interests and needs of all countries', as it states that the 'standards applied by some countries may be inappropriate and of unwarranted economic and social cost to other countries, in particular developing countries'. The above-stated reasoning of Principle 11 is clearly also an echo of Principle 23 of the

Stockholm Declaration. Principle 23 of the Stockholm Declaration makes it clear that 'the extent of the applicability of standards which are valid for the most advanced countries' may be 'inappropriate and of unwarranted social cost for the developing countries'.[274] A practical example of this is that the environmental standard applicable and manageable in Norway or Finland may not be appropriate as an environmental standard in Brazil or Argentina. Similarly, the environmental standard applicable and manageable in Brazil or Argentina may not be a suitable environmental standard in Ecuador or Chad. Therefore, it is understandable that an environmental standard suitable or applicable for an Annex I Party developed country to the Convention is not applicable as an environmental standard for non-Annex I Party least developed countries like Bangladesh.

However, by observing the notions of Principle 6 together with the notions of Principle 11 of the Rio Declaration, one could argue that the differentiated commitments of the states under the Rio Declaration are made on the basis of the 'respective capabilities' of the states. The argument of 'respective capabilities' as the basis for the differentiated commitments seems to be associated with the 'historical contribution', as Principle 7 of the Rio Declaration explicitly acknowledges common but differentiated responsibilities of the states 'in view of the different contributions to global environmental degradation'.[275] The idea of 'different contributions' of Principle 7 clearly indicates that the 'common but differentiated responsibilities' of the states under the Rio Declaration is mainly premised on the 'historical contribution' of the states in causing environmental degradation.

It is relevant to mention here that given the wide range of state practices, although CBDR has been receiving increased normative status in international law, it has yet to receive a legally obligatory status in all countries that are Parties to the Convention.[276]

2.7.2 Realization of the principle of CBDR

The principle of CBDR is mainly realized through the redistribution of resources as a result of allocating different obligations to the participating parties of any treaty or agreement.[277] The effective methods for realizing the redistribution of resources are: 1) financial assistance, and 2) transfer of technology,[278] which are also directly or indirectly linked with the realization of 'intra-generational equity' and of the global sustainable development goals.[279] With

274 Principle 23 of the Stockholm Declaration 1972.

275 Principle 7 of the Rio Declaration 1992.

276 Vito De Lucia, 'Environmental Law & Policy: Common but Differentiated Responsibility', *The Encyclopedia of Earth*, 2012.

277 Tuula Kolari, in Hans Christian Bugge and Christina Voigt (eds.), 2008, 252.

278 See *infra* Chapter 3.2. and Chapter 3.3.

279 Tuula Kolari in Hans Christian Bugge and Christina Voigt (eds.), 2008, 253, see also in-text refs to Figure 2.3.

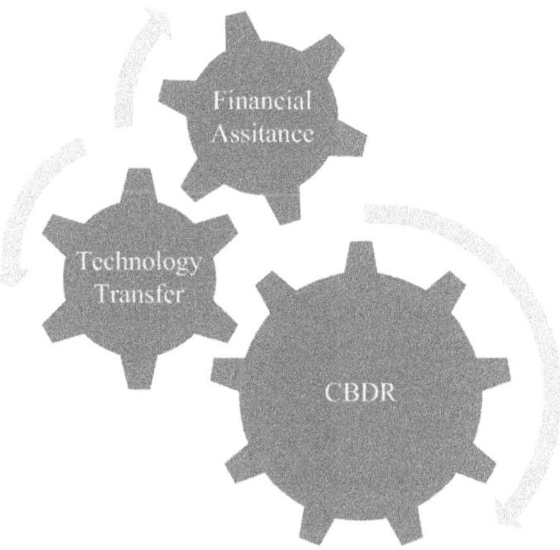

Figure 2.3 Realization of CBDR through financial assistance and technology transfer

regard to international cooperation, the idea of differentiation of the CBDR principle suggests dissimilar obligations for states (based on their capabilities). Hence, through the redistribution of resources, in implementing their own obligations derived from the international environmental agreements, developing and least developed countries are entitled to receive assistance from developed countries.[280]

Among the international environmental instruments, the Stockholm Declaration is the parental international legal instrument that introduced the concepts of transferring environmentally sound technologies and financial aid from developed countries to developing and least developed countries. Principle 9 of the Stockholm Declaration states:

> [e]nvironmental deficiencies generated by the conditions of under-development and natural disasters pose grave problems and can best be remedied by accelerated development *through the transfer of substantial quantities of financial and technological assistance* as a supplement to the domestic effort of the developing countries and such timely assistance as may be required.[281]
>
> (Emphasis added)

Such an assertion in the Stockholm Declaration was also a consequence of the Founex Report.[282] In June 1971 the Founex Report published its opinion that

280 Ibid, 252.
281 Principle 9 of the Stockholm Declaration 1972.
282 The Founex Report was prepared by a panel of experts meeting in Founex, Switzerland in June 1971. It argues for the integration of environment and development strategies. The report stipulates that while concern about the environment sprang from the production and consumption styles of the industrialized world, many of the environmental problems in the world are derived from underdevelopment and poverty. This acknowledgement worked as an influencing factor in persuading

the issues concerning environmental disaster should not merely be considered as development issues. They should be addressed with commitment of flows of international financial aid from developed countries to developing and least developed countries.[283]

However, the direct implication of the realization of the principle of CBDR is found in Principle 12 of the Stockholm Declaration:

> [r]esources should be made available to preserve and improve the environment, taking into account the circumstances and particular requirements of developing countries and any costs which may emanate from their incorporating environmental safeguards into their development planning and the need for making available to them, upon their request, additional international technical and financial assistance for this purpose.

To comply with the 'common responsibility' of taking 'environmental safeguards' developing countries must cooperate with financial and technical assistance. The text of Principle 12 presses for the realization of the principle of CBDR by directly referring to the need for the redistribution of resources for the purpose of giving financial and technical assistance to developing countries. Principle 12 particularly reflects the spirit of the principle of CBDR while it recommends 'taking into account the circumstances and particular requirements of developing countries'.

However, in line with the realization of the principle of CBDR, the introduction of an international financial mechanism was first marked in the 1987 Montreal Protocol. The mechanism was subsequently amended in 1990.[284] In the course of the following decades the issue of integrating a financial mechanism was further developed in various international agreements: the UNFCCC (1992), the CBD (1992) – including subsequent instruments of these Conventions – the Drought and Desertification Convention (1994), the Kyoto Protocol (1997), the Bio-safety Protocol (2000) and the Paris Agreement (2015), etc.

Chapter 33 of Agenda 21, entitled 'Financial Resources and Mechanisms' refers to the need for financing mechanisms to achieve the goals of Agenda 21 and global consensus in integrating environmental issues with development objectives.[285] Generally, the key sources of international financing include bilateral overseas development, funds from multilateral development banks and specialized environmental funds.[286]

many developing countries to attend the 1972 Stockholm Conference. See A. M. Ozorio, *Environment and Development: The Founex Report on Development and Environment,* Carnegie Endowment for International Peace, 1972.

283 Ibid, 4, 8.

284 Art. 10 of the Montreal Protocol on Substances that Deplete the Ozone Layer, 1987.

285 Philippe Sands, 2003, 1021.

286 Philippe Sands, 2003, 1022.

However, as mentioned above, apart from financial assistance, another way of realizing the principle of CBDR through the redistribution of resources is technology transfer.[287] Despite the fact that the inventions of modern science and technology brought about the industrial revolution which has been the major cause of environmental degradation through greenhouse gas emissions in the atmosphere, it is only through the innovations of science and technology the human environment can be preserved and protected from environmental degradation. In this regard, Principle 18 of the Stockholm Declaration states:

> [s]cience and technology, as part of their contribution to economic and social development, must be applied to the identification, avoidance and control of environmental risks and the solution of environmental problems and for the common good of mankind.

Acknowledging the role of science and technology in social and economic development, Principle 18 of the Stockholm Declaration has arguably laid an extra responsibility on the shoulders of science and technology in the form of 'the identification, avoidance and control of environmental risks and the solution of environmental problems'.[288] It means prioritizing environmental responsibility over social and economic advancement, the Stockholm Declaration has given technology the role of achieving sustainable development.

The need for 'the identification, avoidance and control of environmental risks and the solution of environmental problems'[289] is of more importance than social and economic advancement in the context of climate change. Since climate change has diverse adverse effects and the nature of the effects depends on the geographical location, science and technology have a vital role to play in identifying the nature of the problem based on the geographical location concerned. At the same time, it is science and technology that will have to come up with a proposed solution to the negative effects of climate change. For instance, the negative effects of climate change in coastal areas are different from those posed by climate change in a desert area. Accordingly, the nature of the technological solution required for a coastal area is different from that needed for a desert area. It has been predicted that the southern part of Bangladesh which is adjacent to the Bay of Bengal will be inundated with water due to sea level rises and the adjacent areas will suffer from salt water intrusion, but the northern part of Bangladesh is predicted to suffer from more drought and irregular rainfall. Consequently, the role of science and technology is vital in identifying the distinctive pattern of the environmental problems that might hit the northern and southern parts of the country. Science and technology have a further vital role to play in inventing technologies to resolve the identified diverse environmental problems.

287 Tuula Kolari, in Hans Christian Bugge and Christina Voigt (eds.), 2008, 253.
288 Principle 18 of the Stockholm Declaration 1972.
289 Ibid.

However, in the course of drafting the Declaration, the preparatory committee rephrased Chile's proposal to consider science and technology as the 'common property of mankind'[290] as the 'common good of mankind'. One could argue that the inclusion of the phrase 'common good of mankind' is intended to prevent any kind of 'misuse' of science and technology and to promote the use of science and technology for the betterment of mankind. In other words, the Declaration specifies that science and technology should not be employed 'to serve some parochial interest of a nation or an industry but only the interests of the mankind as a whole'.[291]

Though Principle 18 refers to the need for science and technology to address environmental concerns, it does not directly refer to 'the need for international cooperation in the application of modern science and technology and its transfer to developing countries'.[292] The issues concerning distribution of resources in terms of financial and technical aid were more clearly stated under Principle 12 of the Stockholm Declaration. Principle 12 presses for the 'free flow' of scientific information from developed to developing countries, but does not recommend the 'transfer of experiences' for free. Instead, the 'transfer of experiences' is required to 'be supported and assisted' by developed countries coming up with a solution to environmental problems.[293]

Furthermore, Principle 20 of the Stockholm Declaration explicitly addresses the need for technology transfer as follows:

> [s]cientific research and development in the context of environmental problems, both national and multinational, *must be promoted in all countries, especially the developing countries.* In this connection, *the free flow of up-to-date scientific information and transfer of experience must be supported and assisted,* to facilitate the solution of environmental problems; environmental technologies should be made available to developing countries on terms which would encourage their wide dissemination without constituting an economic burden on the developing countries.
>
> (Emphasis added)

It is noticeable that the wording of Principle 20 of the Stockholm Declaration does not only reflect the principle of CBDR by soliciting in favour of the transfer of technology, it further refers to the realization of the principle of CBDR by emphasizing the need to transfer technologies especially from developing countries.

290 U.N. Doc. A/CONF. 48/WG.i/CRP.io, 1972.
291 L. B. Sohn, 'The Stockholm Declaration on the Human Environment', *The Harvard International Law Journal,* Vol. 14(3), 1973, 480; a similar kind of recognition of the need for scientific research in the environmental field can also be found in the UNESCO Conference on the Biosphere; U.N. Doc. A/7291, Annex, 1968, 8–10, 22, 24.
292 U.N. Doc. A/CONF.48/PC. 12, Annex I, 1971, 8.
293 L. B. Sohn, 1973, 485.

Provision concerning technology transfer is also found in the international climate change regime, as Art. 4(1)(h) of the UNFCCC requires the Parties to: 'promote and co-operate in the full, *open and prompt exchange of relevant scientific, technological, technical, socio-economic and legal information* related to the climate system and climate change, and to the economic and social consequences of various response strategies ...'[294] (emphasis added). In addition, Art. 4(3) of the UNFCCC requires the Annex II Parties to the Convention to contribute financially to the cost of the transfer of technologies.[295] Consequently, Art. 11 of the Convention has institutionalized the requirement by establishing financial mechanisms.[296] The purposes of the financial mechanisms established under Art. 11 include the transfer of environmentally sound technologies to non-Annex I Party developing and least developed countries.[297]

2.7.3 CBDR under the UNFCCC

The Preamble to an international treaty or agreement contains the background, aim and context of an agreement,[298] however, it is worth noting that the Preamble to the UNFCCC recognizes global climate change as a 'common concern of humankind'. One could argue, through acknowledging climate change as a 'common concern of humankind', the Preamble to the UNFCCC is declaring that combating climate change is the common responsibility of all states and that international cooperation is essential to deal with global climate change issues.[299]

With regard to global climate change, the Preamble to the UNFCCC clearly states that the measures needed in response to climate change should be based on the 'common but differentiated responsibilities and respective capabilities' and 'social and economic conditions' of the Parties. The Preamble also states the need for differentiated responsibility by acknowledging that the 'standards applied by some countries may be inappropriate and of unwarranted economic and social costs to other countries in particular developing countries'.[300]

The Preamble continues that it is necessary 'to take in to full account the legitimate priority needs of developing countries for the achievement of sustainable economic growth and the eradication of poverty', further acknowledging the need for differentiated responsibility in order to guarantee

294 Art. 4(1)(h) of the UNFCCC 1992.
295 Art. 4(3) of the UNFCCC 1992.
296 Art. 11 of the UNFCCC 1992.
297 Ibid.
298 Vienna Convention on the Law of Treaties, Vienna, 23 May 1969. United Nations, Treaty Series, Vol. 1155, 331, Art. 31(2).
299 L. Rajamani, 'The Principle of Common but Differentiated Responsibility and the Balance of Commitments under the Climate Regime', *Review of European Community & International Environmental Law,* Vol. 9(2), 2000, 120, 125; see also J. Hepburn and I. Ahmad, 'The Principle of Common but Differentiated Responsibilities: A Legal Working Paper', CISDL, 2005, 6.
300 Preamble to the UNFCCC 1992, Para 9.

sustainable economic growth and the eradication of poverty. However, sustainable economic growth and the eradication of poverty are also indirect implications of the realization of the principle of 'intra-generational equity'[301] in non-Annex I Party developing and least developed countries.[302]

Furthermore, the Preamble to the Convention states: 'that per capita emissions in developing countries are still relatively low and that the share of global emissions originating in developing countries will grow to meet their social and development needs'. Such statements in the Preamble recognize that the non-Annex I Parties to Convention are less responsible for the climate change, and these countries may not necessarily reduce their greenhouse gas emissions as they need to fulfil basic social and development needs.

The Convention not only acknowledges the differentiated responsibility of the Parties on the basis of their 'historical responsibilities' for global greenhouse gas emissions into the atmosphere, but it also refers to the 'respective capabilities' of the Parties as a determining factor of differentiation. The implication is found in the Preamble to the Convention, where it calls for 'scientific, technical and economic considerations' for the purpose of adoption of climate change responsive measures.[303] Such differentiation of responsibilities of the Parties to comply with their common responsibility can also be interpreted as a way of ensuring equity and justice in addressing climate change issues.[304] However, the objective clause of the Convention states:[305]

> [t]he ultimate objective of this Convention and any related legal instruments that the Conference of the Parties may adopt is to achieve, in accordance with the relevant provisions of the Convention, stabilization of greenhouse gas concentrations in the atmosphere that would prevent dangerous anthropogenic interference with the climate system.

To attain this objective, Art. 3, which is known as the principle clause of the Convention, confers the leading role on the Annex I developed country Parties: 'the developed country Parties should take the lead in combating climate change and the adverse effects thereof'.[306] Though the reason for conferring the leading role on these Parties is not stated in Art. 3, the reason can be found in paragraph 3 of the Preamble to the Convention in which it states: 'the largest share of historical and current global emissions of greenhouse gases has originated in developed countries'.[307] The aforementioned statements in the Preamble imply that conferring the leading role on the Annex I Parties is based

301 See *supra* Chapter 2.6.
302 Cf. Preamble to the UNFCCC 1992, Para 21.
303 Preamble to the UNFCCC 1992, Para 17.
304 Remarks by C. C. Joyner, 'Common but Differentiated Responsibility', 96 *American Society of International Law Proceedings*, 2002, 358.
305 Art. 2 of the UNFCCC 1992.
306 Art. 3(1) of the UNFCCC 1992.
307 Preamble to the UNFCCC 1992, Para 3.

on the past and current contribution of those Parties to greenhouse gas emissions in the atmosphere. Some scholars argue that the obligation to take the leading role to combat climate change goes to the Annex I developed country Parties not only on the basis of their contribution to 'current and historical global emissions' but also due to their advanced capabilities in taking responsive measures.[308]

Art. 3(1) of the Convention directly refers to the role of the principle of CBDR in combating climate change, when it states: '[t]he Parties should protect the climate system for the benefit of present and future generations of humankind, on the basis of equity and in accordance with their common but differentiated responsibilities and respective capabilities'. Art. 3(2) emphasizes the need for equity and fairness in climate change responsive measures especially for those developing and least developed countries, which are more vulnerable to climate change.[309]

The direct reference to the principle of CBDR can also be found under Art. 4(1) of the Convention, where it requires the Parties to take into account 'their common but differentiated responsibilities and their specific national and regional development priorities, objectives and circumstances' in fulfilling the obligations accorded to them by the Convention. In order to implement the principle of CBDR, Art. 4 differentiated the responsibilities of the Parties by creating differentiated obligations and commitments for the Parties. Accordingly, Art. 4(1) specifies the obligations of all Parties, Art. 4(2) specifies the obligations of the Annex I Parties, and Art. 4(3) together with Art. 4(4) stipulates the obligations of the Annex II Parties to the Convention.

Art. 4(7) of the Convention encourages the realization of the principle of CBDR by stating that the degree of fulfilment of commitments of the non-Annex I Parties are subject to degree of fulfilment of the commitments of the Annex I Parties in transferring technological knowledge and providing financial assistance to the non-Annex I Parties.[310] It stresses the importance of the realization of the principle of CBDR by declaring that the principal obligations of the non-Annex I Parties are the promotion of social and economic development as well as the eradication of poverty.[311]

Furthermore, Art. 4(8) of the Convention follows the spirit of the principle of CBDR by requiring the Parties to 'fully take into account' the needs and concerns of the non-Annex I Party developing and least developed countries, which are particularly vulnerable to climate change. It also requires the Parties to 'fully take into account' the special needs and situation of the least developed countries.[312]

308 A. Chandani, 'Distributive Justice and Sustainability as a Viable Foundation for the Future Climate Regime', *Carbon & Climate Law Review,* Vol. 1(2), 2007, 152, 154.
309 Ibid.
310 Art. 4(7) of the UNFCCC 1992.
311 Ibid, cf. *supra* Chapter 2.7.2.
312 Art.4(8)(a)–(i) of the UNFCCC 1992.

It is arguable that the 'differentiation' in the commitments of the Parties to the Convention not only reflects the spirit of the principle of CBDR, but also facilitates the spirit of the principle of equity by promoting the interest of the poor and vulnerable Parties to the Convention.[313] Since the principle of equity requires that the costs of implementation of legal rules should not be 'unbearable' and bring 'undue' difficulties, one could argue that the aforementioned differentiated obligations of the Annex II Parties to the Convention also imply the realization of the principle of equity in the light of the principle of the CBDR.[314]

2.7.4 Nature of the CBDR in the UNFCCC

While the differential provisions of international agreements prior to the Rio Declaration were based on the different capabilities of the states, the concept of CBDR mentioned in the Declaration and the UNFCCC acknowledged for the first time the responsibility of the states for the harm done in the past (*i.e. historical responsibilities*). Thus, the most important feature of the principle of CBDR in the Convention is building a bridge between the previous economic exploitation of universally common properties and the present responsibility to take steps to mitigate the adverse consequences of the previous exploitation.

In short, under the regime of international climate change, the CBDR principle refers to the assessment of responsibility for the mitigation and remediation of environmental degradation based on the 'historical responsibility' of the states in causing the environmental problem. Such responsibility is further justifiable in the light of the present economic, social and infrastructural capabilities of the states to mitigate the problem. This unique feature of the principle may suggest that it should be considered a 'guiding principle' of international cooperation and solidarity.[315]

However, through adding the phrase 'respective capabilities' in the principle of CBDR, the UNFCCC intends to refer to two kinds of differentiation. One kind of differentiation is possible on the basis of the financial and technological capabilities of the Parties to the Convention. Since those who are better able to deal with a problem should logically contribute more in solving the problem, differentiation on the basis of capability ensures better implementation of the common but differentiated responsibilities of the Parties to the Convention. Another kind of differentiation is possible based on the definition of the differentiation found in Principle 7 of the Rio Declaration which refers to the

313 D. Shelton, 'Equity', in D. Bodansky, J. Brunee and E. Hey (eds.), *The Oxford Handbook of International Law*, 2nd edn, Oxford University Press, 2007, 658.

314 I. H. Rowlands, 'Atmosphere and Outer Space', in D. Bodansky, J. Brunee and E. Hey (eds), *The Oxford Handbook of International Law,* 2nd edn, Oxford University Press, 2007, 316, 329–330.

315 Vito De Lucia, 'Environmental Law & Policy: Common but Differentiated Responsibility', *The Encyclopedia of Earth,* 2012, available at www.eoearth.org/view/article/151320 (last accessed on September 30, 2015).

'historical contribution' of the states to the environmental damage leading to climate change.[316]

Although both the UNFCCC and the Rio Declaration place emphasis on the 'common responsibility' of the states to achieve the chosen goal of protection of the environment or global climate system, the spirit of the principle of CBDR applied in the UNFCCC is different from the spirit accepted by the Rio Declaration.[317] While the Rio Declaration explicitly acknowledges the 'historical contributions' of developed countries to greenhouse gas emissions into the atmosphere or to environmental degradations,[318] such references to the 'historical contribution' of the Annex I Parties are only found in the Preamble to the Convention and not in main body of the Convention.

The Preamble to the Convention states, 'the largest share of historical and current global emissions of greenhouse gases has originated in developed countries'.[319] One could argue that amalgamating historical global emissions with current global emissions and conferring responsibility on only the 'largest share' of both historical and current global emissions to the Annex I Parties implies a 'weaker responsibility' in comparison to the responsibility that would derive from direct reference to 'historical responsibilities' of greenhouse gas emissions into the atmosphere. In other words, though the Preamble to the Convention confers the responsibility of historical global emission on the Annex I Parties, it does not clearly acknowledge the absolute 'historical responsibilities' of global emissions of the Annex I Parties, as did the Rio Declaration.[320]

While an indirect mention of 'historical responsibilities' is found in the Preamble to the Convention, the operational text of the Convention states the principle of CBDR without referring to the notion of 'historical responsibility'. However, the Parties have explicitly acknowledged the issue of 'historical responsibility' in COP 16: '[o]wing to this historical responsibility, developed country Parties must take the lead in combating climate change and the adverse effects thereof'.[321] Although the reference to 'historical responsibility' has not been included in any negotiating texts of the Parties to the Convention, the acknowledgement of the 'historical responsibilities' by the Parties arguably is of considerable importance.

In connection with 'historical responsibilities' and 'respective capabilities', Deleuil (2012) remarks that since the Annex I Parties were reluctant to formally accept their 'historical responsibilities', the Convention had to include the term

316 H. Winkler and L. Rajamani, 'CBDR&RC in a Regime Applicable to All', *Climate Policy*, Vol. 14(1), 102–121, 2014, 104.

317 Cf. *supra* Chapter 2.7.1.

318 Art. 7 of the Rio Declaration 1992. See also *supra* Chapter 2.7.1.

319 Preamble to the UNFCCC 1992, Para 3.

320 Principle 7 of the Rio Declaration 1992 states: 'States shall co-operate in a spirit of global partnership to conserve, protect and restore the health and integrity of the Earth's ecosystem. In view of the different contributions to global environmental degradation, States have common but differentiated responsibilities.'

321 Decision 1/CP 16, FCCC/CP/2010/7/Add.1, 15 March, 2011, 8.

'capabilities' together with the term 'responsibilities'.[322] One could argue that by adding 'respective capabilities', the objective of the Convention aimed to ensure that the Annex I Parties would undertake an additional role in accepting 'common responsibility' for stabilizing greenhouse gas concentrations in the atmosphere on the basis of both 'differentiated historical responsibility' and 'individual capabilities'. Even if any Party to the Convention is reluctant to acknowledge 'historical responsibility', it is possibly more acceptable for the Party to acknowledge the 'respective capabilities'.

However, the notion 'respective capabilities' arguably creates more scope for bringing new Parties, especially the large and advanced developing country Parties that are gradually increasing their capabilities, under binding commitments to emission reduction. Since the capability of countries can change as the income per capita increases, responsibilities and capabilities are also interlinked. While increased capacity that is linked to income per capita may result in increased greenhouse gas emissions,[323] one could argue that the non-Annex I Parties that are increasing their 'capabilities' should also accept increased 'responsibilities'.

Based on the above reasoning, it could be argued that the principle of CBDR of the UNFCCC not only refers to Parties' responsibility for historical emissions but also future emissions. While from a 'historical responsibility' perspective the principle of CBDR under the UNFCCC regime refers to the responsibilities of the Parties on the basis of their past role in global greenhouse gas emissions, which mainly relate to Annex I Party developed countries, the responsibility for future emissions is predicted to mainly relate to non-Annex I Party advanced developing countries. In this connection, it is relevant to mention that the IPCC Report 2007 predicted an increase in carbon dioxide (CO_2) emissions of 45 per cent to 110 per cent between 2000 and 2030, of which two-thirds to three-quarters is projected to come from non-Annex I Party advanced developing countries.[324]

However, as far as historical emission and future emission responsibilities are concerned, one should bear in mind that these two kinds of responsibilities are different. While the amount of past emissions has been proved and measured, the amount of future emissions is still projected and not certain.

The inclusion of the term 'respective capabilities' is also justifiable in the light of the UNFCCC notions of 'developed countries should take the lead'.[325] While the Rio Declaration states 'developed countries acknowledge the responsibility that they bear in the international pursuit of sustainable

322 Pieter Pauw et al., *Different Perspectives on Differentiated Responsibilities A State-of-the-Art Review of the Notion of Common but Differentiated Responsibilities in International Negotiations*, Discussion Paper 6/2014, German Development Institute, 2014, 9.

323 M. A. Aslam, 'Equal Per Capita Entitlements: A Key to Global Participation on Climate Change?' in K. Baumert et al. (eds.), *Building on the Kyoto Protocol: Options for Protecting the Climate*, World Resources Institute, 2002, 175–202.

324 IPCC, 2007, 3.

325 Pieter Pauw et al., 2014, 9.

development', one could argue that the UNFCCC lessens the degree of responsibility of the Annex I developed country Parties by requiring them only to 'take the lead'. This is because the Convention also leaves the option open for the non-Annex I Parties to take the lead in the course of time on the basis of the changed conditions of 'capability' of those countries.[326] Thus, a logical deduction could be that the inclusion of the term 'respective capabilities' with CBDR may also play an important role in balancing the historical environmental degradation responsibility of the Annex I Party developed countries with the potential environmental degradation responsibility of the non-Annex I Party advanced developing countries.

2.7.5 CBDR in mitigation and adaptation

As in applying the principle of CBDR, the UNFCCC also refers to 'respective capabilities', arguably this refers to the provisions concerning finance and technology stipulated in Arts. 4.3–4.7 of the Convention. The obligations of the Parties based on the principle of CBDR under the UNFCCC mainly concern the mitigation activities. Though the purpose of mitigation is not expressly mentioned in the Preamble or in Art. 3(1) of the Convention, the objective of the obligations of the Parties provides a clear indication of the necessity for mitigation.[327]

Although the countries that are most vulnerable to the adverse effects of climate change had a nominal role in the emission of greenhouse gases in to the atmosphere, in realizing the principle of CBDR, Art. 3(1) of the Convention does not contain any specific reference to climate change adaptation. Instead, Art. 3(1) refers to protecting the climate system 'for the benefit of present and future generations of humankind' as the reason for implementing the principle of CBDR.

As a matter of fact, if the 'differentiated responsibilities' of the Parties to the Convention are justified in the objective clause of the Convention,[328] one may think that the differentiation has been allowed only for the purpose of attaining the common goal of the Parties – to reduce and balance the greenhouse gas emissions in the atmosphere, which actually refers to climate change mitigation.[329] Premised on the aforementioned arguments, the scope of application of the principle of CBDR in adaptation activities is not very wide. Some scholars

326 Ibid.

327 Cf. Art. 2 of the UNFCCC 1992, see also D. J. Ciplet et al., 'The Politics of International Climate Adaptation Funding: Justice and Division in the Green House', *Global Environmental Politics*, Vol. 1, 49–68, 2013, cited in Pieter Pauw et al., 2014, 9.

328 Art. 2 of the UNFCCC 1992.

329 L. Rajamani, 'The Doctrinal Basis for and Boundaries of Differential Treatment in International Environmental Law', in L. Rajamani (ed.), *Differential Treatment in International Environmental Law*, Oxford University Press, 129–175, 162, cited in H. Winkler and L. Rajamani, 2014, 108.

have criticized the lack of emphasis on applying CBDR in the adaptation mechanism.[330]

However, in the operational text of the Convention, some provisions are found, though not many, that are aimed at promoting adaptation activities in the light of the principle of CBDR. Art. 3(3) of the UNFCCC includes adaptation issues by requiring all Parties to the Convention to take precautionary measures against the adverse effects of climate change. Although Art. 3 (3) does not explicitly refer to the principle of CBDR, it implies the principle through requiring the Parties to consider the 'different socio-economic contexts' of the Parties.

The 'common responsibility' part of the CBDR principle, though not the 'differentiated responsibility' element, is dealt with in Art. 4(1) of the Convention. Art. 4(1) affirms the obligations of the Parties to take steps to adapt to climate change and to cooperate with each other. Art. 4 (2), which relates to climate change adaptation issues, does also not reflect the spirit of the 'differentiated responsibility' part of the principle of CBDR either, since it does not confer any additional obligations on the Annex II Parties to the Convention for the purpose of adaptation.

However, the application of the principle of CBDR through acknowledging 'differentiated responsibility' of the Parties on adaptation issue is clearly covered by Art. 4(4) of the Convention. Art. 4(4) particularly requires the Annex II Parties to assist in meeting the adaptation costs of the non-Annex I Parties, especially those non-Annex I Parties that are vulnerable to the adverse effects of climate change. Such differentiation of the responsibility of the Parties to meet the adaptation costs has left scope to explore more options that might accelerate financial and technological cooperation with the non-Annex I Parties. In view of the above, the provisions of Art. 4(4) are arguably more helpful to the least developed countries that are vulnerable to climate change.

2.7.6 CBDR in the Berlin Mandate and the Kyoto Protocol

Following the UNFCCC, the first Conference of the Parties (COP 1) to the Convention that was held in Berlin (i.e. the Berlin Mandate)[331] reviewed the adequacy of the obligations specified under Art. 4(2)(a) and 4(2)(b) of the Convention. It was apparently remarked at the Berlin Mandate that the commitments of the Parties were not enough to attain the objective of the Convention. As such, it was suggested that the commitments of the Annex I Parties should be strengthened through the adoption of a legally binding protocol or

330 H. Winkler and L. Rajamani, 2014, 115.

331 UNFCCC, *Report of the Conference of the Parties on its first Session, Berlin 28 March to 7 April 1995 Decision 1/CP.1. The Berlin Mandate: Review of Adequacy of Art.4 Paragraph 2 (a) and (b), of the Convention, Including Proposals Related to a Protocol and Decision on Follow-up*, UN Doc. FCCC/CP/1995/7/Add.1, 6 June 1995.

any similar instrument.[332] The Berlin Mandate pressed for better implementation of the principle of CBDR by strengthening the obligations of the Parties to reduce greenhouse gas emissions through

> taking into account the differences in starting points and approaches, economic structures and resource bases, the need to maintain strong and sustainable economic growth, available technologies and other individual circumstances, as well as the need for equitable and appropriate contributions by each of these Parties to the global effort.[333]

While Art. 3(1) of the UNFCCC explicitly states that the principle of CBDR should guide the implementation of the provisions of the Convention;[334] the Berlin Mandate acknowledges the larger responsibility of developed country Parties in implementing the principle of CBDR.[335] The Mandate reaffirms the leading role of the developed country Parties to the Convention, as such it emphasizes the primary responsibility of the Annex I Parties to take part in mitigation activities.[336]

As a result of the Berlin Mandate pressing for a binding protocol to bring the Annex I Parties to the Convention under a stronger commitment to greenhouse gas emission reduction, the Parties to the Convention agreed on a legally binding Protocol – the Kyoto Protocol at its Third Conference of the Parties (COP 3) held in Kyoto, Japan. Pursuant to the propositions of the Berlin Mandate, with a view to achieving the objective of the Convention, the Kyoto Protocol laid down specific commitments for the Annex I Parties.[337] Since the Preamble to the Protocol explicitly acknowledges the guidance of Art. 3 of the Convention, one could argue that the Protocol also acknowledges the principle of CBDR as its guiding principle.[338]

Since the Convention did not specify the commitments of the Annex I Parties to greenhouse gas emission reduction, pursuant to the principle of CBDR, the Protocol required the Annex I Parties to the Convention to 'individually or jointly, ensure that their aggregate anthropogenic carbon-dioxide equivalent emissions of the greenhouse gases listed in Annex A do not exceed their assigned amounts'.[339] The aim of the commitment was to reduce

332 L. Rajamani, 'The Principle of Common but Differentiated Responsibility and the Balance of Commitments under the Climate Regime', *Review of European Community & International Environmental Law,* Vol. 9(2), 120–131, 2000, 127.
333 UNFCCC, *Report of the Conference of the Parties on Its First Session, Berlin 28 March to 7 April 1995 Decision 1/CP.1. The Berlin Mandate: Review of Adequacy of Art. 4 Para 2 (a) and (b), of the Convention, Including Proposals Related to a Protocol and Decision on Follow-up*, UN. Doc. FCCC/CP/1995/7/Add.1, 6 June 1995, Para 2(a).
334 Art. 3(1) of the UNFCCC 1992.
335 L. Rajamani, 2000, 127.
336 Ibid.
337 Preamble to the Kyoto Protocol 1997, Para 5 and Para 2.
338 Preamble to the Kyoto Protocol 1997, Para 4.
339 Art. 3(1) of the Kyoto Protocol 1997.

'their overall emissions of such gases by at least 5 per cent below 1990 levels in the commitment period 2008 to 2012'.[340]

In line with the spirit of the principle of CBDR, the Protocol did not create any emission reduction obligations for the non-Annex I Parties to the Convention.[341] The Protocol also manifested its role in the implementation of the principle of CBDR by making 'differentiation' between the developed country Parties listed under Annex I to the Convention. Pursuant to the spirit of the principle of CBDR, the Protocol also provided flexibility for the Annex I Party countries whose economies were in transition to a market to select a different base year, if that would be more appropriate than 1990 for them.[342]

The Kyoto Protocol further reflected the principle of CBDR in that it required the compliance with greenhouse gas reduction obligations of the Annex I Parties to be done in such a manner that it would minimize 'adverse social, environmental and economic impacts' on the developing country Parties, especially on the least developed country Parties and on those country Parties to the Convention that were most vulnerable to climate change.[343]

In order to realize the principle of CBDR in greenhouse gas reduction obligations, like the Convention, the Protocol also maintained a 'three-tier' differentiation between the Parties.[344] The 'three-tiers' comprise: developed countries, developed countries with economies in transition to a market and developing countries including the least developed countries. While both the developed country Parties and the developed country Parties with economies in transition to a market (the Annex I Parties) had emission reduction obligations, the financial and technological cooperation with the developing and least developed country Parties (the non-Annex I Parties) obligations were conferred only on the developed country Parties (the Annex II Parties).[345] Pursuant to the principle of CBDR, the Protocol required only the non-Annex I Parties to enhance cooperation 'in relation with the need for them'.[346]

The Kyoto Protocol requirement to cooperate with the developing and least developed country Parties was manifested by introducing CDM which was established in Art. 12 of the Protocol. The CDM certainly reflected the spirit of the principle of CBDR, since its objective was

> to assist Parties not included in Annex I in achieving sustainable development and in contributing to the ultimate objective of the Convention, and

340 Art. 3(1) of the Kyoto Protocol 1997.

341 P. G. Harris, 'Common but Differentiated Responsibility: The Kyoto Protocol and United States Policy', 7 *New York University Environmental Law Journal* 27, 31.

342 Art. 3(5)–Art. 3(6) of the Kyoto Protocol 1997.

343 Art. 3(14) of the Kyoto Protocol 1997.

344 J. Hepburn and I. Ahmad, 'The Principle of Common but Differentiated Responsibilities: A Legal Working Paper' in CISDL, *Recent Developments in International Law Related to Sustainable Development Series,* 2005, 6–7.

345 Arts. 3(1), 11(2) and 11(3) of the Kyoto Protocol 1997.

346 L. Rajamani, 2000, 130.

> to assist Parties included in Annex I in achieving compliance with their quantified emission limitation and reduction commitments under Art.3.[347]

As a method of realization of the principle of CBDR, the non-Annex I Parties were entitled to meet their 'common responsibility' by hosting CDM projects in their territory. At the same time, the Annex I developed country Parties were entitled to perform their 'differentiated responsibilities' through fulfilling their emission reduction obligations by buying certified emission reductions (CERs) generated from the CDM projects.[348] The CDM was denoted as an outcome of the principle of CBDR not only because it reflected the differential commitments of the Parties to the Convention, but also because it promoted cooperation between Annex I Parties and non-Annex I Parties.[349]

Since the purpose of the CDM included assisting the non-Annex I Parties to the Convention to achieve sustainable development, it is arguable that the implementation of the principle of CBDR under the Kyoto Protocol was not limited to mere reduction of global greenhouse gas emissions in to the atmosphere. Rather, the implementation of the principle of CBDR under the Kyoto Protocol was arguably extended to the promotion of global sustainable development.[350]

2.7.7 CBDR under the Post-Kyoto COP Decisions

Although both the UNFCCC and the Kyoto Protocol accepted the principle of CBDR as a guiding principle, the Bali Action Plan concluded in COP 13 also acknowledged the relevance of the principle of CBDR for the purpose of ensuring long-term international cooperation for greenhouse gas emission reduction.

The Bali Action Plan urges Parties to 'launch a comprehensive process to enable the full, effective and sustained implementation of the Convention through long-term cooperative action'. The comprehensive process needs to be 'in accordance with the provisions and principles of the Convention'. It especially requires being prepared 'in accordance with particularly the principle of common but differentiated responsibilities and respective capabilities'.[351]

347 Art. 12(2) of the Kyoto Protocol 1997, Cf. *supra* Chapter 2.5.

348 L. Rajamani, 2000, 130.

349 P. Cullet, 'Equity and Flexibility Mechanisms in the Climate Change Regime: Conceptual and Practical Issues', *Review of European Community & International Environmental Law*, Vol. 8(2), 171–172, 1999, 168; see also M. Rodi, 'Bridging the Divided in Global Climate Policy – Strategies for Enhanced Participation and Integration', *Carbon & Climate Law Review*, Vol. 1(2), 2007, 164, 166.

350 Cf. Art. 12 of the Kyoto Protocol 1997.

351 Decision 1/CP.13: Bali Action Plan in Report of the Conference of the Parties on its Thirteenth Session, FCCC/CP/2007/6/Add.1., Chapeau, and Para 1(a), FCCC/CP/2007/6/Add.1, 14 March 2008.

As part of an 'enhanced national/international action on mitigation of climate change', the Bali Action Plan for the first time calls for the active participation of the non-Annex I Parties by requiring them to prepare Nationally Appropriate Mitigation Activities (NAMAs) taking into account their right to sustainable development.[352] Such a requirement of the Bali Action Plan arguably reflects the principle of CBDR, as a pre-requisite of the preparation of NAMAs by the non-Annex I Parties is that it should be 'supported and enabled by technology, financing and capacity-building, in a measurable, reportable and verifiable manner'.[353] Furthermore, the Bali Action Plan reflects the principle of CBDR as it requires that the 'measurable, reportable and verifiable nationally appropriate mitigation commitments or actions' of the Annex I Parties need to take into account the 'differences in their national circumstances'.[354]

Although it was a global expectation that the Bali Action Plan would be further advanced by COP 15 which was to be held in Copenhagen in 2009, in practice COP 15 did not reach a consensus among all Parties so was not able to conclude any legally binding agreement. Eventually, as a result of Decision 2/CP.15, COP 15 adopted the Copenhagen Accord, which was more likely to achieve a political consensus among the Parties. Since the Copenhagen Accord accepted the principle and provisions of the UNFCCC as its guiding principle, arguably the Accord also acknowledged the principle of CBDR as its guiding principle. In the text of the Accord, the Parties expressed their strong 'political will to urgently combat climate change in accordance with the principle of common but differentiated responsibilities and respective capabilities'.[355]

Under the Copenhagen Accord, the non-Annex I Parties were to submit the mitigation actions they were required to achieve in the context of sustainable development. The Accord created a timeline starting from the calendar year 2010 in order to record the commitments of emission reduction of the Annex I Parties. The Accord also required the Annex I Parties to record the actions taken by them to fulfil their commitments. The Annex I Parties agreed to achieve the 'quantified economy-wide emissions target' by the year 2020.[356]

As the Copenhagen Accord for the first time in the climate change regime pointed out that the non-Annex I Parties should also undergo commitments for emission reduction, it reflects the principle of CBDR, by

> recognizing that the time frame for peaking will be longer in developing countries and bearing in mind that social and economic development and poverty eradication are the first and overriding priorities of developing

352 Decision 1/CP.13, Chapeau, and Para I(b)(ii).
353 Decision 1/CP.13, Para I(b)(ii).
354 Decision 1/CP.13, Para I(b)(i).
355 Decision 2/CP. 15, FCCC/CP/2009/11/Add.1, 30 March 2010, Para 1.
356 John R. Nolon and Patricia E. Salkin, *Climate Change and Sustainable Development Law in a Nutshell,* West Academic Publishing, 2011, 7.

countries and that a low-emission development strategy is indispensable to sustainable development.[357]

In line with spirit of the principle of CBDR, under the Copenhagen Accord the Annex I Parties agreed for the first time to provide reports of their greenhouse gas inventories every two years for the period the Accord was in effect.[358]

In promoting equity by putting the principle of CBDR into practice, the Copenhagen Accord requires Annex II Party countries to 'provide adequate, predictable and sustainable financial resources, technology and capacity-building to support the implementation of adaptation action' of non-Annex I Party countries.[359] One could argue that the said acknowledgements of the requirements of technological and financial cooperation from the developed country Parties with the developing and least developed country Parties in a post-2012 scenario seems an important recognition of the principle of CBDR under the Copenhagen Accord.[360]

Following the Copenhagen Accord, the Cancun Agreement, which was concluded in COP 16, also acknowledges that the Annex I Parties to the Convention should continue to take a leading role in combating climate change.[361] At the same time, the Cancun Agreement reflects the principle of CBDR by stating the need to 'bear[ing] in mind that social and economic development and poverty eradication are the first and overriding priorities of developing countries' in attaining the shared vision of long-term cooperative action against climate change.[362] In taking enhanced action on adaptation, the Cancun Agreement requires the Parties to take into account 'their common but differentiated responsibilities and respective capabilities, and specific national and regional development priorities, objectives and circumstance'.[363]

In order to take enhanced action on mitigation, the Agreement emphasizes 'the need for deep cuts in global greenhouse gas emissions and early and urgent undertakings to accelerate and enhance the implementation of the Convention by all Parties'. Consequently, it suggests that Parties comply with such an obligation 'on the basis of equity and in accordance with their common but differentiated responsibilities and respective capabilities'.[364]

357 Decision 2/CP. 15, FCCC/CP/2009/11/Add.1, 30 March 2010, Para 2.
358 Cf. John R. Nolon and Patricia E. Salkin, 2011, 7; see also Art. 4(1)(a) of the UNFCCC 1992.
359 Decision 2/CP. 15, FCCC/CP/2009/11/Add.1, 30 March 2010, Para 3.
360 H. E. Ott et al., 'The Bali Road Map: New Horizons for Global Climate Policy', *Climate Policy,* Vol. 8(1), 2008, 91–95. For an understanding of the negotiation process before and during the Bali Conference, see C. Spence et al., 'Great Expectations: Understanding Bali and the Climate Change Negotiation Process', *Review of European Community & International Environmental Law,* Vol. 17(2), 2008, 142–153.
361 Decision 1/CMP.6, FCCC/KP/CMP/2010/12/Add.1 recital 5..
362 Decision 1/CP. 16, FCCC/CP/2010/7/Add.1, 15 March 2011, Para 6.
363 Decision 1/CP. 16, Para 14.
364 Decision 1/CP.16, Part III.

In order to attain the objective of the Convention, the Cancun Agreement also acknowledges the principle of CBDR in affirming, 'all Parties share a vision for long-term cooperative action', which should be on the basis of 'equity and in accordance with common but differentiated responsibilities and respective capabilities'.[365]

Moreover, inviting all Parties to enhance action on adaptation under the Cancun Adaptation Framework, the Agreement requires the Parties to take 'into account their common but differentiated responsibilities and respective capabilities, and specific national and regional development priorities, objectives and circumstances'.[366] In addition, in taking 'enhanced action and international cooperation on adaptation', the Cancun Agreement reflects the spirit of the principle of CBDR by requiring the Parties to consider the 'urgent and immediate needs of those developing countries that are particularly vulnerable'.[367] In this regard, the Agreement further calls for 'capacity-building for adaptation, with a view to promoting access to technologies, in particular in developing country Parties'.[368]

In COP 17 (held in 2011 in Durban, South Africa), the Durban Long Term Cooperative Action (LCA) Decision[369] also reflects the principle of CBDR through reaffirming, 'Parties should protect the climate system in accordance with their common but differentiated responsibilities and respective capabilities'.[370] However, the Durban Platform for Enhanced Action did not make any reference to the principle of CBDR, which led to a prediction that the post 2020 climate agreement might bring symmetrical emission reduction commitments for both Annex I and non-Annex I Parties to the Convention.

The spirit of implementation of the principle of CBDR was reaffirmed in COP 18 (held in 2012 in Doha, Qatar), when it stated that the efforts of the Parties 'should be undertaken on the basis of equity and common but differentiated responsibilities and respective capabilities'. The commitment to implementation of the principle of CBDR was further strengthened in that COP 18 made it a requirement that the Parties' efforts should also 'take into account the imperatives of equitable access to sustainable development, the survival of countries and protecting the integrity of Mother Earth'.[371] One could argue that the adoption of a Decision addressing 'loss and damage associated with climate change impacts in developing countries that are particularly vulnerable to the adverse effects of climate change to enhance adaptive capacity' is another instance of the acknowledgement of the principle of CBDR by COP 18.[372] The Decision invites Parties to take into account 'common but

365 Decision 1/CP.16, Para 1.
366 Decision 1/CP.16, Para 14.
367 Decision 1/CP. 16, Para 11.
368 Decision 1/CP.16, Para 14(g).
369 Decision 2/CP.17, FCCC/CP/2011/9/Add.1, 15 March 2012.
370 Decision 2/CP.17, II, E.
371 Decision 1/CP.18, FCCC/CP/2012/8/Add.1, 28 February 2013, Para 2.
372 See generally Decision 3/CP.18.

differentiated responsibilities and respective capabilities and specific national and regional development priorities, objectives and circumstances' with a view to increasing action to address 'loss and damage associated with the adverse effects of climate change'.[373]

While COP 19 (held in 2013 in Warsaw, Poland) made no reference to the principle of CBDR, the Lima Call for Climate Action of COP 20 (held in 2014 in Lima, Peru) explicitly stated the commitment of the Parties to reach 'an ambitious agreement in 2015 that reflects the principle of common but differentiated responsibilities and respective capabilities, in the light of the different national circumstances'.[374]

2.7.8 CBDR in the Paris Agreement

In December 2011, during COP 17, the Parties to the UNFCCC decided to 'launch a process to develop a protocol, another legal instrument or an agreed outcome with legal force under the Convention applicable to all Parties'.[375] This is known as the Durban Platform for Enhanced Action (the Durban Platform), which was mandated to conduct negotiations leading up to COP 21 scheduled to be held in 2015 in Paris.

The Durban Platform made no reference to the principle of CBDR. The desired outcome of the Platform was expected to be 'applicable to all Parties', but made no reference to the formalistic Annex I/non-Annex I division of the countries.[376] While the mandate of the platform was to reach an agreement 'under the Convention', it was an implicit indication that the Platform would necessitate following the principles and guidelines of the Convention. Hence, it indirectly meant that the mandate given to the Durban Platform would necessarily consider the principle of CBDR as a guiding principle for the 'agreed outcome'.

On the one hand, the phrase 'applicable to all'[377] without referring to any division of Parties necessitated enhancing the collective level of ambition as well as 'ensuring the highest possible mitigation efforts by all Parties'.[378] On the other hand, the notions 'under the Convention' required adopting some kind of differential treatment that reflects the principle of CBDR. This tension between 'under the Convention' and 'applicable to all' was not resolved until the end of the negotiation process.[379] This is because one group of negotiators preferred to argue for a diverse 'spectrum' of 'self-differentiated' commitments,

373 Decision 3/CP.18, Para 6.

374 Decision 1/CP.20, FCCC/CP/2014/10/Add.1, 2 February 2015, Para 3.

375 Decision 1/CP.17, FCCC/CP/2011/9/Add.1. 15 March 2012, Para 2

376 Adrian Macey, 'The Road to Durban and Beyond: The Progress of International Climate Change Negotiations', *Policy Quarterly* Vol. 8(2), 23–28, 2012, 27.

377 Decision 1/CP.17, Para 2.

378 Decision 1/CP.17, Para 7.

379 Christina Voigt and Felipe Ferreira, 'Differentiation in the Paris Agreement', *Climate Law* Vol. 6(1–2), 58–74, 2016, 63.

while the other group's preference was 'strict abidance' to the principles, provisions and structure of the UNFCCC that also includes Annexes to the UNFCCC.[380]

The evolution of the differentiation debate received an additional dimension when COP 19 adopted the concept of 'nationally determined contributions', which follows the 'bottom up' approach of the Copenhagen pledges.[381] The concept of the 'nationally determined contributions' as introduced by COP 19 required self-determination of their level of effort. It also provided an assurance that no country would be required to accomplish more than it was prepared to do.[382] This approach arguably failed to reflect 'equitable effort-sharing', as some Parties feared that other Parties might renege on their previous commitments, and some Parties feared that the overall level of ambition of emission reduction would not be adequate and fair.[383] In the above circumstances, while the 'bottom up' approach of commitment through 'nationally determined contributions' left increased possibilities for fluid commitments, the differentiation idea of the principle of CBDR appeared to be 'a vital corrective' to bring 'distributive fairness' to the new regime of climate change.[384]

Consequently, in COP 20 Parties agreed to a kind of differentiation 'in light of different national circumstances'.[385] Under Decision 1/CP.20, Parties committed to reach 'an ambitious agreement in 2015 that reflects the principle of common but differentiated responsibilities and respective capabilities, in light of different national circumstances'.[386] It is noteworthy that this was the first time that the Ad Hoc Working Group on the Durban Platform for Enhanced Action (ADP) explicitly referred to the principle of CBDR.[387] In fact the qualifier 'in light of different national circumstances', which was reflected in the Paris Agreement has changed the meanings and understandings of the principle of CBDR from 'a strict, explicit, differentiation, expressed in annexes' to the UNFCCC to the dynamic and changing context of the Paris Agreement.[388]

Hence, while the Paris Agreement is guided by the principles of the UNFCCC which include the principle of equity, and CBDR,[389] throughout the Agreement these principles are reflected 'in the light of different national circumstances'.[390] Art 2(2) of the Agreement clearly states that the 'Agreement

380 Ibid.

381 Dan Bodansky, 'Reflections on the Paris Conference', *Opinio Juris,* December 15, 2015, available at http://opiniojuris.org/2015/12/15/reflections-on-the-paris-conference (last accessed on August 14, 2020).

382 Christina Voigt and Felipe Ferreira, 2016, 63.

383 Ibid.

384 Ibid.

385 Decision 1/CP.20, Para 3.

386 Ibid.

387 Christina Voigt and Felipe Ferreira, 2016, 64.

388 Ibid.

389 Decision 1/CP.21, FCCC/CP/2015/10/Add.1, 29 January 2016, Annex, Preamble to the Paris Agreement 2015.

390 Arts. 2(2), 4(3), 4(4) and 4(19) of the Paris Agreement 2015.

will be implemented to reflect equity and the principle of common but differentiated responsibilities and respective capabilities, in the light of different national circumstances'.

The type of differentiation in the Paris Agreement is clearly dynamic and more diversified than that of the UNFCCC. While the division of developed and developing countries remains relevant for the purpose of the Agreement, it makes no reference as to how this division will be measured. In this regard, it has not even referred to Convention's Annexes, which signifies that the Agreement aims to reflect 'responsibilities, capacities, and circumstance' of all Parties to the Agreement.[391] However, it implements the differentiation concept of the principle of CBDR in diverse explicit and implicit ways. The degree and type of differentiation in the Paris Agreement varies in accordance with the various elements and/or topics of the Agreement. Since the Agreement addresses what is common and what needs to be differentiated in a more careful manner than the previous regime, one can observe that each section of the Agreement adopts a different approach to the compact of differentiation.[392]

2.7.8.1 Nationally determined contributions

The binary distinction of the Parties (e.g. Annex I, non-Annex I) became blurred in the Cancun Agreement.[393] However, the distinction still existed and in the run up to Paris the real challenge was designing an agreement which would go beyond the binary distinction.[394] Finally, in Paris, Parties agreed on 'self-differentiation' based on the tool of the 'intended nationally determined contributions', which was adopted in Warsaw. In adopting the tool, the Paris Agreement discarded the term 'intended' and the tool was referred to as 'nationally determined contributions'. The 'nationally determined contributions' became the central piece of the Agreement as Art. 3(1) states: 'As nationally determined contributions to the global response to climate change, all Parties are to undertake and communicate ambitious efforts as defined in Arts. 4, 7, 9, 10, 11 and 13 with the view to achieving the purpose of this Agreement as set out in Article 2'.[395]

The Agreement requires that 'the efforts of all Parties will represent a progression over time'. While all parties are required to submit their nationally determined contributions, the Agreement offers developing countries preferential treatment through 'recognizing the need to support developing country Parties for the effective implementation of this Agreement'.[396]

391 Christina Voigt and Felipe Ferreira, 2016, 65.
392 See generally Sandrine Maljean-Dubois, 'The Paris Agreement: A New Step in the Gradual Evolution of Differential Treatment in the Climate Regime?', *Review of European, Comparative & International Environmental Law*, Vol. 25(2), 2016, 151–160.
393 Ibid, 155.
394 Ibid.
395 Art. 3(1) of the Paris Agreement 2015.
396 Ibid.

Under the Agreement each Party is required to 'prepare, communicate and maintain successive … nationally determined contributions' which 'it intends to achieve'.[397] After communicating their 'nationally determined contributions', all Parties are also required to 'pursue domestic mitigation measures, with the aim of achieving the objectives of such contributions'.[398]

The Agreement aims to ensure fairness by requiring that Parties' successive 'nationally determined contributions' will 'represent a progression beyond the Party's then current … nationally determined contributions'. It observes differentiation and the principle of CBDR through requiring that each Party's 'nationally determined contributions' will 'reflect its highest possible ambition, reflecting its common but differentiated responsibilities and respective capabilities, in the light of different national circumstances'.[399]

In terms of coverage of global emissions, the idea of 'nationally determined contributions' seems to have been successful, as 188 countries communicated their respective 'nationally determined contributions' just after COP 21 which covers more than 98 per cent of global emissions, which is far more than the commitments made under second phase of the Kyoto Protocol and also more than the mitigation commitments made under the Cancun Agreements.[400]

The Paris Rulebook leaves Parties with extensive discretion to define their 'nationally determined contributions'.[401] During the negotiations of the Paris Rulebook, in COP 24 (held in Katowice, Poland, in December 2018) in order to bring some discipline into the 'nationally determined contributions' process by limiting the extensive substantive liberty that Parties currently enjoyed, some countries argued for the introduction of some additional features.[402] Other countries argued that conferring any additional features to 'nationally determined contributions' would be contrary to the self-determined feature of Parties' mitigation contributions.[403] It is not surprising that ultimately the latter view prevailed.[404]

2.7.9 Differentiation as reflected in the provisions of the Paris Agreement

2.7.9.1 Mitigation

The Paris Agreement's subtle approach to differentiation can be found in its mitigation related provisions enumerated in Art. 4 of the Agreement. Under

397 Art. 4(2) of the Paris Agreement 2015.
398 Ibid.
399 Art. 4(3) of the Paris Agreement 2015.
400 Sandrine Maljean-Dubois, 2016, 155.
401 Lavanya Rajamani and Daniel Bodansky, 'The Paris Rule Book: Balancing International Perceptiveness with National Discretion', *International and Comparative Law Quarterly,* Vol. 68(4), 1023–1040, October 2019, 1025.
402 Ibid, 1029.
403 Ibid.
404 Ibid.

this provision, which states 'Parties aim to reach global peaking of greenhouse gas emissions as soon as possible', a requirement that is applicable to all Parties, guidance is given as to how this aim can be attained in that the developing country Parties are allowed flexibility: 'recognizing that peaking will take longer for developing country Parties'.[405]

In line with the differential treatment element of the principle of CBDR, the Agreement requires the developed country Parties 'continue taking the lead by undertaking economy-wide absolute emission reduction targets'.[406] On the other hand, although Art. 4 of the Agreement requires the developing country Parties to 'continue enhancing their mitigation efforts' and encourages them 'to move over time towards economy-wide emission reduction or limitation targets', they are requested to do so in 'in the light of different national circumstances'.[407] Since developing country Parties have diverse kinds of national capacity and circumstances, the nature of differentiation mentioned under Art. 4 is undoubtedly dynamic, as it intends to consider the individual circumstances of each developing country Party.

Although the requirement of preparing, communicating and maintaining 'successive nationally determined contributions' is applicable to all Parties,[408] the requirement is followed by some adjustors which permit differentiation 'in the content (i.e. level of ambition) and form (i.e. type of target)' of Parties' 'nationally determined contributions'.[409]

In Art. 4(3), the 'common responsibilities' element of the principle of CBDR is reflected while Parties' 'nationally determined contributions' require them to 'represent a progression beyond the Party's then current … nationally determined contributions' and reflect their 'highest possible ambition' in the 'nationally determined contributions'. The 'differentiated responsibility' element of the principle of CBDR can also be found, as those 'nationally determined contributions' are also required to reflect Parties' 'common but differentiated responsibilities and respective capabilities, in the light of different national circumstances'.[410]

Hence, Voigt and Ferreira (2016) have accurately figured out that reading Art. 4(4) together with Art. 4(3) of the Agreement leads us to the fact that '[d]ifferentiation applies both to the content (i.e. ambition, or "how much") and to the form (i.e. type of target, or "what") of parties' mitigation efforts'.[411]

However, it is important to note that the mitigation requirements of the Agreement further promote the principle of CBDR by giving preferential treatment to the least developed and small island developing countries. Under Art. 4(6), these countries, 'may prepare and communicate strategies, plans and

405 Art. 4(1) of the Paris Agreement 2015.
406 Art. 4(4) of the Paris Agreement 2015.
407 Art. 4(4) of the Paris Agreement 2015.
408 Art 4(2) of the Paris Agreement 2015.
409 Christina Voigt and Felipe Ferreira, 2016, 68.
410 Art. 4(3) of the Paris Agreement 2015.
411 Christina Voigt and Felipe Ferreira, 2016, 68.

actions for low greenhouse gas emissions development reflecting their special circumstances'.

2.7.9.2 Adaptation

Art. 7 of the Agreement establishes 'the global goal on adaptation of enhancing adaptive capacity, strengthening resilience and reducing vulnerability to climate change'[412]. It does not confer any specific obligation or reference to developed country Parties. But it offers preferential treatment to developing country Parties as it acknowledges that 'continuous and enhanced international support shall be provided to developing country Parties'.[413] It further acknowledges that in implementing the Agreement's obligations, it is essential to take into account 'the urgent and immediate needs of those developing country Parties that are particularly vulnerable to the adverse effects of climate change'.[414]

Under the Agreement, Parties' strengthening cooperation on enhancing action on adaptation also requires 'assisting developing country Parties in identifying effective adaptation practices, adaptation needs, priorities, support provided and received for adaptation actions and efforts, and challenges and gaps'.[415] While the Agreement requires Parties to 'submit and update periodically an adaptation communication' it privileges developing countries by giving them immunity from additional reporting burdens.[416] The Agreement's provisions on adaptation show that the differentiation on adaptation related commitments are based on Parties' capacities and vulnerabilities.[417] However, the Agreement is silent as to how the particular vulnerability of developing countries will be measured or identified.[418]

2.7.9.3 Finance and support

Differential treatment is clear in the Paris Agreement's provisions regarding financial support. Art. 9(1) clearly states: '[d]eveloped country Parties shall provide financial resources to assist developing country Parties with respect to both mitigation and adaptation'. 'Other Parties' are merely 'encouraged to provide or continue to provide such support voluntarily'.[419] In line with the principle of CBDR, the Agreement requires the developed country Parties to 'take the lead in mobilizing climate finance from a wide variety of sources'.[420] Such effort of developed countries needs to 'represent a progression beyond

412 Art. 7(1) of the Paris Agreement 2015.
413 Art. 7(13) of the Paris Agreement 2015.
414 Art. 7(2) of the Paris Agreement 2015.
415 Art. 7(7)(d) of the Paris Agreement 2015.
416 Art. 7(10) of the Paris Agreement 2015.
417 Christina Voigt and Felipe Ferreira, 2016, 69.
418 Ibid.
419 Art. 9(2) of the Paris Agreement 2015.
420 Art. 9(3) of the Paris Agreement 2015.

previous efforts' and at the time of mobilizing climate finance, the developed country Parties are also required to take 'into account the needs and priorities of developing country Parties'.[421]

In line with the spirit of the principle of CBDR, it can be observed that the Agreement's provisions regarding 'scaled-up financial resources' require achieving 'a balance between adaptation and mitigation' and the measures also need to take into account the needs of particularly vulnerable countries like the least developed countries and small island developing states.[422]

In addition to the provisions related to financial support, Art. 3 of the Agreement also recognizes the need to support the developing country Parties to achieve the effective implementation of the Agreement. It is important to notice that unlike the UNFCCC,[423] the developing country Parties' efforts are not dependent on the support provided by the developed country Parties. Instead of that, under Art. 4(5) of the Agreement, 'enhanced support for developing country Parties will allow for higher ambition in their actions'.[424]

2.7.9.4 Transparency

As far as transparency is concerned, differentiation of obligations between developed and developing countries are more subtle than other provisions.[425] This is because the ultimate purpose of transparency is 'to build mutual trust and confidence and to promote effective implementation'.[426] The differentiation enumerated for the 'enhanced transparency framework for action and support' is based on 'Parties' different capacities'.[427] Art. 13(2) clearly states: '[t]he transparency framework shall provide flexibility in the implementation of the provisions of this Article to those developing country Parties that need it in the light of their capacities'.[428] It also recognizes 'the special circumstances of the least developed countries and small island developing States'.[429]

Under the 'enhanced transparency framework for action and support', all Parties (regardless of whether they are developed or developing country Parties) have an obligation to submit 'a national inventory report of anthropogenic

421 Art. 9(3) of the Paris Agreement 2015.
422 Art. 9(4) of the Paris Agreement 2015.
423 Article 4(7) of the UNFCCC states: 'The extent to which developing country Parties will effectively implement their commitments under the Convention will depend on the effective implementation by developed country Parties of their commitments under the Convention related to financial resources and transfer of technology and will take fully into account that economic and social development and poverty eradication are the first and overriding priorities of the developing country Parties'.
424 Sandrine Maljean-Dubois, 2016, 157–158.
425 Cf. Christina Voigt and Felipe Ferreira, 2016, 70.
426 Art. 13(1) of the Paris Agreement 2015.
427 Art. 13(1) of the Paris Agreement 2015.
428 Art. 13(2) of the Paris Agreement 2015.
429 Art. 13(3) of the Paris Agreement 2015.

emissions'[430] and information which is 'necessary to track progress made in implementing and achieving its nationally determined contribution'.[431] But differentiation can also be found within this framework as distinct kinds of transparency requirements are set for 'different types of commitments and obligations under the agreement'.[432] For example, developed country Parties have mandatory reporting obligations as to the 'financial, technology transfer and capacity-building support provided to developing country Parties'.[433] But, instead of having mandatory reporting obligation, 'other Parties' only 'should' report.[434]

2.8 Conclusion

While the international legal regime on climate change has a clear goal to promote global sustainable development, it is the principles of equity and CBDR which will facilitate reaching the goal both globally and locally. Accordingly, the principles of equity and CBDR have been adopted as the guiding principles of the international legal regime on climate change. However, success in attaining sustainable development through observing the principle of equity and CBDR mostly depends on developed and developing countries' cooperation to observe the provisions adopted based on these principles. Under the Paris Agreement, while the dynamic approach of the principle of CBDR requires all Parties to set their own emissions target, it is the developed country Parties that are still required to take the lead in providing financial support and other assistance to the developing country Parties. Although, the Paris Agreement does not link developing country Parties' efforts to comply with the Agreement's provisions with developed country Parties' support, one could argue that developed country Parties' full support and assistance might enable other Parties to comply with the provisions of the Agreement in a smoother manner as such attain sustainable development.

430 Art. 13(7)(a) of the Paris Agreement 2015.
431 Art. 13(7)(b) of the Paris Agreement 2015.
432 Christina Voigt and Felipe Ferreira, 2016, 70.
433 Art. 13(9) of the Paris Agreement 2015.
434 Art. 13(9) of the Paris Agreement 2015.

3 Technology transfer under the global climate regime

3.1 Introduction

Technology transfer and financial assistance are known to be tools of intra-generational resource distribution but are also considered to be tools of the realization of the principle of CBDR.[1] Moreover, the transfer of environmentally sound technologies to the developing and least developed countries is a method of bringing intra-generational equity and attaining sustainable development by combating climate change and facilitating the eradication of poverty. For this reason, as Figure 3.1 shows, the principles of equity and CBDR, the concept of sustainable development and the issue of the transfer of environmentally sound technologies all are interconnected.[2]

As an important tool in combating climate change the transfer of environmentally sound technologies under the international legal regime on climate change takes place through financial mechanisms[3] established by the Parties to the Convention. The flexible mechanisms such as CDM established under the Kyoto Protocol are also considered to be a means of transferring environmentally sound technologies to non-Annex I Party developing and least developed countries.[4] In addition to the direct and indirect (i.e. flexible mechanisms) financial mechanisms, the UNFCCC has also established technology mechanisms[5] in order to facilitate the transfer of environmentally sound technologies in the developing and least developed countries. The Paris Agreement endorses all the financial mechanisms under the UNFCCC regime: '[t]he Financial

1 See *supra* Chapter 2.7, *infra* Chapter 3.2 and Chapter 3.3; see also Figure 3.1.
2 See Figure 3.1; see also *supra* Figure 2.2.
3 UNFCCC, *Introduction to Climate Finance,* available at https://unfccc.int/topics/climate-finance/the-big-picture/introduction-to-climate-finance (last accessed on September 2, 2019).
4 The *chapeau* of Decision 17/CP.7 on 'Modalities and Procedures for a CDM' explicitly states that the CDM project activities 'should lead to the transfer of environmentally safe and sound technology and know-how in addition to that required under Art.4, paragraph 5, of the Convention and Art.10 of the Kyoto Protocol', see Decision 17/CP.7, FCCC/CP/2001/13/Add.2, 21 January 2002.
5 UNFCCC, *Technology Mechanism,* available at https://unfccc.int/ttclear/support/technology-mechanism.html (last accessed on September 2, 2019).

DOI: 10.4324/9781003056416-3

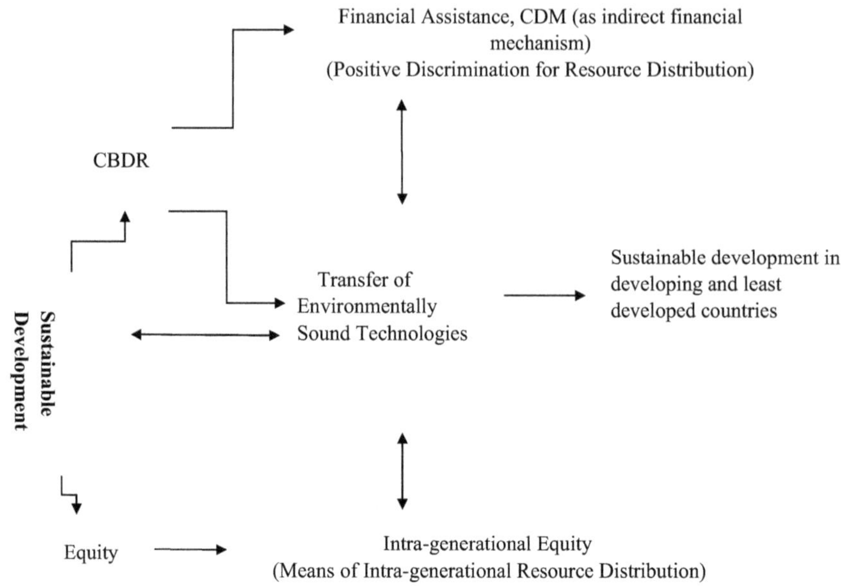

Figure 3.1 Principles of sustainable development in the transfer of environmentally sound technologies in the developing and least developed countries

Mechanism of the Convention, including its operating entities, shall serve as the financial mechanism of this Agreement'.[6]

3.2 The UNFCCC financial mechanisms

Parties to the UNFCCC acknowledged that they did not have equal capacities to achieve the goals of the Convention with respect to the mitigation of greenhouse gases and adaptation to climate change. Hence, the Convention introduced methods that include commitments for the Annex II Parties to assist the non-Annex I Parties (developing and least developed countries) in meeting their UNFCCC obligations through financial assistance and technology transfer cooperation.[7] In line with the promotion of equity through the realization of the principle of CBDR,[8] Art. 4.9 of the Convention explicitly requires the Annex II Parties to fully consider 'the specific needs and special situations' of the least developed countries at the time of fulfilling financial cooperation and technology transfer obligations. The requirement to consider the special needs of the least developed countries was reaffirmed by Art. 2(3) of the Kyoto Protocol.[9] More recently, 'with regard to funding and transfer of technology', the

6 Art. 9(8) of the Paris Agreement 2015.
7 Art. 4(3) of the UNFCCC 1992.
8 Cf. *supra* Chapter 2.6. and Chapter 2.7.2.
9 Art. 4(9) of the UNFCCC 1992; Art. 2(3) of the Kyoto Protocol 1997.

Preamble to the Paris Agreement also urges Parties to take full account of 'the specific needs and special situations' of the least developed countries'.[10]

In relation to the financial cooperation obligation, Art. 4(3) of the UNFCCC explicitly requires 'the developed country Parties and other developed Parties included in Annex II' to 'provide new and additional financial resources to meet the agreed full costs incurred by developing country Parties in complying with their obligations'. The 'new and additional' terms of the provision requires that the financial cooperation obligation of the Annex II Parties should be additional to the existing ODAs.[11] Art. 4(3) facilitates the realization of the principle of CBDR by requiring the Annex II Parties to take into account the 'need for adequacy and predictability in the flow of funds' and ensure the principle of equity by acknowledging 'the importance of appropriate burden sharing among developed country Parties'.[12]

The inclusion of the phrase 'new and additional' is intended to make sure that the contribution of the developed countries to climate financing should not be just be a rescheduling of official ODA.[13] Since the Convention has not explained the term 'new and additional' finance, it has left open the possibility of different interpretations. The interpretation of 'additionality' in terms of the financial contribution of the developed countries is difficult for diverse political and technical reasons.[14] From the political perspective, for the purpose of ensuring that the financial contributions of the Annex II Parties are 'new and additional', it is arguable that the countries are required to agree on a common baseline in order to determine what constitutes 'climate finance'.[15] From the technical perspective, it is also important to ensure that financial data from various government departments and international organizations are effectively collected or gathered.[16]

Concerning the establishment of a 'base line' scale for 'new and additional' finances, some indications have been found under a Decision of COP 7. In the context of the establishment of the SCCF and the LDCF, the Decision 7/CP.7 states:

> there is a need for funding, including funding that is new and additional to contributions which are allocated to the climate change focal area of the

10 Preamble to the Paris Agreement 2015, Para 6.
11 Cf. G-77 and China Proposal, *Financial Mechanism for Meeting Financial Commitments under the Convention*, Para 5, available at http://unfccc.int/files/kyoto_protocol/application/pdf/g77_china_financing_1.pdf (last accessed on July 30, 2020).
12 Cf. *supra* Chapter 2.6 and Chapter 2.7.2.
13 Yulia Yamineva and Kati Kulovesi, 'The New Framework for Climate Finance Under the United Nations Framework Convention on Climate Change: A Breakthrough or an Empty Promise?', in Erkki J. Hollo et al. (eds), *Climate Change and the Law*, Springer-Verlag, 2013, 196.
14 Farhana Yamin and Joanne Depledge, *The International Climate Change Regime: A Guide to Rules, Institutions and Procedures*, Cambridge University Press, 2004, 276.
15 Ibid.
16 Ibid.

> Global Environment Facility and to multilateral and bilateral funding, for the implementation of the Convention.[17]

In addition, Decision 10/CP.7 states, 'an adaptation fund shall be established to finance concrete adaptation projects and programmes in developing country Parties that are Parties to the Protocol'.[18]

Given the texts of the aforementioned two Decisions of COP 7, it could be said that the phrase 'new and additional' climate finances indicates the increased amount of the financial contribution of the non-Annex II Parties to the implementation of the provisions of the Convention.

From the Reports submitted by the Annex I Parties as part of their National Communication, it is clear that all Annex I Parties have not adopted the definition of 'new and additional' in the same manner.[19] Different Annex I Party countries have adopted different approaches to explain the meaning of 'new and additional'.[20] Some Annex I Party countries considered the increasing climate related funding over a reporting period of time as 'new and additional financial resources'. Other Annex I Party countries considered the financial contribution in relation to the pledges made in the Bonn Agreements on the implementation of the Buenos Aires Plan of Action as 'new and additional financial resources'.[21] Moreover, some Annex I Party countries also suggested that the 'new and additional' should be measured on the basis of the addition of the official development assistance resulting in a target of providing 0.7 per cent of their gross national income by 2013.[22]

The 'new and additional financial resources' contributed by the Annex II Party countries are required to be spent on setting up both adaptation and mitigation policies as well as the implementation of the policies in non-Annex I Party countries. Since the implementation of adaptation and mitigation policies is in many cases dependent on the development of proper technologies and access to those technologies, the 'financial resources' are also meant to be spent on the development and promotion of the transfer of environmentally sound technologies to the non-Annex I Party developing and least developed countries.[23] In order to provide financial assistance specifically for the purpose of

17 Decision 7/CP.7, FCCC/CP/2001/13/Add.1, 21 January 2002, Para 1(a).

18 Ibid.

19 *Guidelines for the Preparation of National Communications by Parties Included in Annex I to the Convention,* UN Doc. FCCC/CP/1999/7, 16 February 2000, Paras 50–56 (Guidelines for Annex I National Communications).

20 *Compilation and Synthesis of Fifth National Communications. Note by the Secretariat. Addendum. Financial Resources, Technology Transfer, Vulnerability, Adaptation and Other Issues Relating to the Implementation of the Convention by Parties Included in Annex I to the Convention,* UN Doc. FCCC/SBI/2011/INF.1/Add.2, 20 May 2011, Paras 45–47.

21 Decision 5/CP.6, FCCC/CP/2001/5, 25 September 2001.

22 *Compilation and Synthesis of the Fifth National Communications,* FCCC/SBI/2011/INF.1/Add.2, 20 May 2011, Para 46.

23 Cf. ibid, Para 12.

technology transfer, Art. 4(3) of the UNFCCC further states that the Annex II Parties shall 'provide such financial resources, including for the transfer of technology, needed by the developing country Parties to meet the agreed full incremental costs of implementing measures'.

However, the term 'incremental cost' refers to the difference between the 'base line cost' or costs of the 'business as usual scenario' and the actual cost of implementation of a climate friendly project.[24] For this purpose, the 'base line cost' refers to the usual cost of a project planned by a state taking into consideration its national benefit, not necessarily taking into account the environmental benefit.[25] For example, if a non-Annex I Party developing country or least developed country, for instance, Bangladesh, receives economic assistance for a solar energy project as the technology needed for energy production from any of the UNFCCC financial mechanisms, and the project substitutes a coal or diesel plant in the energy production, it will be more costly for Bangladesh to generate a similar amount of electricity on the basis of solar panels than it would be using conventional energy technology. The extra costs required to transfer solar energy technologies should be considered to be 'incremental costs'.

Debate also exists over the definition of the term 'incremental cost', as it excludes the base line costs of any project and allows financing only to the extent the project ensures benefit to the global environment. Though for many mitigation projects, it is easy to calculate the incremental cost of the environmentally sound technologies involved, the same is not possible in the case of adaptation projects that are only intended to be of local benefit.[26]

Ever since the adoption of the Convention, the COP and the GEF have tried to clarify the meaning of the term 'incremental costs' and simplify its application. The GEF has played a noteworthy role in bringing the concept in to operation through its funding decisions like the Resource Allocation Framework.[27] The objective of the Resource Allocation Framework was to allocate resources among countries on the basis of country performance and potential to generate global environmental benefits.[28] Gomez-Echeverri and Müller (2009) have criticized the system for not taking into consideration vulnerability to the effects of climate change and adaptation needs.[29] The system has recently been replaced by a new GEF policy, which in line with the

24 Cf. Ken King, *The Incremental Costs of Global Environmental Benefits,* GEF, 1993, 5.
25 Ibid.
26 Erik Haites, *Development Perspectives for a Post-Copenhagen Climate Financing Architecture,* OECD, 2010, 12–13.
27 GEF, *The GEF Resource Allocation Framework,* GEF/C.27/Inf.8/Rev.1, October 17, 2005, available at https://www.thegef.org/sites/default/files/council-meeting-documents/C.27.Inf_.8.Rev_.1_RAF_1.pdf (last accessed on August 14, 2020).
28 Ibid, Para 4.
29 Luis Gomez-Echeverri and Benito Müller, 'The Financial Mechanism of the UNFCCC: A Brief History', *ECBI Policy Brief,* April 2009, 3.

implementation of the principle of CBDR takes countries' GDP into account in the allocation of funds.[30]

However, Art. 4(4) of the UNFCCC requires the Annex II Parties to 'assist the developing country Parties that are particularly vulnerable to the adverse effects of climate change in meeting costs of adaptation to those adverse effects'. Emphasizing the need to assist the non-Annex I Parties, which are 'particularly vulnerable to the adverse effects of climate change,' can be taken as a reflection of the spirit of the principle of CBDR.[31]

Although the Convention does not specify the level of resources that should be contributed by the Annex II Parties, Art. 11(3)(d) obliges the COP to work with the operating entity of the financial mechanism to decide 'in a predictable and identifiable manner of the amount of funding necessary and the conditions under which that amount shall be periodically reviewed'.[32] The non-Annex I Parties to the Convention were not happy for the Annex II Parties to be in a position to assess the resources required for them (non-Annex I Parties). The non-Annex I Parties therefore proposed that the COP should make the assessment. The proposal was strongly opposed by the Annex II Parties.[33]

As a result, the GEF Council and the COP are now jointly responsible for determining the total GEF financial requirement for the purpose of the implementation of the provisions of the Convention.[34] One could argue that the process of joint assessment by the GEF Council and the COP is in compliance with the realization of the principle of intra-generational equity, since it gives all the concerned Parties the opportunity to participate in the decision-making process of the GEF financial requirement assessment.[35]

COP 3 adopted supplementary guidance requiring the COP to make an assessment of the amount of support required to assist the non-Annex I Parties.[36] The COP assessment of the required support needs to take into account: the agreed full costs of preparing national communications; the agreed full incremental costs of the other commitments of the Annex II Parties; relevant information from the GEF about approved projects and programmes; and other financial sources that are available for the implementation of the Convention.[37] In practice, it is 'the GEF Secretariat and the Trustee, who make assessments and funding scenarios on the basis of estimates of what the donors are willing to contribute'.[38]

30 Yulia Yamineva and Kati Kulovesi, 'The New Framework for Climate Finance Under the United Nations Framework Convention on Climate Change: A Breakthrough or an Empty Promise?' in Erkki J. Hollo et al. (eds), 2013, 196.
31 Cf. *supra* Chapter 2.7.
32 Art. 11(3)(d) of the UNFCCC 1992.
33 Farhana Yamin and Joanne Depledge, 2004, 276.
34 Ibid.
35 Cf. *supra* Chapter 2.6, see also Sharon Beder, 2000, 230.
36 FarhanaYamin and Joanne Depledge, 2004, 268, see also Decision 12/CP.3, FCCC/CP/1997/7/Add.1, 25 March 1998, available at https://unfccc.int/resource/docs/cop3/07a01.pdf (last accessed on March 23, 2021).
37 FarhanaYamin and Joanne Depledge, 2004, 268.
38 Luis Gomez-Echeverri and Benito Müller, April 2009, 6.

However, regarding the financing of technology transfer, more specific and elaborate instructions are found under Art. 4(5) of the Convention. It requires the Annex II Parties to 'take all practicable steps to promote, facilitate and finance, as appropriate, the transfer of, or access to, environmentally sound technologies and know-how to other Parties, particularly developing country Parties, to enable them to implement the provisions of the Convention'.[39]

Since Art. 4(5) has not elaborated on the term 'all practicable steps', one could arguably explain the term in the light of the guiding principles of the Convention – the principles of equity and CBDR.[40] Accordingly, one could maintain the level of practicable steps to be taken by the Annex II Parties needs to be determined on the basis of the socio-economic capabilities of the concerned Party.

In requiring the Annex II Parties to take 'all practicable steps' to provide financial assistance as well as to transfer environmentally sound technologies and know-how in particular to developing countries (that also includes the least developed countries), the Convention explicitly refers to the 'differentiated responsibility' of the Parties and reflects the spirit of the principle of CBDR. At the same time, it promotes equity by implementing the 'common responsibility' part of the principle of CBDR. Because, it requires the non-Annex I Parties to implement the provisions of the Convention with 'required' financial assistance and technological cooperation of the Annex II Parties.[41]

However, to institutionalize the substantive requirement of financial cooperation that also results in technological cooperation, Art. 11(1) of the UNFCCC has defined a formal financial mechanism.[42] The involvement of all Parties in a climate finance mechanism was ensured by requiring that the financial mechanism established under the Convention 'shall function under the guidance of and be accountable to the Conference of the Parties'.[43] Accordingly, the Conference of the Parties has also been entitled to decide the 'policies, programme priorities, and eligibility criteria' of the UNFCCC climate finance mechanisms.[44] Through ensuring the participation of all Parties, the UNFCCC financial mechanism has arguably guaranteed the realization of intra-generational equity as well as the implementation of the principle of CBDR.[45] The Convention also states that the operation of the financial mechanism 'shall be entrusted to one or more existing international entities'.[46] As a result, COP 9 established the GEF Trust Fund through Decision 9/CP.1.[47]

39 Art. 4(5) of the UNFCCC 1992.
40 Since equity and CBDR are two guiding principles of the Convention, see *supra* Chapter 2.7.3.
41 Cf. *supra* Chapter 2.6, and *supra* Chapter 2.7.
42 Art. 11(1) of the UNFCCC1992.
43 Ibid.
44 Ibid.
45 Cf. *supra* Chapter 2.6, and *supra* Chapter 2.7.
46 Art. 11(1) of the UNFCCC 1992.
47 Decision 9/CP.1, FCCC/CP/1995/7/Add.1, 6 June 1995.

Moreover, in 2001 the Marrakech Accords (adopted in a COP 7 Decision) established three special funds: 1) the Special Climate Change Fund (SCCF) under the Convention; 2) the Least Developed Countries Fund (LDCF) under the Convention; and 3) the Adaptation Fund (AF) under the Kyoto Protocol.[48]

In addition, in COP 16 the Parties also established a new fund – the Green Climate Fund (GCF). The GCF was entrusted as an operating entity of the financial mechanism mentioned in Art. 11(1) of the UNFCCC.[49]

The previously mentioned funding facilities are illustrated in Figure 3.2.

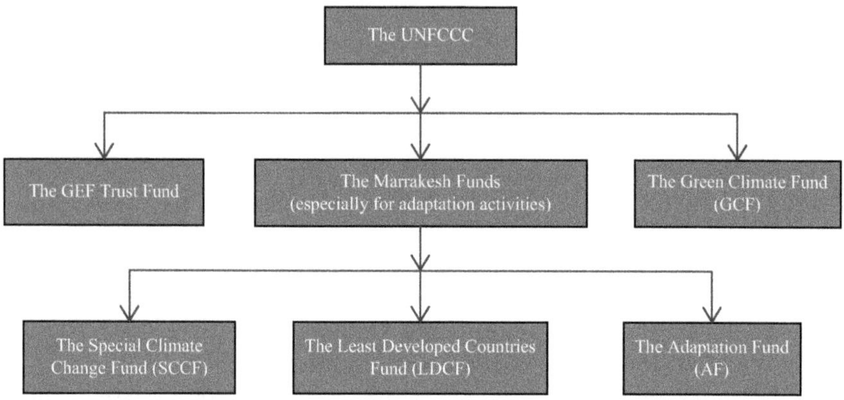

Figure 3.2 Financial mechanisms under the UNFCCC

Art. 11(5) of the Convention also acknowledged the possibility of realizing the provisions of the Convention through financial cooperation between the developed countries (Annex II Parties) and the developing countries (non-Annex I Parties) through bilateral, regional and other multilateral channels. The suggestion of bilateral, regional and multilateral approaches also exists in the Paris Agreement, where the suggestion is made of 'enhancing the capacity of developing country Parties to implement' the Agreement.[50]

One could argue that the inclusion of the possibility of bilateral or regional cooperation was intended to complement the UNFCCC climate finance mechanism in fulfilling the 'common responsibility' of the Parties to combat climate change by taking climate change adaptation and mitigation measures. Since the range of negative effects brought about by climate change is huge, Art. 11(5) of the Convention has implicitly encouraged the Parties to take voluntary financial cooperation measures to deal with the global climate change issue. In this regard, the bilateral or multilateral agreements concerning CDM projects between developed and developing countries could also be argued to

48 UNFCCC, *United Nations Framework Convention on Climate Change (UNFCCC): Handbook*, UNFCCC, 2006, 114, 132.
49 Decision 1/CP.16, FCCC/CP/2010/7/Add.1, 15 March 2011.
50 Art. 11(4) of the Paris Agreement 2015.

be an instance of the realization of Art. 11(5) of the Convention and Art. 11(4) of the Paris Agreement.

As a voluntary measure of financial cooperation, Japan, for instance, has initiated the Bilateral Offset Credit Mechanism (BOCM) under which it can invest in emission reduction projects in the developing or least developed countries and obtain carbon credit units. It has been claimed that the BOCM has a simpler process than that of the CDM. This is because the method of establishment of the BOCM is specified through a bilateral agreement whereas the CDM is administered by an international body under the authority of the UNFCCC.[51]

As in the case of the UNFCCC, the Paris Agreement realizes the principle of equity and CBDR by requiring developed country Parties to the Agreement to provide financial resources to assist the adaptation and mitigation activities of the developing country Parties.[52] Arguably, the Paris Agreement is more successful in realizing the principle of CBDR since it not only assures financial support from the developed country Parties but also encourages '[o]ther Parties to provide or continue to provide' financial support voluntarily.[53] In 'mobilizing climate finance from a wide variety of sources, instruments and channels',[54] the Paris Agreement requires developed country Parties to play the leading role, which in other words is an instance of the realization of the principle of equity and CBDR. As with the 'incremental cost' requirement of the Art. 4(3) of the UNFCCC, Art. 9(3) of the Paris Agreement clarifies that developed country Parties' mobilization of climate finance 'should represent a progression beyond previous efforts'.[55] The Paris Agreement further realizes the principle of equity and CBDR by requiring the 'scaled-up financial resources' to not only 'aim to achieve a balance between adaptation and mitigation', but also to take into account the special needs and priorities of those developing countries which are 'particularly vulnerable to the adverse effects of climate change'.[56] Such developing countries mainly include the least developed countries and small island developing states.[57]

However, a knowledge and understanding of the UNFCCC climate finance mechanisms which were later endorsed by the Paris Agreement is important in order to understand the differences and similarities in general legal conditions in the transfer of environmentally sound technologies under the UNFCCC through direct finance mechanisms and through indirect finance mechanisms (e.g. the CDM)[58] or through newly established similar mechanisms.[59]

51 Hanh Le and Anais Delbosc,'Japan's Bilateral Offset Crediting Mechanism: A Bilateral Solution to a Global Issue?', *Climate Brief*, No. 11, January, 2012, 3.
52 Art. 9(1) of the Paris Agreement 2015.
53 Art. 9(2) of the Paris Agreement 2015.
54 Art. 9(3) of the Paris Agreement 2015.
55 Art. 9(3) of the Paris Agreement 2015.
56 Art. 9(4) of the Paris Agreement 2015.
57 Ibid.
58 See *infra* Chapter 3.4.1 and *infra* Chapter 3.4.2.
59 Art. 6 of the Paris Agreement 2015.

3.2.1 The Green Environment Facility and the Green Environment Facility Trust Fund

In line with the realization of equity on the basis of the principle of CBDR, the financial mechanism under the climate change regime is designed to ensure 'equitable and balanced representations' of the Parties to the Convention and it is also required to take place within 'a transparent system of governance'.[60] The special requirement of 'equitable and balanced representations' of the Parties is a clear reflection of the principle of equity.[61] Since it is required to have a working agreement between the COP and the concerned entity for the operation of the mechanism, the COP has authorized the Green Environment Facility (GEF) to be an international entity responsible for the operation of the financial mechanism.[62] The establishment of the GEF is vital because it stands at the edge of 'positive discrimination and resource distribution', which is important for its role in bringing 'intra-generational equity' and eradicating poverty on the basis of the realization of the principle of CBDR through ensuring the transfer of environmentally sound technologies.[63]

In 1991, the World Bank first established the GEF with a view to financing activities that concern the protection of the environment and promotion of sustainable development. The initial aim of the GEF was to provide 'new and additional grants and concessional funding to cover the "incremental" or "additional" costs associated with transforming a project with national benefits into a project with global environmental benefits'.[64]

In order to determine the 'incremental' or 'additional' costs, the GEF requires five consecutive steps to be followed: determining the 'business as usual scenario'; ascertaining the global environmental benefits (GEBs) and matching this with the GEF priorities under the GEF focal areas and themes; making a framework about the outcome of the transformation of the technologies to this project; providing the incremental reasoning and role of the GEF; and negotiating the method of co-financing between the GEF and the recipient country.[65]

After being restructured in 1994, the GEF was separated from the World Bank structure and started working as an individual and permanent organization. Since then the World Bank, as a trustee for the GEF Trust Fund, has also been providing administrative services. During its reorganizing period, the GEF

60 Art. 11 of the UNFCCC 1992.
61 See *supra* Chapter 2.6.
62 Art. 21(3) of the UNFCCC 1992. See also Philippe Sands, 2003, 1036.
63 Philippe Cullet, 2003, 95.
64 GEF, *About Us,* available at www.thegef.org/gef/whatisgef (last accessed on July 30, 2020).
65 GEF, *Operational Guidelines for the Application of the Incremental Cost Principle,* GEF/C.31/12 May 14, 2007, available at https://www.thegef.org/ sites/default/files/documents/C.31.12 _Operational _Guidelines_ for_ Incremental_Costs-2007_0.pdf (last accessed on July 30, 2020).

became the financial mechanism for both the UNFCCC and the CBD.[66] In line with compliance of differentiated obligations, the Annex II Parties to the Convention are required to make a contribution to the GEF Trust Fund every four years.[67] The initial implementing partners of the GEF projects are the United Nations Development Programme (UNDP), the United Nations Environment Programme (UNEP) and the World Bank.[68]

The option of submitting project proposals seeking financial assistance from the GEF is open to national governments, national institutions, local communities, academic institutions, international organizations, non-governmental organizations (NGOs) and private sector entities.[69] Hence, all climate change vulnerable developing and least developed countries are entitled to seek financial assistance from the GEF. In addition, any national institution, academic institution, NGO or private entity of those countries is also entitled to apply and receive funding from the GEF.

The GEF project cycle includes: concept development, preparation, appraisal, approval, implementation supervision, a closing inspection and an evaluation. The projects that follow all these steps are called full-size projects (FSPs). Usually it takes approximately a year to a year and a half to develop an FSP, while implementation of these projects takes 3–6 years. In addition to FSPs, other available funding options under the GEF are: medium-sized projects (MSPs), Enabling Activities and the Small Grant Programme.[70]

3.2.1.1 Organizational structure of the GEF

As restructured in March 1994,[71] the GEF is comprised of three main organs: the Council, the Assembly and the Secretariat.[72] The Council is the main governing body of the GEF. It is responsible for development, adaptation and evaluation of the implementation of the GEF programmes. The Council consists of 32 members. Of the 32 members of the GEF Council, 16 members

66 In 2001, GEF was entrusted as financial mechanism for the Stockholm Convention on Persistent Organic Pollutants and in 2003 was entrusted as financial mechanism for the United Nations Convention to Combat Desertification. Acting as a partner of the Montreal Protocol, GEF also started financing projects in phasing out the use of ozone-destroying chemicals in the Russian Federation, Eastern Europe and Central Asia. The important changes during the restructuring of GEF of 1994 resulted in more involvement in the developing countries in policy-making and the implementation of projects.

67 UNFCCC, 2006, 128.

68 GEF, *About Us,* available at www.thegef.org/gef/whatisgef (last accessed on July 30, 2020).

69 UNFCCC, 2006, 130.

70 Ibid, 130–131.

71 GEF, *Instrument for the Establishment of the Restructured Global Environmental Facility,* Washington, October 2011, 12, available at https://www.thegef.org/sites/default/files/publications/GEF_Instrument_Oct2011_final_0_1.pdf (last accessed on September 30, 2015).

72 Ibid, 15–18.

come from the non-Annex I Party developing countries, 14 members come from the developed country Parties and the other 2 members come from countries with transitional economies. One could argue that the distribution of the GEF Council membership among the different groups of the Parties to the Convention follows the principle of equity. The principle of equity is reflected because the process ensures the largest representation comes from the largest group of the Convention – non-Annex I developing country Parties, followed by representation from the developed country Parties and the countries with Economies in Transition (EIT) Parties respectively.

Since the process of taking decisions in the GEF Council is based on the consensus of the GEF members, it arguably promotes the principle of equity on the basis of the realization of the principle of CBDR.[73] Similarly, the option to participate of NGOs and civil societies in the GEF Council is arguably another important feature of the Council that ensures the realization of procedural equity in the decision-making process.[74]

In line with the realization of the principle of equity, the GEF Assembly is comprised of representatives from all Parties.[75] The Assembly meets once every four years at the ministerial level.[76] Representatives from Parties to the Convention of the GEF Assembly include ministers and high-level government delegations. The Assembly participants also include parliamentarians, business leaders, scientists and NGO leaders. Hence, the GEF Assembly, like the GEF Council, reflects the principle of equity by ensuring the participation of all its stakeholders.[77]

Headed by the Chief Executive Officer and the Chairperson, the GEF Secretariat is responsible for reporting to the GEF Council and the GEF Assembly. It assesses the implementation success of the Decisions taken by the GEF Council and the GEF Assembly. The GEF Secretariat is also responsible for coordinating the design of projects included in the work programmes, supervising their implementation and ensuring that the operational methods and policies are properly followed.[78]

3.2.1.2 Contributions to financial mechanisms by the Parties

While Arts 4(1) and 4(2) of the Convention have set a list of duties and obligations for the Parties in tackling climate change issues, Art. 4(3) of the Convention requires that the commitments of the Parties 'shall take into account the need for adequacy and predictability in the flow of funds and the importance of appropriate burden sharing among the developed country Parties'. The

73 See *supra* Chapter 2.6 and Chapter 2.7.
74 Cf. GEF, 2011, 19, 21, 36. See also *supra* Chapter 2.6 and Chapter 2.7.
75 GEF, 2011, 15.
76 GEF, *The GEF Assembly,* available at https://assembly.thegef.org/assembly/overview (last accessed on August 14, 2020).
77 Cf. *supra* Chapter 2.6.
78 GEF, 2011, 18.

cited 'need for adequacy and predictability in the flow of funds' should be evaluated in the light of the provisions of Art. 11 of the Convention. Art. 11 states that an individual entity should be authorized to operate the financial mechanism and that the authorized entity should be accountable to the COP.[79]

At the time of making an agreement between the COP and the entrusted entity, it is also required to determine the necessary amount of funding in a 'predictable' and 'identifiable' manner. The purpose of determining the 'predictable' and 'identifiable' manner is to assist the concerned Parties in fulfilling their obligations derived from the Convention. The amount granted under the financial mechanism should also be periodically reviewed for the sake of proper fulfilment of the purpose of the funding mechanism.[80]

The phrase 'the importance of appropriate burden sharing among the developed country Parties' of Art. 4(3) reflects the underlying spirit of the principle of CBDR, through aiming to share the 'burden' between the Annex II Party developed countries. Since all Annex II Party countries do not have the same capability, one could argue that the more capable Annex II Parties should take more 'burden' and the less capable Annex II Parties should take less 'burden' on their shoulders. By giving the opportunity to share the 'burden' the Convention has made it easier for the Annex II Parties to fulfil their aggregated obligations. Hence, one could say that the Convention's requirement to consider the importance of sharing the burden appropriately between the Annex II Parties reflects the principle of CBDR based on the 'respective capabilities' of the Annex II Parties.[81]

However, paragraph 9 of the Memorandum of Understanding (MOU) between the COP and the Council of the GEF requires them jointly to determine 'the aggregate GEF funding requirements for the purpose of the Convention'.[82] The annex attached to the said MOU requires the COP to assess the amount required to assist the developing and least developed countries to fulfil their commitments under the Convention. It also requires the GEF to take into account the assessment done by the COP.[83] As the task of assessing the amount required for the developing and least developed countries is conferred on the COP, the assessment process ensures the participation of all Parties to the Convention. By ensuring the participation of all Parties it realizes the principle of equity in the decision-making process of the GEF funding.[84]

79 Art. 11 of the UNFCCC 1992.
80 Art. 11.3(d) of the UNFCCC 1992.
81 Cf. *supra* Chapter 2.7.4.
82 *Draft Memorandum of Understanding between the Conference of the Parties and the Council of the Global Environment Facility: Annex on the Determination of Funding, Necessary and Available for the Implementation of the Convention*, FCCC/CP/1996/9, 21 May 1996, Para 9, available at http://unfccc.int/cop3/resource/docs/cop2/09.pdf (last accessed on July 30, 2020).
83 UNFCCC, 2006, 118.
84 Cf. *supra* Chapter 2.6.

3.2.1.3 The COP guidance to the GEF

The COP guidance to the GEF under the UNFCCC is entitled 'Guidance to the operating entity of the financial mechanism'. Further guidance is also found in the COP Decisions on thematic work areas like national communications from the developing and least developed countries, implementation of Art. 4(8) and 4(9) of the Convention, capacity building and technology transfer. One of the most important guiding principles of the GEF in providing funding is to distinguish between the local or national benefits of a project and the global environmental benefit.[85]

The concept of 'incremental cost'[86] is applied to apportion the national development and international environmental benefit as well as determine the actual cost of global environmental protection.[87] It means that after determining the actual cost of global environmental protection, the GEF provides only the amount of funding that the operator of a project needs to spend to achieve global environmental benefit. One could say that the requirement to differentiate between the national benefits of a project and the global environmental benefit is intended to make sure that the climate finance is used properly to achieve the objective of the Convention. Besides, arguably the objective of the requirement of said differentiation is to make sure that the climate finance is used solely to assist the Parties to fulfil their obligations derived from the Convention.

It is important to note that the GEF funding is intended to promote national sustainable development by requiring that the only projects entitled to receive funding are those that are designed in compliance with national priorities in meeting national sustainable development goals.[88] Therefore, if any developing or least developed country government or any national or private entity or NGO of those countries applies to receive financial aid from the GEF for any project, the project must be in line with the concerned country's priorities in attaining national sustainable development goals.

By introducing a novel financial mechanism, which is different from traditional development aid mechanisms, the GEF promotes equal partnership between donor and recipient states, which realizes the principle of intra-generational equity – an important element of the sustainable development concept.[89] The way in which the principles of equity and CBDR guide the GEF structure are to be seen in two ways. The implication and realization of the principle of CBDR is depicted in its role in assisting the Parties to the Convention to fulfil their international obligations.[90] Another important role of the principle of CBDR in

85 UNFCCC, 2006, 118.
86 See *supra* Chapter 3.2.1.
87 Ken King, 1993, 5 ff, see also GEF, *Funding,*https://www.thegef.org/about/funding (last accessed on August 20, 2020).
88 Philippe Cullet, 2003, 119.
89 Philippe Cullet, 2003, 112 ff.. Cf. *supra* Chapter 2.6.
90 Ibid.

guiding the GEF is that the financial assistance under this mechanism is meant to assist only those countries that plan to spend the fund on fulfilling their international environmental obligations derived from international environmental or climate change conventions. Through receiving assistance from the GEF funding, the developing and least developed countries can fulfil their common responsibilities to take care of the global environment. At the same time, through financial contributions to the GEF, the Annex II Parties can fulfil their differentiated responsibilities of financial cooperation derived from the Convention.[91] The implication and realization of procedural equity is depicted through the GEF's special governance structure which involves the accelerated participation of the developing and least developed countries. Thus, through redistributing resources from the Annex II Parties to the non-Annex I Parties, the legal structures of the GEF promotes fairness and justice in the international climate regime in the light of the realization of the principle of equity on the basis of the principle of CBDR.[92]

Besides the above issues, through offering financial aid, the GEF attracts more states to enter into international environmental obligations and to sign and ratify the relevant treaties.[93] Assurance of a wide level of participation of the states in the UNFCCC enhances the possibility of realizing the principle of intra-generational equity. At the same time, it enhances the possibility of accelerated commitment to the common responsibility of the world community to combat climate change and prevent environmental degradation. Recently, COP 25 (held in 2019 in Madrid, Spain) requested the GEF to provide adequate support to developing country Parties to prepare their 'first and subsequent biennial transparency reports'.[94]

Based on the above arguments, it can justifiably be said that while realization of equity on the basis of the principle of CBDR is the legal-philosophical basis of the GEF, it functions as an important tool to promote and observe the principle of equity and CBDR under the UNFCCC regime.

3.2.2 The Marrakech Funds

Since the financial support from the GEF Trust Fund was principally intended to be disbursed for mitigation purposes, and not essentially for adaptation purposes, the Parties to the UNFCCC at COP 7 (held in Marrakech, Morocco) requested a kind of financial cooperation mechanism that would only support an adaptation mechanism including the transfer of adaptation technologies.[95] Thus, the Parties established the AF in order to support concrete adaptation activities, the LDCF in order to support the preparation and

91 Ibid.
92 Cf. *supra* Chapter 2.6 and Chapter 2.7.
93 Ibid.
94 Decision 7/CMA.2, FCCC/PA/CMA/2019/6/Add.1, March 16, 2020.
95 Decision 5/CP.7, FCCC/CP/2001/13/Add.1, 21 January 2002.

implementation of the National Adaptation Programmes of Action (NAPAs) and the SCCF with a special focus on adaptation and the transfer of adaptation technology.[96] The Paris Rulebook has confirmed that the LDCF, the SCCF and the AF will serve the Paris Agreement.[97]

3.2.2.1 The AF

In line with promotion of equity through the realization of the principle of CBDR, the UNFCCC established the AF in order to finance the concrete adaptation projects in climate change vulnerable developing and least developed countries.[98] It is managed and supervised by the Adaptation Fund Board (AFB).[99] The AFB is composed of 16 members and 16 alternatives, which seat at least twice a year.[100]

The AF provides the option of direct access to its Fund for the concrete adaptation projects of the non-Annex I Party developing countries, which are Parties to the Kyoto Protocol.[101] The direct access means that the accredited implementing agencies of a country can gain access to the AF directly to implement approved projects or programmes. The non-Annex I Parties are eligible to apply for funding directly through the nominated National Implementing Entity. The National Implementing Entity is a kind of national legal entity, which can be nominated by any non-Annex I Party and then recognized by the AFB after fulfilling the fiduciary standard set by the Board. If the AFB does not accredit the National Implementing Entity, the funding will have to be disbursed through multilateral institutions or regional banks, that are accredited by the AFB.[102]

Müller (2010) describes the aforementioned flexible path of direct access to the AF as 'one of the most lucid examples of devolution of decision-making in international fund structuring to date'. It is obvious that by allowing a national implementing entity of a non-Annex I Party to receive funding, the AF has avoided the conventional lengthy bureaucratic process of access to any international funding. Arguably its advantages are twofold.

96 L. Christiansen et al. (eds.), *Technologies for Adaptation: Perspectives and Practical Experiences,* UNEP Risø, 2011, 8.
97 *Proposal by the President Informal Compilation of L-Documents*, Version 15/12/2018, 13, 48, available at https://unfccc.int/sites/default/files/resource/Informal%20Compilation_proposal%20by%20the%20President_rev.pdf (last accessed on July 31, 2020).
98 See also Decision 1/CMP.3, FCCC/KP/CMP/2007/9/Add.1, 14 March 2008, See also *supra* Chapter 2.7.2.
99 *Adaptation Fund,* available at https://www.adaptation-fund.org/about/governance/board/ (last accessed on August 10, 2020).
100 Ibid.
101 Decision 1/CMP.3, FCCC/KP/CMP/2007/9/Add.1, 14 March 2008.
102 Benito Müller, *The Reformed Financial Mechanism of the UNFCCC: Part II The Question of Oversight Post Copenhagen Synthesis Report,* Oxford Institute for Energy Studies, 2010, 35.

First, it avoids time and resources that might be spent following a conventional bureaucratic process. Second, it creates a sense of 'national ownership of initiatives' that might facilitate the pace and quality of implementation of the project.[103]

The eligible non-Annex I Parties need to comply with the *Adaptation Funds Operational Policies and Guidelines* of the AF.[104] As per the *Adaptation Funds Operational Policies and Guidelines*, the eligible non-Annex I Party developing and least developed countries need to obtain the endorsement of a designated authority, chosen by the government of the state concerned.[105] The eligible non-Annex I Party country has to include a baseline and a results framework with its final project submission.[106] In addition, the eligible country needs to submit its proposals through an accredited National Implementing Entity or through a Multilateral Implementing Entity.[107]

Although the AF is mainly available for concrete adaptation projects and programmes, it may also provide funding for projects and programmes that contain elements of capacity building or policy mainstreaming. However, funding for the projects and programmes that contain elements of capacity building or policy mainstreaming is restricted to about 10–12 per cent of the project budget.[108]

The World Bank is acting as an interim trustee of the AF. The main source of finance of the AF comes from the amount gained through trading CERs generated from the CDM projects. This is because 2 per cent of CER units issued to CDM projects are required to donate to the AF.[109]

The requirement to donate 2 per cent of the income generated from CER units derived from the CDM projects to the AF has an indirect impact on the promotion of equity based on the realization of the principle of CBDR in the climate finance mechanism of the UNFCCC. Such a requirement encourages the non-Annex I Parties to host more CDM projects, since hosting more CDM projects will result in increased funding of the AF.

Since one of the main objectives of the CDM is to promote local sustainable development,[110] the increased number of CDM projects can arguably play an

103 Ibid, 36.
104 AFB, *Operational Policies and Guidelines for Parties to Access Resources from the Adaptation Fund* (amended in October, 2017), available at https://www.adaptation-fund.org/wp-content/uploads/2017/08/OPG-amended-in-October-2017-1.pdfhttps://www.adaptation-fund.org/about/governance/board (last accessed on August 10, 2020).
105 Ibid, 22.
106 Ibid, 25.
107 Ibid, 31.
108 N. C. Trujillo and S. Nakhooda, *The Effectiveness of Climate Finance: A Review of the Adaptation,* Working Paper 373, U.K. Aid, March 2013, 4ff.
109 For more about the CDM see *infra* Chapter 3.4.1.
110 Art. 12(3) of the Kyoto Protocol 1997.

enhanced role in promoting the sustainable development of the hosting countries. At the same time, the increased number of CDM projects can assist the Annex I Parties to meet their emission reduction obligation of the Convention on a greater scale and at cheaper cost. Besides, the increased number of CDM projects would generate an increased number of CER units, which would result in increased donations to the AF. If the AF contains more funds, the non-Annex I Parties will gain more access to the funding, as such they will be better able to implement the adaptation obligation derived from the Convention. Therefore, one could argue that the link between the CDM projects and the AF has a positive impact on the fulfilment of the mitigation obligation of the Annex I Parties as well as the adaptation obligation of the non-Annex I Parties to the Convention.

Besides, the requirement to donate 2 per cent of the income generated from CER units issued under the CDM projects to the AF arguably promotes the principle of equity on the basis of the realization of the principle of CBDR for its 'resource redistribution' impact.[111] In practice, it is clear that the proponents of the CDM projects choose a handful of non-Annex I Party developing countries that contain favourable conditions for hosting projects. For this reason, a large proportion of the total benefit of hosting CDM projects goes to only a few developing countries.[112] As a consequence, most other non-Annex I Party developing and least developed countries are deprived of the benefit of hosting CDM projects, which is contrary to the aim of the introduction of the CDM.[113] This disparity between the non-Annex I Party developing and least developed countries in the quantity of CDM projects they host may arguably be balanced to a certain extent by way of a redistribution of the benefits generated from the CDM projects by donating to the AF.

However, the AF also receives donations from governments, the private sector and individuals.[114] One could argue that by providing the aforementioned stakeholders with the source of finance, the AF provides them with an opportunity to fulfil the global 'common responsibility' to combat climate change. From this point of view, it is possible to remark that being guided by the principle of CBDR, the AF also promotes equity in the international climate change regime.[115]

111 Cf. *supra* Chapter 2.7.2.

112 For example, Brazil, China, India, South Africa, etc.

113 Art. 12(2) of Kyoto Protocol states the objective of introducing CDM as: 'The purpose of the clean development mechanism shall be to assist Parties not included in Annex I in achieving sustainable development and in contributing to the ultimate objective of the Convention, and to assist Parties included in Annex I in achieving compliance with their quantified emission limitation and reduction commitments under Article 3'.

114 GEF, *Climate Change Adaptation,* available at www.thegef.org/gef/adaptation (last accessed on August 9, 2020).

115 See *supra* Chapter 2.6 and *supra* Chapter 2.7.

3.2.2.2 The LDCF

In order to support the least developed countries to carry out a special work programme that includes the preparation and implementation of the NAPAs, COP 7 established the LDCF.[116]

GEF is responsible for managing the LDCF as per the request of the COP. The GEF is 'guided by and accountable to' the COP. The governing body of this Fund is the LDCF Council. The Council meets twice a year.[117]

As a first step to utilization of the fund, COP 7 requested the GEF to employ the LDCF to meet the agreed full costs of preparation of the NAPA.[118] Hence, in 2002 the GEF issued the *Operational Guidelines for Expedited Funding for the Preparation of National Adaptation Programmes of Action by Least Developed Countries.*[119] The main objectives of the preparation and implementation process of the NAPAs include identification of adaptation priorities at the national level and facilitating access to the funds for the least developed country non-Annex I Parties to the Convention to address the most urgent and essential needs.[120]

Considering the urgent need of the least developed countries, the LDCF follows a comparatively simplified procedure of fund distribution in comparison with the traditional procedure of fund disbursement of the GEF funds. However, like the SCCF, the LDCF also follows the GEF's fiduciary standards, result-based frameworks and monitoring and evaluation practices for ensuring sound financial management. Unless the LDCF Council decides otherwise as a response to the COP guidance, the Fund also follows the GEF operational policies.[121]

To comply with common but differentiated responsibility derived from the Convention, the Annex II Party developed countries (along with some Annex I Party countries as well as some non-Annex I Party developing countries, which are voluntarily interested in donating to the Fund) are required to donate to the LDCF.[122] Pursuant to the realization of equity based on the realization of the principle of CBDR, any non-Annex I Party least developed country that has already completed its NAPA is entitled to receive funding from the LDCF. This Fund reflects the principle of CBDR due to its special favours to the least developed countries. It is an example of the implementation

116 Decisions 5/CP.7 and 7/CP.7, FCCC/CP/2001/13/Add.1, 21 January 2002.
117 GEF, *Accessing Resources Under the Least Developed Countries Fund*, May 2, 2011, 7.
118 Decision 27/CP.7, FCCC/CP/2001/13/Add.4, 21 January 2002.
119 GEF, *Operational Guidelines for Expedited Funding for the Preparation of National Adaptation Programs of Action by Least Developed Countries*, April 2002, available at https://unfccc.int/sites/default/files/gefsecnapaguideeng.pdf (last accessed on August 9, 2020). See *supra* Chapter 2.6 and Chapter 2.7.
120 GEF, May 2, 2011, 7.
121 Ibid.
122 Ibid.

of the substantive requirement of the Convention to take ‘full account of the specific needs and special situations of the least developed countries’.[123]

However, to apply for funding from the LDCF, a non-Annex I Party least developed country has to prepare its NAPA and send the same to the UNFCCC Secretariat for web publication. The LDCF divides the projects eligible for receiving fund into FSPs and MSPs. Projects with a value of more than US$ 2 million are categorized as FSPs, and projects with a value of US$ 2 million or less are categorized as MSPs.[124]

After developing a concept, the proponents of the projects that wish to receive financial assistance from the LDCF have to request assistance from any of the ten implementing agencies of the GEF. The project proponents can choose the most appropriate of the ten implementing agencies to fund their project.[125] It is quite possible that the agency chosen will be different from the agency that supported the project in preparing the NAPA. The LDCF project proponents are required to receive endorsement from the national GEF Operational Focal Point.[126]

The steps involved in the LDCF project cycle for an FSP include submission of a Project Identification Form, and a Project Preparation Grant (if needed). If the LDCF Council approves the Project Identification Form, then the chosen GEF agency helps the project proponent to develop the project into a detailed Full Project Document. Thereafter, if the GEF Chief Executive Officer endorses the project, it is ready to receive funding.[127]

For the MSPs the project proponents can directly submit the Full Project Document. If it is approved and endorsed by the GEF Chief Executive Officer, the project is ready for implementation.[128]

The LDCF has some unique characteristics that make it different from the traditional GEF trust funds. To be eligible to receive money from this Fund it is not essential that the proposed project generates global environmental benefits. While no precondition of generation of adaptation benefit exists to receive funding from the GEF Trust Fund, generation of adaptation benefit is an essential precondition to receive money from the LDCF.[129]

While funds from the GEF Trust Fund are allocated according to the Resource Allocation Framework, this is not the case for financial assistance from the LDCF. Financial assistance from the GEF Trust Fund has to follow

123 Cf. Art. 4(9) of the UNFCCC 1992.
124 GEF, May 2, 2011,7.
125 Ibid, 9. GEF guidelines are available online to assist in the selection of the appropriate agency according to its comparative advantage in climate change adaptation: www.thegef.org/gef/gef_agencies (last accessed on July 3, 2020).
126 GEF, May 2, 2011, 8.
127 Ibid, 9.
128 Ibid, 9.
129 Cf. GEF, May 2, 2011, 8.

the concept of the 'incremental cost'.[130] Financial assistance from the LDCF does not need to comply with the 'incremental cost' concept.

Furthermore the LDCF also involves the option of approving projects on a rolling basis, which is not available under the GEF Trust Fund. In line with the promotion of the principle of equity, the LDCF has accepted a provision to fund projects in accordance with 'balanced accesses' approach.[131]

Moreover, the ceiling for an MSP under the GEF Trust Fund is US$ 1 million, whereas the ceiling for an MSP under the LDCF is US$ 2 million.[132]

3.2.2.3 The SCCF

The SCCF was designed to complement other funds established under the GEF's climate change focal area as well as other bilateral and multilateral funds. It works as a catalyst to leverage the funding from other bilateral and multilateral funding systems. In line with implementation of the principle of CBDR the Annex II Party countries to the UNFCC are required to contribute to this Fund along with some Annex I Party countries/ non-Annex I Party countries that may voluntarily be interested in contributing to the Fund. Any non-Annex I Party developing or least developed country to the Convention is eligible to receive financial aid from this Fund.[133]

Though adaptation activities have been set as the top priority to receive funding from the SCCF, technology transfer associated with 'capacity building' for technology transfer are two other important areas that are also eligible to receive funding from the SCCF. Moreover, the initial aims of this UNFCCC fund included funding projects involving energy, transport, industry, agriculture, forestry and waste management. Another initial aim of the SCCF was to facilitate the economic diversification of fossil fuel dependent countries. However, as of today the options for funding adaptation and technology transfer related projects are active.[134]

As per the COP guidelines, lists of the areas of adaptation eligible to receive funding from the SCCF include: water resource management, land management, agriculture, health, infrastructure development, fragile ecosystems, integrated coastal zone management and climatic disaster risk management. In relation to the transfer of technology, the SCCF particularly favours, but is not restricted to, those environmentally sound technologies that focus on the reduction of emissions or atmospheric concentrations of greenhouse gases. In this regard, the SCCF is entitled to provide funding to implement the results of the Technology Needs Assessment (TNA) of the relevant non-Annex I Party

130 Ibid.
131 Ibid.
132 Ibid.
133 Decision 7/CP.7, FCCC/CP/2001/13/Add.1, 21 January 2002.
134 Ibid.

country. Besides, it can also provide funding for technological information, capacity building for technology transfer and for enabling the environment of any non-Annex I Party developing or least developed country.[135]

By providing fund for not only the transfer of environmentally sound technologies, but also for building capacity in the state receiving the technology, the SCCF plays a twofold role in technology transfer. This is because 'capacity building' is not only an important element in the promotion of intra-generational equity, but also it facilitates technology transfer by creating a favourable environment in a non-Annex I Party developing or least developed country.[136]

The SCCF is managed by the GEF. In this regard, the GEF receives guidance from the COP. The GEF also reports to the COP. The governing body of the SCCF is called the SCCF Council, which meets twice a year.[137]

For the purpose of securing financial management, the GEF also follows the GEF's fiduciary standards, result-based frameworks and monitoring and evaluation practices. The SCCF also follows the GEF operational policies unless the SCCF Council needs to take a different decision in response to the COP guidance.[138]

Projects eligible to receive funding from the SCCF are divided into two kinds. Projects that are of more than US$ 2 million in value, which are known as FSPs, and projects that are of US$ 2 million or less in value, which are known as MSPs.[139] The steps involved in the project cycle of an FSP for the SCCF include submission of a project identification form (PIF) which also entails a project preparation grant (if desired). If the SCCF Council grants the PIF, then the GEF agency works in collaboration with the project proponent to develop the project and convert it into a detailed project document. The project is eligible to receive funding once it has been endorsed by the GEF

135 Climate Funds Update, Special Climate Change Fund, available at https://climatefundsupdate.org/the-funds/special-climate-change-fund (last accessed on March 22, 2021).

136 See *supra* Chapter 2.6 and Chapter 2.7.

137 Global Environment Facility, *Programming to Implement the Guidance for the Special Climate Change Fund Adopted by the Conference of the Parties to the United Nations Framework Convention on Climate Change at Its Ninth Session*, GEF/C.24/12 October 15, 2004, page 1 ff, available at https://www.thegef.org/sites/default/files/council-meeting-documents/C.24.12_5.pdf (last accessed on March 23, 2021), see also LDCF/SCCF Council Meetings, available at https://www.thegef.org/council-meetings/ldcf-sccf (last accessed on March 22, 2021).

138 Global Environment Facility, *Programming to Implement the Guidance for the Special Climate Change Fund Adopted by the Conference of the Parties to the United Nations Framework Convention on Climate Change at Its Ninth Session*, GEF/C.24/12 October 15, 2004, page 6, available at https://www.thegef.org/sites/default/files/council-meeting-documents/C.24.12_5.pdf (last accessed on March 22, 2021),

139 Climate Funds Update, Special Climate Change Fund, available at https://climatefundsupdate.org/the-funds/special-climate-change-fund (last accessed on March 22, 2021).

Chief Executive Officer. For MSPs, the project proponent needs to submit a detailed full project document and it can come into operation after being endorsed by the GEF Chief Executive Officer.[140]

The application for funding needs to be submitted through the selected GEF agency.[141] The SCCF is unique and different from the conventional GEF trust funds for several reasons. It is not essential to prove that the project will generate global benefit to receive funding from the SCCF.[142] This provision of receiving finance from the SCCF is different from the GEF Trust Fund, which requires that the proposed project to generate global environmental benefit.[143] Furthermore, except for mitigation related technology transfer project, any proposed project must prove that it generates adaptation benefit in order to receive funding from the SCCF.[144]

Although funding from the GEF Trust Fund is allocated in accordance with the Resource Allocation Framework, the funding from the SCCF does not follow any Resource Allocation Framework.[145] The non-Annex I Parties and civil society groups have strongly criticized the SCCF because of this. In addition, finance from the SCCF is not allocated according to the 'incremental cost' principle.[146] This should also be noted as a 'difference' from the system of the GEF Trust Fund, which allocates funding based on the 'incremental cost' principle.

The objective of the SCCF is to 'serve as a catalyst to leverage additional resources from bilateral and other multilateral sources'. In line with the

140 UN Environment Programme, Financing Opportunities, Special Climate Change Fund (SCCF), available at https://cambioclimatico-regatta.org/index.php/en/financing-opportunities/item/fondo-especial-para-el-cambio-climatico-fecc-2 (last accessed on March 22, 2021).

141 The 18 institutions which act as GEF agencies are: Asian Development Bank (ADB), African Development Bank (AfDB), European Bank for Reconstruction and Development (EBRD), Food and Agriculture Organization of the United Nations (FAO), Inter-American Development Bank (IDB), International Fund for Agricultural Development (IFAD), United Nations Development Programme (UNDP), United Nations Environment Programme (UNEP), United Nations Industrial Development Organization (UNIDO), The World Bank Group (WBG), Conservation International (CI), Development Bank of Latin America (CAF), Development Bank of Southern Africa (DBSA), Foreign Economic Cooperation Office, Ministry of Environmental Protection of China (FECO), Brazilian Biodiversity Fund (FUNBIO), International Union for Conservation of Nature (IUCN), West African Development Bank (BOAD) and World Wildlife Fund (WWF-US), see GEF, *GEF Agencies*, available at https://www.thegef.org/partners/gef-agencies (last accessed on September 4, 2020)

142 Please note that this provision is not applicable to projects relating to the transfer of mitigation technology.

143 Cf. *supra* Chapter 3.2.1.

144 GEF, Accessing Resources under the Special Climate Change Fund (SCCF), May 2011, p 8, available at https://www.thegef.org/sites/default/files/publications/23470_SCCF_1.pdf (last accessed on March 23, 2021).

145 Ibid.

146 Ibid.

promotion of equity on the basis of the realization of the principle of CBDR, the SCCF gives funding to those projects that are prepared on the basis of a 'country-driven' approach and take into consideration national sustainable development and poverty-reduction strategies. At the time of providing financial assistance, the SCCF considers whether the proposed project or programme is 'cost-effective', and whether it complies with National Communications or NAPA and other relevant studies and information provided by the relevant non-Annex I Party. One could argue that such consideration of compliance with the NAPA and other relevant studies and information facilitates implementation of the principle of CBDR by assisting the Parties to act in accordance with obligations derived from the UNFCCC.[147]

Hence, non-Annex I Party developing and least developed countries can benefit from the SCCF implementing their adaptation related projects or projects involving energy, transport, industry, agriculture, forestry and waste management, etc. Through implementing these projects with assistance from the SCCF, these countries can also ensure transferring environmentally sound technologies to the relevant adaptation sectors. These countries can also receive financial assistance from the SCCF to implement projects specifically focusing on technology transfer or capacity building. The promotion of the transfer of environmentally sound technologies or capacity building (with financial assistance from the SCCF) will *de facto* facilitate local sustainable development in the non-Annex I Party developing and least developed countries concerned.

Based on the above discussions, it is evident that while the texts of the Convention implemented the principle of CBDR mainly for mitigation purposes,[148] the adoption of the Marrakech Accords which introduced the Marrakech Funds have in practical terms brought the adaptation issues under the financial mechanism of the Convention. By financing adaptation related projects, the Marrakech Funds arguably facilitate the transfer of adaptation related technologies in non-Annex I Party developing and least developed countries. Accordingly, these countries can obtain better access to the required adaptation technologies by seeking financial cooperation from the Marrakech Funds.

Hence, through financing adaptation related projects and facilitating the transfer of adaptation technologies, the Marrakech Funds have implemented the principles of equity and CBDR in the climate change adaptation sector.

3.2.3 The Fast Start Finance and the GCF

In line with promotion of equity based on the principle of CBDR, under the Copenhagen-Accord (an outcome of COP 15, held in 2009 in Copenhagen, Denmark), the Annex II Parties agreed to mobilize US$ 100 billion a year as

147 Cf. Decision 5/CP.9, FCCC/CP/2003/6/Add.1, 22 April 2004.

148 Mizan R. Khan and J. Timmons Roberts, 'Adaptation and International Climate Policy', *WIREs Climate Change,* Vol. 4, 2013, 171–189, 172.

climate finance by the year 2020. The aim of such finance was to ensure a balanced distribution between mitigation and adaptation. This collective commitment of the Copenhagen-Accord was later formally established by the Cancun Agreement and named the Fast Start Finance (FSF). Under the FSF, the Annex II Parties (not specified in the text) made a collective commitment to supply new and additional resources of US$ 30 billion for the period 2010–2012 to address the needs of the non-Annex I Parties to the Convention.[149]

As a reflection of the principle of equity on the basis of the principle of CBDR, the Cancun Agreement (an outcome of COP 16, held in 2010 in Cancun, Mexico) reaffirmed that the most vulnerable (to climate change) developing and least developed countries would get preferential treatment in receiving funding from the FSF.[150] The fund of the FSF is disbursed through the GCF.[151]

COP 17 (held in 2011 in Durban, South Africa) welcomed the FSF contributed by the Annex II Parties as fulfilment of their collective commitment to provide 'new and additional' finance of around US$ 30 billion for the period 2010–2012.[152] COP 17 also took note of the information given by the Annex II Parties about their contribution to the FSF and suggested the Annex II Parties should continue to increase the transparency of their reporting on fulfilling their FSF commitments.[153]

The suggestion of enhanced transparency in reporting by the Annex II Parties has practical implications. Because, although the pledge of the FSF was agreed to be 'new and additional', a study by Oxfam (2012) reported a different state affairs. The Oxfam study observed that in practice only 33 per cent of the claimed FSF was 'new'. The rest of the disbursed amount was agreed before the Copenhagen Accord and therefore before the establishment of the FSF. It was also observed that only 24 per cent of the amount disbursed under the FSF was 'additional' to the existing promises. Moreover, only 43 per cent of the amount disbursed was disbursed as a grant, and the remainder was given as loan, which has to be repaid with interest by the non-Annex I Party countries.[154]

Another study conducted by Oxfam (2013) stated that although the Annex II Parties claimed to have disbursed US$ 16.3 billion as grants, the actual amount of grant was US$ 7.6 billion. The remainder was distributed as a loan that had to be repaid with interest. The disbursed amount is far less than the

149 Decision 1/CP.16, Para 95.
150 Decision 1/CP.16, Para 95.
151 Oxfam, *Climate 'Fiscal Cliff' Looms for Developing Countries if Leaders Come to Doha with No New Money,* available at https://www.oxfam.org/en/press-releases/climate-fiscal-cliff-looms-developing-countries-if-leaders-come-doha-no-new-money (last accessed on April 15, 2020).
152 Decision 2/CP.17, Para 125–126.
153 Ibid.
154 Ibid.

amount predicted as essential (more than US$ 100 billion per year) for the adaptation and mitigation needs of the non-Annex I Party countries.[155]

However, as an open operating entity of the financial mechanism under the UNFCCC, the Cancun Agreement introduced the GCF.[156] The GCF was later officially established by way of a Decision of COP 17.[157] It is noteworthy that the GCF was designed to help to achieve the ultimate goals of the Convention which also include the transfer of environmentally sound technologies and the promotion of sustainable development.

The GCF is intended to promote equity on the basis of the realization of the principle of CBDR by considering the special needs of the climate change vulnerable developing and least developed countries (at the time of promoting the transfer of environmentally sound technologies to those countries).[158] The GCF could play an important role in climate change mitigation as well as attaining the sustainable development objectives of the Convention through its vision of promoting a low carbon development strategy. Moreover, the GCF requirement to involve relevant stakeholders realizes procedural intra-generational equity in decision-making, which is an essential element of the realization of sustainable development.[159]

It should be pointed out that while developing and least developed countries are only entitled to receive funding for mitigation related projects from the GEF Trust Fund and only for adaptation related projects from the Marrakech Funds, those countries are entitled to receive funding from the GCF for both adaptation and mitigation related projects.

In COP 17, the Durban Platform took the decision to form the GCF Board. In line with the principle of equity, the Durban Platform required an equal number of representations from the Annex II, and non-Annex I Parties on the GCF Board.[160] In order to select trustees, the Durban Platform also required a methodology to be followed, which is in line with the realization of the procedural equity. The Platform required the GCF Board to initiate a transparent and competitive bidding process intending either to replace or to continue with the World Bank as its interim trustee.[161]

COP 19 (held in 2013 in Warsaw, Poland) adopted official guidance on policies, programme priorities and eligibility criteria for receiving funding from the GCF.[162] The guidelines ensured substantive equity in fund distribution by

155 Oliver Tickell, 'COP 19: Poor countries left in the dark on climate finance', *Ecologist,* November 14, 2013, available at https://theecologist.org/2013/nov/14/cop19-poor-countries-dark-climate-finance (last accessed on April 15, 2014).

156 Decision 1/CP.16.

157 Decision 1/CP.16. and Decision 3/CP.17, FCCC/CP/2011/9/Add.1, 15 March 2012

158 Cf. *supra* Chapter 2.6 and Chapter 2.7.

159 Cf. Decision 3 /CP.17, Para 31; see also *supra* Chapter 2.6.

160 Decision 3/CP.17, Annex, Para 9.

161 Decision 3/CP.17, Para 16.

162 Decision 4/CP.19, FCCC/CP/2013/10/Add.1, 31 January 2014, Para 9.

requiring a balance of resource distribution between adaptation related projects and mitigation related projects.[163] Moreover, the guidelines promote equity through realizing the principle of CBDR while pursuing 'country-driven' approaches.[164] The guidelines further facilitate an intra-generational approach to equity on the basis of the realization of the principle of CBDR through requiring assurance that all non-Annex I Parties will have access to the resources of the GCF.[165] Facilitating the 'differentiated responsibilities' of financial contribution of the Annex II Parties, COP 19 called for 'ambitious and timely contributions' by Annex II Parties by COP 20.[166] The requirement of 'country-driven' approaches for the GCF can arguably result in accelerated assistance to the small island and least developed countries, which are especially affected by the negative effects of climate change.

COP 25 (held in 2019 in Madrid, Spain) encouraged the GCF to continue to enhance its support for the climate change adaptation of developing countries. It has further requested the GCF to rapidly accomplish 'its work on guidance on the approach and scope for providing support to adaptation activities'.[167]

In connection with technology transfer, COP 25 encouraged the GCF to 'continue to collaborate with the Climate Technology Centre and Network (CTCN) and the Technology Executive Committee (TEC) with a view to both strengthening cooperative action on technology development and transfer at different stages of the technology cycle'.[168] In relation to the promotion and realization of equity and CBDR it further encouraged the GCF to continue its collaboration with the CTCN and the TEC to achieve 'a balance between support for mitigation and support for adaptation'.[169]

Although it has a separate board, trustee and secretariat, the legal structure of the GCF requires it to remain under the auspices of the UNFCCC. One could argue that since the GCF is placed under the auspices of the UNFCCC, it also needs to accept the principles of equity and CBDR as its guiding principles. By remaining under the auspices of the UNFCCC, the GCF ensures the wide-ranging involvement of all Parties in the GCF activities. While involving all stakeholders in the decision-making process is an essential condition of the realization of procedural equity, it could be said that putting the GCF under the auspices of the UNFCCC is in line with the realization of the principle of equity.

However, the governing legal structure of the GCF is more like the governing legal structure of the GEF, and less like the governing legal structure of the AF. While the governing structure of the AF obliges it to remain

163 Decision 4/CP.19, Para 9.
164 Decision 4/CP.19, Para 9.
165 Decision 4/CP.19, Para 9.
166 Decision 4/CP.19, Para13.
167 Decision 6/CMA.2, FCCC/PA/CMA/2019/6/Add.1, 16 March 2020, Para 6.
168 Ibid, Para 7.
169 Ibid.

'accountable to and function under the guidance and authority of the Conference of Parties', the governing structure of the GCF requires it to remain 'accountable to and function under the guidance of the Conference of Parties'.[170] Realizing the spirit of the procedural intra-generational equity, the GCF governing legal structure ensures that the GCF Board is equally represented by both Annex I and non-Annex I Parties to the Convention.[171]

The GCF was officially started in September 2014.[172] One of the most important issues for the GCF is the sources of finance. Though as per provisions of the Convention, the Annex II Parties are under a commitment to provide financial assistance and technology transfer cooperation to the non-Annex I Parties,[173] clarification is needed as to how or in what manner the GCF will receive funds from the Annex II Parties. The Cancun Agreement did not make any decision about how finances would flow to the GCF. The Cancun Agreement merely took note of

> relevant reports on the financing needs and options for mobilization of resources to address the needs of developing country Parties with regard to climate change adaptation and mitigation, including the report of the High-level Advisory Group on Climate Change Finance [AGF].[174]

The governing instrument of the GCF provided little elaboration on the source of finances. It stated that the fund 'would receive financial inputs from developed country Parties to the Convention'. In addition, it stated that the GCF 'may also receive financial inputs from a variety of other sources, public and private, including alternative sources'.[175]

COP 19 (held in 2013 in Warsaw, Poland) further supported the aforementioned requirements of the GCF governing instrument. COP 19 called for 'ambitious and timely contributions by developed countries', as such it invited financial cooperation from 'a variety of other sources, public and private, including alternative sources'.[176] One could argue that because of the amount of funding necessary for climate change adaptation and mitigation globally; the inclusion of 'a variety of other sources' has important implications in the climate finance mechanism. The inclusion of 'a variety of other sources' as a source of finance for the GCF has arguably important implications, especially in the promotion of procedural equity through involving mass participation in contributing to climate finances.[177]

170 Decision 3/CP.17, Annex, Para 4.
171 Decision 7/CP.18, FCCC/CP/2012/8/Add.1, 28 February 2013, Para 1.
172 Congressional Research Service, *The Green Climate Fund (GCF),* available at https://fas.org/sgp/crs/misc/IF10382.pdf (last accessed on July 30, 2020).
173 Cf. Art. 4 of the UNFCCC 1992.
174 Decision 1/CP.16, Para 101.
175 Decision 3/CP.17, Annex, Para 29–30.
176 Decision 1/CP.19, FCCC/CP/2013/10/Add.1, 31 January 2014, Para 13, and Para 15.
177 Cf. *supra* Chapter 2.6 and Chapter 2.7.2.

3.2.4 Mechanism for Loss and Damage

COP 19 (held in 2013 in Warsaw, Poland) established the Warsaw International Mechanism for Loss and Damage associated with Climate Change Impacts.[178] This mechanism has been established in order to 'address loss and damage associated with impacts of climate change, including extreme events and slow onset events' in developing countries particularly vulnerable to the adverse effects of climate change.[179] The Paris Agreement endorses this mechanism and requires Parties to 'recognize the importance of averting, minimizing and addressing loss and damage associated with the adverse effects of climate change'.[180] The Mechanism realizes the principle of equity and CBDR by requiring Parties to cooperate and collaborate to enhance understanding, action and support on the following issues: 1) Early warning systems; 2) Emergency preparedness; 3) Slow onset events; 4) Events that may involve irreversible and permanent loss and damage; 5) Comprehensive risk assessment and management; 6) Risk insurance facilities, climate risk pooling and other insurance solutions; 7) Non-economic losses; and 8) Resilience of communities, livelihoods and ecosystems.[181] No doubt, the above-required cooperation and collaboration will automatically require financial or technological cooperation between Parties.

The Mechanism explicitly requires the Parties to take into account 'common but differentiated responsibilities and respective capabilities and specific national and regional development priorities'.[182] The promotion of the principle of equity on the basis of the principle of CBDR is also found in the Loss and Damage Mechanism's function of resource redistribution through assistance in finance and technology transfer. In addition, it realizes the principle of intra-generational equity through assisting Parties in capacity building.[183]

In 2019, COP 25 reaffirmed the Warsaw International Mechanism's role 'in promoting the implementation of approaches to avert, minimize and address loss and damage associated with climate change impacts in a comprehensive, integrated and coherent manner'.[184] Moreover, it invited the GCF to 'continue providing financial resources for activities relevant to averting, minimizing and addressing loss and damage in developing country Parties'.[185]

However, since different funds under the Convention have been established to fulfil different purposes, all these Convention funds follow different methodologies and different strategic objectives. As a result of the diversities in

178 UNFCCC, *Warsaw Outcomes,* available at https://unfccc.int/process/conferences/the-big-picture/milestones/outcomes-of-the-warsaw-conference (last accessed on August 21, 2020).
179 Decision 2/CP.19, FCCC/CP/2013/10/Add.1, Para 1.
180 Art. 8(1) of the Paris Agreement 2015.
181 Art. 8(3) and Art. 8(4) of the Paris Agreement 2015.
182 Decision 3/CP.18., Para 6.
183 Cf. *supra* Chapter 2.6 and Chapter 2.7.
184 Decision 2/CMA.2, FCCC/PA/CMA/2019/6/Add.1, 16 March 2020, *Chapeau.*
185 Ibid, Para 8.

methodologies and strategies between funds, the non-Annex I Party developing and least developed countries are required to adjust their priority needs and implementation plans in order to maintain their eligibility to apply for financial cooperation from different funds. This imposes an extra load on developing and least developed countries as they have to go through extra administrative and bureaucratic procedures in order to secure the necessary urgent financial funds. For this reason, the COP entrusted the SCCF to come up with a suggestion as to how to improve harmonization, coherence and coordination between the different funds established under the Convention.[186]

During COP 20, the Parties requested the SCCF to consider issues in relation to establishing possible future institutional linkages between the AF and other institutions under the Convention.[187] The functions of the SCCF include working to ensure coherence and coordination in the disbursement of the different sources of climate financing.[188]

3.3 The UNFCCC Technology Transfer Mechanisms

Apart from establishing a financial mechanism that facilitates the transfer of environmentally sound technologies in non-Annex I Parties to the Convention, the UNFCCC has also established mechanisms for facilitating the transfer of environmentally sound technologies in developing and least developed countries (non-Annex I Parties to the Convention). Like climate finance, direct technology transfer mechanisms of the UNFCCC are also considered to be a tool in the realization of equity based on the principle of CBDR.[189] The key provision for the need for technology transfer has been specified in Art. 4.5 of the Convention:

> [t]he developed country Parties and other Parties included in annex II shall take all practicable steps to promote, facilitate and finance, as appropriate, the transfer of, or access to, environmentally sound technologies and know-how to other Parties, particularly developing country Parties.[190]

This means that the obligations imposed on the Annex II Parties to take 'all practicable steps' including financial cooperation is intended to promote the transfer of environmentally sound technologies to other Parties to the UNFCCC. In line with the implementation of the principle of CBDR, Art. 4.5 required special focus to be given to the non-Annex I Parties to the Convention. Hence, through the compliance with such obligations by the Annex II

186 Oumar Kaloga with contribution by David Eckstein, *Rationalization of the Financial Mechanism of the UNFCCC: Options for Adaptation Finance,* Briefing Paper, Bonn, German Watch, 2015, 8.
187 Decision 2/CMP.10, FCCC/KP/CMP/2014/9/Add.1, 2 February 2015, Para 7.
188 Decision 2/CP.17, Para 121.
189 See *supra* Chapter 3.2 and Chapter 2.7.2.
190 Art. 4(5) of the UNFCCC 1992.

Parties, the climate change vulnerable developing and least developed countries have become better able to adapt to and mitigate the adverse effects of climate change, which will allow them to meet their 'common responsibility' of combating climate change and preventing environmental degradation. As the transfer of technology cannot truly take place through transferring only equipment or products, Art. 4(5) requires not only the transfer of environmentally sound technologies but also the transfer of know-how associated with the concerned technologies.

As complete transfer of environmentally sound technologies needs not only the transfer of the product and know-how associated with the product, but also the creation of a favourable environment as well as building capacity in the technology receiving state,[191] the Convention also requires the Annex II Parties to 'support the development and enhancement of endogenous capacities and technologies of developing country Parties'.[192] Arguably, such a requirement by the Convention is aimed at facilitating technology transfer in non-Annex I Party countries in a complete manner so that it complies with the definition of technology transfer specified under Agenda 21.[193] As consequences of such a requirement of the Convention, 'capacity building' and 'enabling environments' have been included as two main themes of the UNFCCC Technology Transfer Framework.[194] The requirement to promote 'capacity building' and an 'enabling environment' can be very important for the non-Annex I Party developing and, especially, least developed countries.

Art. 4(5) of the UNFCCC also requires that all Parties and not merely the Annex II Parties 'may' take part in facilitating the development and transfer of environmentally sound technologies in the least developed countries, if possible.[195] Consequently, the non-Annex I Party advanced developing countries may also be required to help other non-Annex I Party developing and least developed countries on a voluntary basis.

Art. 4(1) of the Convention requires all Parties to 'promote and cooperate in the development, application and diffusion, including transfer of technologies' on the basis of the 'common but differentiated responsibilities' of the Parties and also on the basis of 'specific national and regional development priorities' of the Parties.[196] To realize the principle of CBDR, the requirements of Art. 4(1) are not limited to only requiring the Annex II Parties to transfer environmentally sound technologies to the non-Annex I Parties. Instead, Art. 4(1) arguably extends the obligation on the Parties to require them to innovate and develop new environmentally sound technologies, which might be essential for climate change adaptation and mitigation.

191 See *supra* Chapter 1.3.
192 Art. 4(5) of the UNFCCC 1992.
193 See *supra* Chapter 1.3.
194 See *infra* Chapter 3.3.1.1, and Chapter 3.3.1.2.
195 Art.4.5. of the UNFCCC 1992.
196 Art 4(1)(c) of the UNFCCC 1992.

As most of the non-Annex I Party developing and least developed country Parties do not have the ability to develop the new environmentally sound technologies that they urgently need, the Annex II Parties to the Convention need to take the leading role in the research and development of new environmentally sound technologies. Such an obligation on the Annex II Parties can take on a broader meaning if it is read in conjunction with the principle clause of the Convention that requires the Annex II Parties to take 'the lead in combating climate change and the adverse effects thereof' on the basis of 'equity and in accordance with their common but differentiated responsibilities and respective capabilities'.[197]

Art. 4(1) of the Convention arguably supports the provision requiring the Annex II Parties to take 'leading role'. Art. 4(1) requires the Parties to the Convention to accomplish their obligations on the basis of the principle of CBDR as well as on the basis of 'the specific national and regional development priorities'.[198] In accordance with the spirit of the principle of CBDR, one could say that since the Annex II Parties are more capable of combating climate change and since these Parties have more historical responsibility for emitting greenhouse gases into the atmosphere, the 'leading role' has *de facto* been conferred on the Annex II Parties.[199]

Art. 4(8) of the Convention requires the Parties to 'give full consideration to what actions are necessary to the Convention' in 'the implementation of the commitments'. The necessary actions mentioned under Art. 4(8) of the Convention include actions related to 'funding, insurance, and the transfer of technology'. Art. 4(8) reflects the spirit of the principle of CBDR in stating its purpose as: 'to meet the specific needs and concerns of developing country Parties arising from the adverse effects of climate change and/or the impact of the implementation of response measures'.[200] The realization process of the principle of CBDR is further geared up while the purpose of Art. 4(8) also includes meeting in particular 'the specific needs and concerns' of the group of countries that are most vulnerable to the adverse effects of climate change in various ways.[201]

As with the UNFCCC, Art. 10(c) of the Kyoto Protocol required all Parties to:

> cooperate in the promotion of effective modalities for the development, application and diffusion of, and take all practicable steps to promote, facilitate and finance, as appropriate, the transfer of, or access to, environmentally sound technologies, know-how, practices and processes pertinent to climate change, in particular to developing countries ....

197 Art. 3(1) of the UNFCCC 1992.
198 Art. 4(1) of the UNFCCC 1992.
199 Cf. *supra* Chapter 2.7.3.
200 Art. 4(8) of the UNFCCC 1992.
201 Ibid.

In complying with the aforementioned requirements for development of new environmentally sound technologies and facilitating the transfer of environmentally sound technologies, Art. 10 (c) required the Parties to take account of 'their common but differentiated responsibilities and their specific national and regional development priorities, objectives and circumstances'.

Thus, the Kyoto Protocol obliged all Parties to cooperate with each other to promote the transfer of environmentally sound technologies and know-how associated with the environmentally sound technologies among its Parties. For this reason, it certainly promoted equity in the light of the realization of the principle of CBDR by putting special emphasis on the transfer of environmentally sound technologies to the non-Annex I Party developing countries (which also includes the least developed countries). To express the importance of addressing the issue of transfer of environmentally sound technologies, Art. 10(c) of the Kyoto Protocol required the Parties to take 'all practicable steps'.

One could argue that the obligations of Art. 10(c) of the Kyoto Protocol referred to the realization of the 'common responsibility' part of the principle of CBDR by requiring all Parties to cooperate with each other to promote the transfer of or access to environmentally sound technologies.[202] The transfer of environmentally sound technologies or ensuring all Parties have access to environmentally sound technologies is essential to achieve the 'common responsibility' of all Parties to preserve the global environment as well as combat climate change. Art. 10(c) of the Kyoto Protocol also referred to the 'differentiated responsibility' part of the CBDR principle by requiring the transfer of environmentally sound technologies especially to the developing and least developed countries, which are not capable of buying or developing environmentally sound technologies on their own.

It could also be said that the notion of 'promotion of effective modalities for the development, application and diffusion' of Art. 10(c) implicitly refers to the issues of promotion of 'capacity building' and an 'enabling environment' of the technology receiving developing and least developed countries.[203] For technology transfer to take place in a complete manner, it is essential to create an enabling environment and building capacity in the technology receiving state.[204] Accordingly it is possible to remark that the above-mentioned Kyoto encouragement of 'capacity building' and an 'enabling environment' was intended to ensure the transfer of environmentally sound technologies in a full manner.[205]

However, Art. 10(c) of the Kyoto Protocol divided the environmentally sound technologies into two broad divisions: technologies that are already in the public domain meaning they are not protected by intellectual property rights, and environmentally sound technologies that are not in the public domain meaning that they are protected by intellectual property rights. While

202 Cf. *supra* Chapter 2.7.
203 See *supra* Chapter 3.2.1.1 *supra* Chapter 3.2.1.2.
204 See *supra* Chapter 1.3.
205 Ibid.

the public domain environmentally sound technologies are not owned by any private entity, Art. 10(c) required the Parties to lay down appropriate policies in order to make sure that these technologies are transferred to the most climate change vulnerable developing and least developed countries. In order to ensure access to the environmentally sound technologies that are protected by intellectual property rights and are owned by the private sector, Art. 10(c) required the Parties to create a favourable environment encouraging the private sector to engage in transfer of environmentally sound technologies and make them available more cheaply to the climate change vulnerable developing and least developed countries.

This means that the Parties should decide and lay down policies on how the transfer of publicly owned environmentally sound technologies can be enhanced and facilitated. At the same time, the Parties need to create an 'enabling environment' for the private sector so that the non-Annex I Party developing and least developed countries can have access to their required technologies.

Apart from the aforementioned provisions, the Kyoto Protocol directly or indirectly promoted the transfer of environmentally sound technologies through the introduction of three flexible mechanisms: the emission trading mechanism,[206] the joint implementation (JI) mechanism[207] and the clean development mechanism (CDM).[208]

However, to institutionalize the requirements of financial cooperation and technology transfer, Art. 3(14) of the Kyoto Protocol required the COP serving as the meeting of the Parties to this Protocol to consider at its first session how a mechanism for funding, insurance and transfer of technology could be established.[209] Accordingly, several policies were adopted under the UNFCCC regime with a view to facilitating the realization of the technology transfer obligation of the UNFCCC and the Kyoto Protocol – the Technology

206 'Emissions trading, as set out in Article 17 of the Kyoto Protocol, allows countries that have emission units to spare – emissions permitted them but not "used" – to sell this excess capacity to countries that are over their targets.' See https://unfccc.int/process/the-kyoto-protocol/mechanisms/emissions-trading (last accessed on August 20, 2020).

207 'The mechanism known as "joint implementation", defined in Article 6 of the Kyoto Protocol, allows a country with an emission reduction or limitation commitment under the Kyoto Protocol (Annex B Party) to earn emission reduction units (ERUs) from an emission-reduction or emission removal project in another Annex B Party, each equivalent to one tonne of CO_2, which can be counted towards meeting its Kyoto target.' See https://unfccc.int/process/the-kyoto-protocol/mechanisms/joint-implementation (last accessed on August 20, 2020).

208 'The Clean Development Mechanism (CDM), defined in Article 12 of the Protocol, allows a country with an emission-reduction or emission-limitation commitment under the Kyoto Protocol (Annex B Party) to implement an emission-reduction project in developing countries. Such projects can earn saleable certified emission reduction (CER) credits, each equivalent to one tonne of CO_2, which can be counted towards meeting Kyoto targets.' See https://unfccc.int/process-and-meetings/the-kyoto-protocol/mechanisms-under-the-kyoto-protocol/the-clean-development-mechanism (last accessed on August 20, 2020).

209 Art. 3(14) of the Kyoto Protocol 1997.

Transfer Framework, the Technology Mechanism, and the Poznan Strategic Programme on Technology Transfer.

The Technology Transfer Framework of the UNFCCC comprises five main themes: Technology Needs and Needs Assessment; Technology Information; Enabling Environments for Technology Transfer; Capacity Building for Technology Transfer; and Mechanisms for Technology Transfer.[210]

The institutional structure of the Technology Mechanism is composed of two components – the Technology Executive Committee (TEC) and the Climate Technology Centre and Network (CTCN).[211]

3.3.1 The Technology Transfer Framework

In order to implement the substantive requirements derived from Art. 4(5) of the Convention,[212] and from Art. 10(c) of the Kyoto Protocol,[213] the Parties to the Convention established the Technology Transfer Framework. In line with the promotion of equity and of sustainable development in the light of the principle of CBDR, the main task of the Technology Transfer Framework is to assist the Parties in their initiatives and cooperation with the transfer of environmentally sound technologies and the relevant know-how.[214]

The Technology Transfer Framework is composed of five main themes or pillars established under the Marrakech Accords of COP 7. Since building capacity in the technology receiving country to improve, adapt or innovate environmentally sound technologies is an essential condition for the transfer of environmentally sound technologies,[215] the Marrakech Accords has accepted the Capacity Building as a theme of the Technology Transfer Framework.[216] Similarly, as Art. 10(c) of the Kyoto Protocol pressed for the creation of an 'enabling environment' to encourage the private sector to get involved in the development as well as the transfer of environmentally sound technologies, the Marrakech Accords accepted the Enabling Environment as another important

210 UNFCCC, *Technology Framework,* available at https://unfccc.int/ttclear/tec/tech-transfer-framework.html (last accessed on August 31, 2020).

211 Gabriel Blanco et al., *The Technology Mechanism under the UNFCCC: Ways Forward,* Climate and Development Knowledge Network, Policy brief, October 2012, 4, available at https://cdkn.org/wp-content/uploads/2014/07/policy_brief_-_the_technology_mechanism_under_the_unfccc_-_ways_forward.pdf (last accessed on August 31, 2020).

212 Art. 4(5) of the Convention requires the Parties to take all possible initiatives in the promotion and facilitation of the transfer of environmentally sound technologies and know-how.

213 Art. 10(c) of the Kyoto Protocol urged the Parties to formulate 'policies and programmes for the effective transfer of environmentally sound technologies'.

214 UNFCCC, *Technology Transfer Framework,* available at http://unfccc.int/ttclear/templates/render_cms_page?TTF_home (last accessed on August 3, 2020).

215 See *supra* Chapter 1.3.

216 The Marrakech Accords and the Marrakech Declaration, available at https://www.preventionweb.net/files/5646_accordsdraft.pdf (last accessed on July 15, 2020).

theme of the Technology Transfer Framework.[217] The Marrakech Accords also included the Mechanisms for Technology Transfer, Technology Information and the TNA as themes of the Technology Transfer Framework of the Convention.

The aforementioned Technology Transfer Framework of the Convention and its five themes are shown in Figure 3.3.

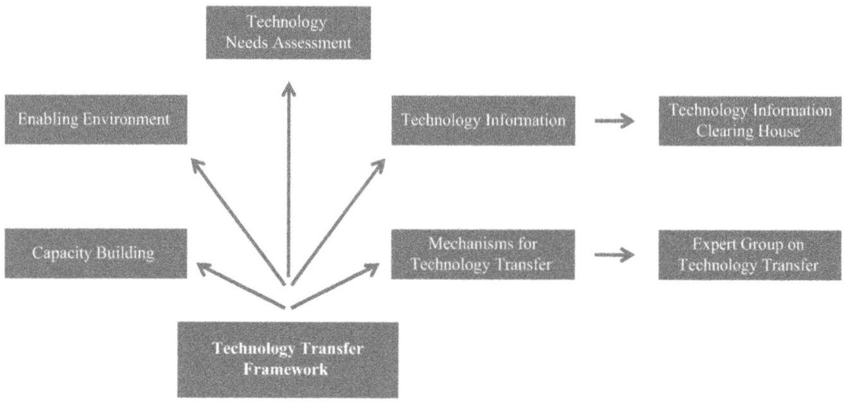

Figure 3.3 The UNFCCC Technology Transfer Framework and its five themes

During COP 16 the Parties established another mechanism for technology transfer which was called the Mechanisms for Technology Transfer. It comprises the TEC and the CTCN. The 'authority' to implement the Technology Transfer Framework was conferred on the TEC.[218]

3.3.1.1 Capacity Building

Art. 10(c) of the Kyoto Protocol requires the Parties to 'cooperate in the promotion of effective modalities for the development, application and diffusion' of 'environmentally sound technologies, know-how, practices and processes pertinent to climate change, in particular to developing countries'.[219] The encouragement of 'promotion of effective modalities for the development, application and diffusion' are certainly an indication of the need for capacity building in non-Annex I Parties to the Convention.

In accordance with Art. 10(c) of the Kyoto Protocol, the Capacity Building theme of the Technology Transfer Framework refers to a process, 'which seeks to build, develop, strengthen, enhance and improve existing scientific and technical skills, capabilities and institutions particularly in developing countries, to enable them to assess, adapt, manage and develop technologies'.[220] As technology development

217 Ibid.
218 Decision 1/CP.16.
219 Art. 10(c) of the Kyoto Protocol 1997.
220 Decision 4/CP.7, FCCC/CP/2001/13/Add.1, 21 January 2002, Para 15.

and transfer does not refer to the mere installation of a new technology, but to the transfer of relevant knowledge to make the technology workable, it is essential to build and enhance the capacity of the technology receiving developing countries or least developed countries. Enhancing capacity in technology receiving countries is essential so that the technology can be used properly and modified to meet the needs of the receiving country, if necessary. Capacity building refers to transferring knowledge, experiences, skills and practices relevant to any specific technology or group of technologies.[221]

The aim of the Capacity Building theme is to assist the non-Annex I Parties to the Convention to build and develop their competence in the adoption and transfer of environmentally sound technologies. Since the socio-economic circumstances and conditions of all non-Annex I Parties are not same, the Capacity Building theme needs to follow a 'country-specific' approach, which involves a country specific in-depth study.[222] One could argue that by taking a 'country-specific' approach the Capacity Building theme reflects the 'differentiated responsibility' element of the principle of CBDR.[223]

The Capacity Building theme of the Technology Transfer Framework is mainly guided by Decision 2/CP.7,[224] and Decision 3/CP.7[225] of COP 7. For the purpose of promotion of equity through the realization of the principle of CBDR, the contents of Decision 2/CP.7 focus particularly on the transfer of environmentally sound technologies to the developing and least developed countries. They provide guidance on building capacity in the developing and least developed countries in order to 'implement the Convention and to effectively participate in the Kyoto Protocol process'.[226]

Although there are very dissimilar socio-economic circumstances in the various developing and least developed countries, the disparities are most explicit between the large developing countries and the small least developed countries. Acknowledging such dissimilar circumstances among the non-Annex I Parties, the Capacity Building theme requires a special focus on the least developed countries.[227] It acknowledges the 'differentiated responsibilities' of the Parties on the basis of their 'respective capabilities'.[228] Due to dissimilar socio-economic circumstances amongst the non-Annex I Parties, it is not possible to apply any uniform methodology to them for building capacity.[229] In this regard, a Decision of 2/CP.7 states, 'the special circumstances of least

221 *Capacity Building in the Development and Transfer of Technologies,* Technical Paper, FCCC/TP/2003/1 26 November 2003, Para 10, available at http://unfccc.int/resource/docs/tp/tp0301.pdf (last accessed on January 23, 2019).

222 Decision 2/CP.7, FCCC/CP/2001/13/Add.1, 21 January 2002, Annex, Para 17.

223 Cf. *supra* -Chapter 2.7.1.

224 About capacity building in developing countries (non-Annex I Parties).

225 About capacity building in countries with economies in transition.

226 Decision 2/CP.7, Para 3.

227 Decision 2/CP.7, Annex, Para 17.

228 Cf. Decision 2/CP.7, Annex, Para 5, and Para 9.

229 Decision 2/CP.7, Annex, Para 5.

developed countries and small-island developing states need to be taken into account in the implementation of this framework'.[230]

Thus, the guiding Decision of the Capacity Building theme reflects the underlying spirit of the principle of CBDR by suggesting the Parties need to consider the special circumstances of the least developed countries. Such special circumstances include:

> a. fragile ecosystems; b. high population pressure and isolated geographical locations; c. weak economies, low incomes, high levels of poverty and lack of foreign investment; d. land degradation, desertification; e. undeveloped services, *inter alia,* meteorological and hydrologic services and water resources management; f. lack of early warning systems for natural disaster management; g. inadequate food security.[231]

The Capacity Building theme has an inherent co-relationship with the other themes of the Framework. Hence, any initiative in the realization of the other themes relating to technology transfer is automatically connected to the realization of the Capacity Building theme of the Convention.[232]

3.3.1.2 Enabling Environment

Art. 10(c) of the Kyoto Protocol urges the Parties to the Convention to formulate 'policies and programmes for the effective transfer of environmentally sound technologies that are publicly owned or in the public domain'.[233] It further requires 'the creation of an enabling environment for the private sector, to promote and enhance the transfer of, and access to, environmentally sound technologies'.[234] Accordingly, the Enabling Environment theme of the Technology Transfer Framework refers to the acts of laying policy, law and praxis by the Parties to motivate both the public and private sectors in the transfer of environmentally sound technologies.

Since the Enabling Environment, especially to assist the private sector to innovate and transfer environmentally sound technologies, is an essential requirement of the Kyoto Protocol, the Parties' obligations under the Enabling Environment theme include laying down trade policies that promote the transfer of environmentally sound technologies, or removing any existing trade policy or regulatory frameworks that may hinder the transfer of environmentally sound technologies.[235] The aim of the Enabling Environment theme is to make the Technology Transfer Framework more efficient by recognizing the policies that should be adopted, demolished or

230 Decision 2/CP.7, Annex, Para 9.
231 Ibid.
232 UNFCCC, *Technology Transfer Framework,* available at http://unfccc.int/ttclear/templates/render_cms_page?TTF_cpb (last accessed on July 30, 2020).
233 Art. 10(c) of the Kyoto Protocol 1997.
234 Art. 10(c) of the Kyoto Protocol 1997.
235 The Marrakech Accords and the Marrakech Declaration, Para 12, available at https://www.preventionweb.net/files/5646_accordsdraft.pdf (last accessed on July 15, 2020).

reconsidered to facilitate the transfer of environmentally sound technologies.[236] The Enabling Environment can be an important theme for those developing and least developed countries where the local legal and policy issues are identified as a barrier to the transfer of environmentally sound technologies.

Due to the emerging necessity of involving the private sector in combating climate change,[237] the Enabling Environment theme also has direct implications for promoting equity. The objective of this theme is to ensure the participation of the private sector in dealing climate change, which is already acknowledged as a global 'common responsibility' (i.e. preventing environmental degradation or combating climate change).[238] In view of this, the Enabling Environment theme also promotes the 'common responsibility' part of the principle of CBDR.[239]

3.3.1.3 The Mechanisms for Technology Transfer

In order to promote the transfer of environmentally sound technologies among the Parties to the Convention, the Mechanisms for Technology Transfer are aimed at promoting assistance in the financial, institutional and methodological activities of the Technology Transfer Framework in coordination with different stakeholders in different regions and countries. Since the Mechanisms for Technology Transfer promote the transfer of environmentally sound technologies by promoting financial cooperation in transferring environmentally sound technologies to the non-Annex I Parties, it promotes the realization of 'intra-generational equity' by engaging itself in cooperative efforts in the development, diffusion and transfer of environmentally sound technologies by building technology cooperation and partnerships (e.g. public-public, private-private, public-private).[240]

In line with the realization of the spirit of the principle of CBDR, the Mechanisms for Technology Transfer further engage in developing projects and programmes to realize the aforementioned issues.[241] The compliance with the principle of CBDR of the Mechanisms for Technology Transfer is premised on a Decision of COP 7. Decision 4/CP.7 requires that the Mechanisms for Technology Transfer should focus especially on the technology transfer needs of the developing and least developed countries.[242] In order to achieve the goals of the Technology Transfer Framework, COP 7 also formed an institutional organ – the Expert Group on Technology Transfer under the theme of the Mechanisms for Technology Transfer.[243] Hence, the Mechanism for

236 The Marrakech Accords and the Marrakech Declaration, Para 13, available at https://www.preventionweb.net/files/5646_accordsdraft.pdf (last accessed on July 15, 2020).
237 See *infra* Chapter 3.6.
238 Cf. *supra* Chapter 2.7, see also Sharon Beder, 2000, 230.
239 Cf. *supra* Chapter 2.7.1.
240 Decision 4/CP.7, Annex, Para 22; see also *supra* Chapter 2.6.
241 Ibid.
242 Ibid.
243 Decision 4/CP.7, Para 2.

Technology Transfer is especially helpful in promoting the transfer of environmentally sound technologies in non-Annex I Parties to the Convention.

The Expert Group on Technology Transfer is also intended to function in line with the spirit of the principle of CBDR. This is clear from its stated objective: 'enhancing the implementation of Art. 4, paragraph 5, of the convention'.[244] As mentioned earlier, Art. 4(5) of the Convention reflects the promotion of equity in the light of the principle of CBDR by requiring the Annex II Parties to take steps to promote the transfer of environmentally sound technologies in non-Annex I Parties.[245] The force of the obligations derived from Art. 4(5) of the Convention has been enhanced since COP 7 requires the Expert Group on Technology Transfer to analyse and identify 'ways to facilitate and advance technology transfer activities and, making recommendations to the Subsidiary Body on Scientific and Technological Advice'.[246]

However, COP 13 included four sub-themes under the Mechanisms for Technology Transfer: International Cooperation, which is a precondition of the realization of 'intra-generational equity';[247] Endogenous Development of Technologies, which is an essential precondition of technology transfer; Innovative Financing, which is an effective tool for the promotion of equity on the basis of the realization of the principle of CBDR;[248] and Collaborative Research and Development, which is also a tool for technology transfer as well as the promotion of sustainable development.[249]

The four sub-themes of the Mechanisms for Technology Transfer are shown in Figure 3.4.

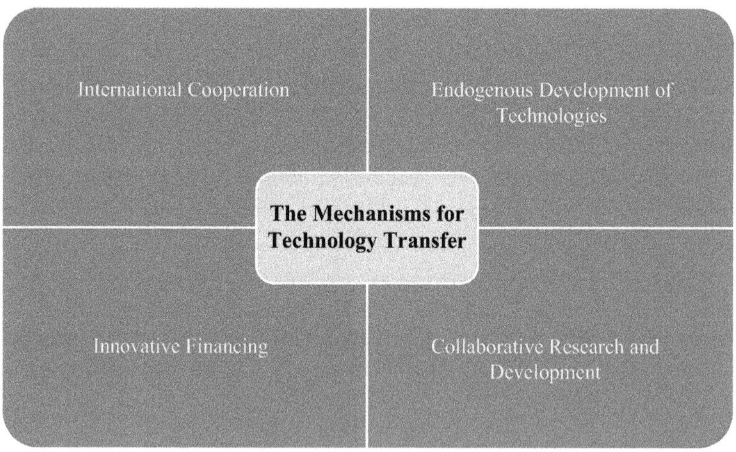

Figure 3.4 The four sub-themes of the mechanisms for technology transfer

244 Ibid.
245 See *supra* Chapter 2.6.2 and Chapter 2.7.3.
246 Decision 4/CP.7, Para 2.
247 See *supra* Chapter 2.6.
248 Cf. *supra* Chapter 2.6 and Chapter 2.7.2.
249 Decision 3/CP.13.

The objective of the International Cooperation sub-theme is to assist in identifying ways of facilitating cooperation between the relevant conventions and intergovernmental processes involved with the development and transfer of environmentally sound technologies. In line with the realization of the principle of equity,[250] in order to promote International Cooperation for the cross-border transfer of environmentally sound technologies, COP 13 recommended that the Expert Group on Technology Transfer should not only consider the international environmental treaties, but also look for synergies with the intergovernmental processes of other regimes like international trade regime, international energy regime, etc.[251]

At the time of establishing the International Cooperation sub-theme, COP 13 recommended that the UNFCCC should share its experiences and information relating to the transfer of environmentally sound technologies. COP 13 also suggested that the Parties to the Convention should look for inspiration at other international or multinational environmental agreements at the time of laying down their national climate change strategies.[252] Furthermore, to implement the sub-theme, COP 13 advocated that the Parties should decide on prospective areas of cooperation and formulate specific objectives for that cooperation.[253] One could say that identifying the specific areas of cooperation and the specific goals thereof is important in ensuring the best possible outcome of the cooperation.

Since the Annex II Parties are required to 'support the development and enhancement of endogenous capacities and technologies of developing country Parties',[254] COP 13 established the sub-theme Endogenous Development of Technologies.[255] To realize the aims of the Endogenous Development of Technologies sub-theme, Decision 3/CP.13 recommended that the developing and least developed countries should share the difficulties they encountered in developing endogenous technologies and suggested all Parties to share their experiences in facilitating endogenous technologies in the developing and least developed countries.[256] This Decision also encouraged the Parties to establish institutes to promote a national innovation system in order to develop endogenous technologies and also to share the experiences of development of endogenous technologies through publishing under the Technology Transfer Clearing House (TT:Clear).[257] Hence, as per the requirement of the sub-theme Endogenous Development of

250 Cf. *supra* Chapter 2.6.
251 Decision 3/CP13, Annex 1, Para 19(a).
252 Decision 3/CP.13, Annex 1, Para 19(b) and Para 19(c).
253 Ibid, Para 19(d).
254 Ibid, see also Art. 4(5) of the UNFCCC 1992.
255 Decision 3/CP.13.
256 Ibid, Para 21(a).
257 Ibid, Para 21(b) and Para 21(c).

Technologies, non-Annex I Party developing and least developed countries need to share the experiences of the difficulties they face in developing endogenous technologies. These countries also need to establish institutes to promote national innovation systems for the purpose of developing endogenous technologies.

Decision 3/CP.13 of COP13 established the sub-theme Innovative Financing under the Mechanisms for Technology Transfer theme. The objective of Innovative Financing is to promote access to finance for the development and transfer of environmentally sound technologies. To implement the Innovative Financing sub-theme, Decision 3/CP.13 suggested the Expert Group on Technology Transfer should 'promote success stories in financing technology transfer projects in emerging markets involving the private sector, including carbon funds, corporate-social-responsible, and triple-bottom-line investor'.[258] The most important role of the Innovative Financing sub-theme is to inspire the Parties to motivate private sector investment, and to develop innovative public-private mechanisms, so that the private sector can play a substantial role in innovating and transferring environmentally sound technologies in the developing and least developed countries by operating projects in those countries.[259]

Encouraging the private sectors is important because in many cases the work processes of the private sector are less bureaucratic and more quickly expedited than those of the public sector. Besides, as combating climate change globally requires innovation, development and transfer of environmentally sound technologies on a large scale, the Innovative Financing sub-theme can play an important role in involving the private sector in developing and innovating new environmentally sound technologies as well as transferring those technologies to the climate change vulnerable developing and least developed countries. The function of the Innovative Financing sub-theme could be seen as complimentary to the Enabling Environment theme of the Technology Transfer Framework. Because, the Enabling Environment theme has also been established in line with the Kyoto Protocol's requirement of the 'creation of an enabling environment for the private sector'.[260] The role of the sub-theme Innovative Financing is important to emerging developing and least developed countries where the potential for private sector investment is high.

However, in order to implement the Collaborative Research and Development sub-theme, Decision 3/CP13 recommended motivating the relevant intergovernmental organizations[261] to provide information about climate

258 Ibid, Para 17(c).

259 Ibid, Annex 1, Para 21(d) and Para 21(d) and (e).

260 Art. 10(c) of the Kyoto Protocol 1997.

261 For example: The Inter-governmental Panel on Climate Change, the UNDP, UNEP, the United Nations International Development Organization, the Food and Agriculture Organization of the United Nations and other international organizations (e.g., International Energy Agency).

change related research and development activities.[262] Decision 3/CP13 also recommended facilitating regional research collaboration by using the existing research centres.[263]

For regional research collaboration, the aforementioned COP decision suggested motivating governments to inspire industries and academics to develop research programmes on climate change issues.[264] In this regard, the governments of developing and least developed countries could offer incentives to the public universities and the national scientific research institutes to focus on the development and innovation of environmentally sound technologies required for those countries.

As the research and development capabilities of the Parties to the Convention differ from Party to Party, Collaborative Research and Development can assist the research and development organizations of the non-Annex I Party developing and least developed countries to develop and innovate their required environmentally sound technologies. Such assistance can be given in association with the support of the research organizations of the Annex II Parties that have a proven record of advanced research capabilities. In this connection, one could argue that since Art. 3(1) of the Convention requires the Annex II Parties to take 'the lead in combating climate change and the adverse effects thereof' on the basis of the principle of equity and CBDR, the Annex II Parties may also take the leading role in implementing 'the collaborative research and development' through collaborating with the research and development organizations of the non-Annex I Party developing and least developed countries.

In short, to achieve the overarching goal of the transfer of environmentally sound technologies among the Parties to the Convention, the objective of the Mechanisms for Technology Transfer is to promote assistance in the financial, institutional and methodological activities of the Technology Transfer Framework in coordination with different stakeholders from different regions and countries. The aim of the mechanisms is to fulfil their objective by dividing its task between its four branches. By ensuring the combined efforts of these four sub-themes, the Mechanisms for Technology Transfer of the UNFCCC can promote the transfer of environmentally sound technologies in climate change vulnerable developing and least developed countries. This role of the Mechanisms also leads to the promotion of equity based on the realization of the principle of CBDR. The Mechanisms for Technology Transfer therefore also play a role in the promotion of sustainable development in non-Annex I Party least developed countries.[265]

262 Decision 3/CP13, Annex 1, Para 23(c).
263 Ibid, Para 21(d).
264 Ibid, Para 21(f).
265 Cf. *supra* Chapter 2.5.

3.3.1.4 Technology Information

In order to facilitate the development and transfer of environmentally sound technologies among Parties to the Convention, the Technology Information theme of the Technology Transfer Framework is intended to create a freely flowing interchange of information about environmentally sound technologies. The theme reflects the spirit of the principle of CBDR while providing a special focus on transferring information from the Annex II Parties to the non-Annex I Parties to the Convention. The flow of information under the UNFCCC may take different forms. It includes all hardware, software and networking. In order to implement the Technology Information theme, the Parties to the Convention also established a technology information clearing house, which is designed to work as a hub for information concerning the transfer of environmentally sound technologies.[266]

3.3.1.5 The TNA

In line with the guidance of the principle of CBDR,[267] the TNA is a country driven theme that is aimed at assessing the need to transfer adaptation and mitigation technologies to the climate change affected non-Annex I Party developing and least developed countries.[268] This theme promotes the realization of the principle of equity at the procedural level by confirming that the TNA process of any particular country involves consultancy from various relevant stakeholders.[269] The reason for consulting various stakeholders is to identify the nature of the climate change related problems as well as viable solutions to them.[270]

As a part of the global TNA project, the Parties that need environmentally sound technologies also need to prepare a Technology Action Plan (TAP). The content of the TAP is a group of measures to deal with the barriers identified by the TNAs in the development and transfer of prioritized environmentally sound technologies in the developing and least developed countries.[271]

It is noteworthy that conducting a TNA is also one of the key components of the Poznan Strategic Programme on Technology Transfer adopted by COP 14.[272]

266 The Marrakech Accords and the Marrakech Declaration, Paras 8, 9, 10 and 11, available at https://www.preventionweb.net/files/5646_accordsdraft.pdf (last accessed on July 15, 2020).

267 Cf. *supra* Chapter 2.7.

268 UNDP, *Handbook for Conducting Technology Needs Assessment for Climate Change*, UNDP, Nov. 2010, IX.

269 Ibid.

270 Ibid.

271 TEC, *Enhancing Implementation of Technology Needs Assessments: Guidance for Preparing a Technology Action Plan*, UNEP-DTU, 2016, 9 ff.

272 See also *infra* Chapter 3.3.3.

3.3.2 The Technology Mechanism

Aiming 'to support action on mitigation and adaptation in order to achieve the full implementation of the Convention',[273] in 2010, COP 16 established the Technology Mechanism, which became fully operational in 2012.[274] It is guided by and obliged to the COP that ensures realization of the principle of equity at the procedural level through involving all Parties in the governing process of the mechanism.[275] The Paris Agreement endorses this mechanism as a mechanism to serve the Agreement.[276]

The Technology Mechanism reflects the principle of CBDR while one of its functional bases is 'capacity building', which is also based on the TNA of the non-Annex I Party developing and least developed countries.[277] Pursuant to the principle of the CBDR, the Technology Mechanism aims to promote the transfer of environmentally sound technologies through promoting increased public-private partnerships, encouraging innovation and promoting joint research and development, which are based on the environmentally sound technology related requests of the developing and least developed countries.[278] Promotion of public-private partnerships, and joint research and development through the Technology Mechanism has a twofold impact on local sustainable development. First, it enhances local capacity which creates a meaningful environment for technology transfer. Secondly, it ensures the involvement of more stakeholders, which is in line with the realization of the principle of CBDR and the promotion of the principle of equity.

The way in which the Technology Mechanism functions is arguably similar to the functions of Innovative Financing, Endogenous Development of Technologies and Collaborative Research and Development sub-themes of the Mechanisms for Technology Transfer. The institutional support of the Technology Mechanism theme comprises two components: the TEC and the CTCN.[279] COP 16 mandated the TEC and the CTCN to work to expedite the 'effective implementation' of the Technology Mechanism.[280]

273 Decision 1/CP.16, FCCC/CP/2010/7/Add.1, 15 March 2011, Para 113.
274 Ibid, Para 117.
275 Ibid.
276 Art. 10(3) of the Paris Agreement 2015.
277 See generally UNFCCC, *Technology Mechanism Enhancing Climate Technology Development and Transfer,* available at https://unfccc.int/ttclear/ misc_/StaticFiles /gnwoerk_static/ TEM/0e7cc25 f3f9843ccb9 8399df4d47 e219/174ad939936746b6bfad76e30a324e78.pdf (last accessed on August 15, 2015).
278 Cf. Gabriel Blanco & Heleen de Coninck, *The Technology Mechanism under the UNFCCC: Ways Forward*, Policy brief, Climate & Development Knowledge Network, October 2012, 4.
279 Decision 1/CP.16, Para 117.
280 Decision 1/CP.16, Para 118. see also UNFCCC, *Technology Mechanism,* available at http://unfccc.int/ttclear/templates/render_cms_page?TEM_home (last accessed on August 3, 2020), the composition of the institutional relationships under the Technology Mechanism is shown in Figure 3.5.

The structure of the branches of the Technology Mechanism are shown in Figure 3.5.

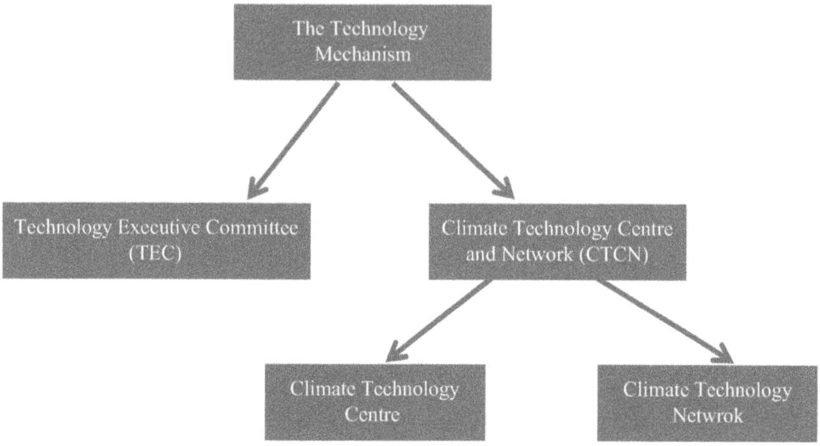

Figure 3.5 The institutional composition of the Technology Mechanism

3.3.2.1 The Technology Executive Committee

As a policy component of the Technology Mechanism, in 2010, the Parties to the Convention established the Technology Executive Committee (TEC).[281] The TEC was designed to work together with the CTCN under the guidelines of the COP.

While the texts of the UNFCCC and the Kyoto Protocol emphasized mitigation activities, Decision 1/CP.16 of COP 16 mandated the TEC to analyse the needs of both adaptation and mitigation technologies.[282] One could argue that the aforementioned mandates that are conferred on the TEC were designed to ensure equity in the sense of equal distribution between the transfer of adaptation technologies and the transfer of mitigation technologies.

In addition to identifying needs, the TEC is also required to 'seek cooperation with relevant international technology initiatives, stakeholders and organizations, and promote coherence and cooperation across technology activities, including activities under and outside of the Convention'.[283] The requirement of such cooperation also arguably reflects the principles of equity and CBDR by facilitating the transfer of environmentally sound technologies in those developing and least developed countries that need international cooperation to avail themselves of the technologies for climate change adaptation and mitigation activities.[284]

281 Decision 1/CP.16, Para 117.
282 Decision 1/CP.16, Para 121.
283 Decision 1/CP.16, Para 121(f).
284 Cf. *supra* Chapter 2.6 and *supra* Chapter 2.7.2.

The TEC is required to give 'special consideration' to the least developed country Parties when recommending 'guidance on policies and programme priorities related to technology development and transfer'.[285] This TEC 'special consideration' requirement arguably reflects the guidance of the principle of CBDR.

3.3.2.2 The Climate Technology Centre and Network

Being the implementing organ of the Technology Mechanism, the main mandate of the Climate Technology Centre and Network (CTCN) includes facilitating cooperation between the Parties in the development and transfer of environmentally sound technologies.[286] Its objective is to assist the developing and least developed countries in gaining access to the technologies they need on request.[287]

COP 19 adopted the modalities and procedures of the CTCN and the rules of procedure of the Advisory Board of the Climate Technology Centre and Network.[288] The tasks of the CTCN stipulated under its modalities and procedures include managing the requests from the Nationally Designated Entities of the developing and least developed countries. The tasks include providing technical support and suggestions as to how to develop the TNA as well as 'national technology road maps and action plans', providing technical aid and suggestions on 'tools for identifying, planning, and implementing climate technologies', and, in particular, providing guidance on 'policies and measures in support of implementation of climate technologies'.[289]

Another important task of the CTCN is to promote collaboration and access to information and knowledge for the purpose of promoting the transfer of environmentally sound technologies. This includes catalysing and developing information and knowledge regarding environmentally sound technologies, assessing support available for 'identifying gaps' and 'opportunities for helping developing countries access support', assessing the 'needs and opportunities' for technology cooperation, and recommending 'policies and programme priorities related to technology development' to the Advisory Board. The CTCN is also guided by the principle of CBDR, whilst it is required to give special consideration to the needs of the least developed countries.[290]

The tasks of the CTCN also include strengthening 'networks, partnership and capacity-building for climate technology transfer'.[291] This task refers to catalysing and developing programmes with a view to strengthening the

285 Decision 1/CP.16, Para 121(c).
286 Cf. Decision 1/CP.16, Para 123.
287 CTCN, *About the Climate Technology Centre and Network (CTCN),* available at https://www.ctc-n.org/about-ctcn (last accessed on August 14, 2020).
288 Decision 25/CP.19, FCCC/CP/2013/10/Add.3, 31 January 2014.
289 Decision 25/CP.19, Annex I, Para 4.
290 Ibid, Para 5, cf. *supra* Chapter 2.7.2.
291 Decision 25/CP.19, Para 4(d).

institutions and institutional capacities of the developing and least developed countries. It also includes catalysing and developing 'capacity-building programmes targeted at developing technology cooperation and partnership forming capabilities of technology centres and institutes' in the developing and least developed countries.[292] One could argue that the Climate Technology Centre and Network's task of building capacity is intended to make sure that technology transfer takes place as effectively as possible.[293]

The CTCN reflects the principle of CBDR, by giving special consideration to the least developed countries.[294] Besides, reflection of the principle of equity is found in that the CTCN is required to promote public-private partnerships, partnerships amongst the organizations involved in advancing environmentally sound technologies, and technology related research and development.[295]

3.3.3 The Poznan Strategic Programme on Technology Transfer

In 2007 (during COP 13) the Parties to the Convention requested the GEF to initiate a programme to promote investment in technology transfer in order to promote access to environmentally sound technologies by the non-Annex I Parties to the Convention.[296] In 2008 the GEF Council and the LDCF/the SCCF discussed and approved the Strategic Programme on Technology Transfer. COP 14 accepted the Programme on technology transfer and renamed it the Poznan Strategic Programme on Technology Transfer.[297]

COP 14 requested the GEF to outline the long-term implementation of the Programme.[298] Hence, in line with the principle of CBDR in order to attain the technology transfer objective of the Convention, the Poznan Strategy has been designed as shown in Figure 3.6.

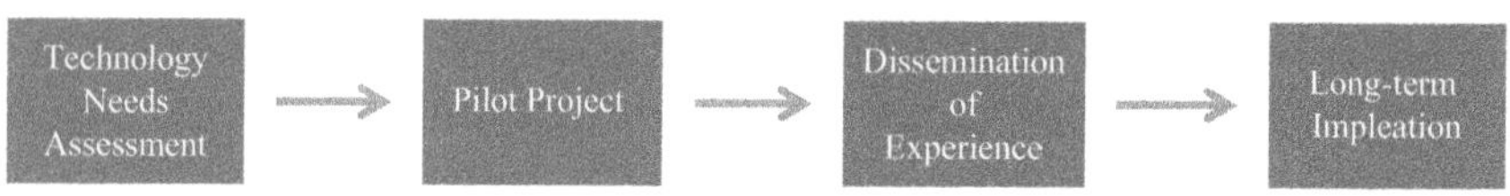

Figure 3.6 Chronological stages of the Poznan Strategic Programme

As an initial step the Poznan Strategic Programme on Technology Transfer requires the developing and least developed countries undergo a TNA with a view to prioritizing the technologies required for climate change adaptation and mitigation.[299] Once the TNA is completed, the Programme expects that

292 Decision 25/CP.19, Para 6(c).
293 Cf. *supra* Chapter 1.3.
294 Decision 25/CP.19, Annex 1, Para 5(d), cf. *supra* Chapter 2.7.2.
295 Decision 25/CP.19, Annex I, Para 6, cf. *supra* Chapter 2.6.
296 GEF, *Poznan Strategic Program,* available at https://www.thegef.org/content/poznan-strategic-program (last accessed on August 5, 2020).
297 Decision 2/CP.14. FCCC/CP/2008/7/Add.1, 18 March 2009, Para 1.
298 Decision 2/CP.14, Para 2(c).
299 For a detailed discussion about the TNA see *supra* Chapter 3.3.1.5.

the GEF will initiate pilot projects to promote the transfer of environmentally sound technologies to the developing and least developed countries. After implementation of the pilot project, the Poznan Strategy requires the GEF to share the experiences gained from transferring environmentally sound technologies by arranging different events like workshops, seminars, etc. or through publication of successful case studies, guidebooks, etc.[300]

As part of the long-term implementation stage of the strategy, the GEF is entrusted to assist the climate technology centres and the climate technology network to promote private-public partnerships for the transfer of environmentally sound technologies.[301] By promoting private-public partnerships for the transfer of environmentally sound technologies, it arguably promotes both the principle of equity and the principle of CBDR.[302]

3.3.4 The Technology Framework

In 2015, the Paris Agreement established the Technology Framework.[303] The purpose of the Framework is 'to provide overarching guidance to the work of the Technology Mechanism in promoting and facilitating enhanced action on technology development and transfer in order to support the implementation of the Paris Agreement in pursuit of the long-term vision'.[304] In this regard, the long-term vision of the Paris Agreement is to 'fully realiz[e] technology development and transfer in order to improve resilience to climate change and to reduce greenhouse gas emissions'.[305] The Framework is aimed to 'play a strategic role in improving the effectiveness and efficiency of the work of the Technology Mechanism'.[306] The vision of playing a strategic role is intended to be carried out 'by addressing the transformational changes envisioned in the Paris Agreement and the long-term vision for technology development and transfer'.[307]

The Paris Rule Book states the principles of the Framework as: coherence, inclusiveness, a results-oriented approach, a transformational approach and transparency.[308] Accordingly, the Framework is required to guide the Technology Mechanism in realizing 'the long-term vision for technology development and transfer and other provisions of the Paris Agreement, national plans and strategies under the Convention and actions undertaken by relevant

300 GEF, *Poznan Strategic Program*, https://www.thegef.org/content/poznan-strategic-program (last accessed on August 5, 2020).
301 Ibid.
302 Cf. *supra* Chapter 2.6.
303 Art. 10(4) of the Paris Agreement 2015.
304 Decision 15/CMA.1, Annex, Technology Framework under Article 10, paragraph 4, of the Paris Agreement I. Purpose, FCCC/PA/CMA/2018/3/Add.2, Para 1, available at https://unfccc.int/sites/default/ files/resource /cma2018_3_add2_new_advance.pdf#page=4 (last accessed on August 10, 2020).
305 Art. 10(1) of the Paris Agreement 2015.
306 Decision 15/CMA.1, Annex, Para 2.
307 Ibid.
308 Ibid, Para 3.

institutions in the international climate regime and beyond'.[309] The Rule Book also requires the Technology Framework to guide the Technology Mechanism in a way 'that facilitates the active participation of all relevant stakeholders and takes into account sustainable development, gender, the special circumstances of the least developed countries and small island developing States'.[310] In terms of output, outcome and impact, the guidance needs to be results-oriented.[311]

The Framework is required to address 'the transformational changes envisioned in the Paris Agreement'.[312] The Technology Framework's guidance to Technology Mechanism needs to be planned and implemented in a way which will enhance 'the transparency of the results, costs and process'.[313] The key themes of the Technology Framework are: Innovation; Implementation; Enabling Environment and Capacity Building; Collaboration and Stakeholder Engagement; and Support.[314]

The Innovation theme requires the Framework to accelerate and scale up innovation at a different phase of its cycle, which should also address both adaptation and mitigation in a balanced way.[315] It needs to be conducted in a way that ensures the participation of developing countries as well as the promotion of the sustainable development and gender responsiveness in those countries.[316] With these requirements the Innovation theme clearly promotes the principle of CBDR based on equity. However, the Innovation theme requires the Technology Framework to foster the innovation through: adopting new collaborative approaches to environmentally sound technology research, development and demonstration; creating relevant enabling policies to assist and encourage a favourable environment for innovation; and actively engaging the private sector and building 'closer collaboration between the public and private sector'.[317]

The Implementation theme requires the Framework to facilitate the implementation of past and ongoing collaborative technology development and transfer activities that must include all kinds of collaboration between countries including regional collaboration.[318] It further requires facilitating the implementation of:

> mitigation and adaptation action identified using planning tools and processes such as nationally determined contributions, long-term low greenhouse gas emission development strategies, technology needs assessments

309 Ibid, Para 3(a).
310 Ibid, Para 3(b).
311 Ibid, Para 3(c).
312 Ibid, Para 3(d).
313 Ibid, Para 3(e).
314 Ibid, Para 4.
315 Ibid, Para 6.
316 Ibid.
317 Ibid, Para 7.
318 Ibid, Para 10.

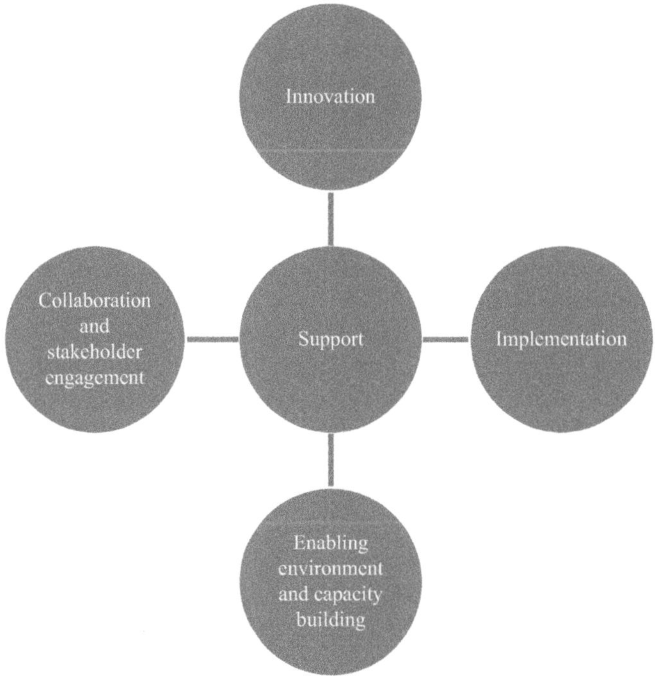

Figure 3.7 Key themes of the Technology Framework

> (TNAs), national adaptation plans, technology road maps and other relevant policies, and facilitat[ing] overcoming challenges by implementing such action, as appropriate.[319]

The Enabling Environment and Capacity Building theme requires fostering the creation and improvement of an enabling environment such as 'policy and regulatory environments for technology development and transfer'.[320] It also requires strengthening countries' capacity to address various challenges in an effective manner.[321] The required activities under this theme include: raising public awareness of the development and transfer of environmentally sound technologies; assisting countries to create an investment-friendly environment; assisting countries to create a favourable environment to promote endogenous and gender-responsive technologies for both mitigation and adaptation activities; assisting countries to create a favourable environment to incentivize both the public and private sector to fully realize the development and transfer of environmentally sound technologies; assisting countries to create a favourable environment by enacting relevant laws and policies that create favourable market

319 Ibid, Para 11.
320 Ibid, Para 15.
321 Ibid, Para 15.

conditions for environmentally sound technologies and encourage the private sector's involvement in developing and transferring these technologies, etc.[322]

Actions and activities under the Collaboration and Stakeholder Engagement theme include augmenting engagement and collaboration with diverse relevant stakeholders such as local communities and authorities, national level planners, the private sector, civil society; nationally designated entities, relevant international organizations, institutes and initiatives; and the academic and scientific community. The objective of the collaboration is to leverage the relevant stakeholder's 'expertise, experience, knowledge and information, particularly on new and innovative technologies'.[323]

The Support theme of the Technology Framework refers to a broader idea than just providing financial support. Instead, it refers to all kinds of support which is essential to realize the goals envisioned in Art. 10 of the Paris Agreement.[324] The support needs to be offered to all the other key themes of the Framework, which must also take into account 'the gender perspective and endogenous and indigenous aspects'.[325] Since successful technology development and transfer requires a diverse set of support, the actions and activities of this theme include: augmenting the collaboration between the Technology Mechanism and the Financial Mechanism; identifying and encouraging innovative finance and investment at diverse phases of the technology cycle; providing developing countries with enhanced technical support such as facilitating those countries' access to climate finance for innovation, research and development, as well as assisting those countries in creating an enabling environment and capacity building; creating or augmenting a system for monitoring and tracking actions and activities undertaken and receiving support from the Technology Mechanism in order to implement the Technology Framework.[326]

3.4 Indirect financial mechanisms

3.4.1 Kyoto flexible mechanism: the clean development mechanism

Despite some disagreement, market-based approaches to carbon emission reduction and forming an efficient 'carbon market' are considered to be an essential tool for mitigating greenhouse gas emissions in the global atmosphere.[327] At present the international carbon market consists of various kinds of carbon reducing mechanisms, which can broadly be divided into two kinds:

322 Ibid, Para 16(a)–16(e).
323 Ibid, Para 20(a)–20(d).
324 Ibid, Para 22.
325 Ibid.
326 Ibid, Para 25(a)–25(e).
327 Cf. Center for Climate and Energy Solutions, *Market-Based Strategies,* available at https://www.c2es.org/content/market-based-strategies (last accessed on August 10, 2020).

1) cap-and-trade schemes, and 2) baseline-and-credit schemes.[328] The cap-and-trade schemes offer carbon emission allowances free of charge or carbon emission allowances based on auctioning.[329] The baseline-and-credit schemes offer a transfer of reduction units that are derived from individual projects and calculated as the quantitative reduction of carbon, where the approval of a hypothetical base line plays a key role.[330]

The Kyoto Protocol established the cap-and-trade scheme for Annex I Parties by issuing Assigned Amount Units (AAUs). The clean development mechanism (CDM) and the JI are the baseline-and-credit schemes established under the Kyoto Protocol. The carbon reduction unit derived from the CDM is called the Certified Emission Reduction (CER) unit and the reduction unit derived from the JI is called the Emission Reduction Unit (ERU). Kyoto member states can authorize private entities of their own territory to take part in the trading mechanism, but they cannot do so without an agreement between the donor and the host country. This is because the countries that are Parties to the UNFCCC are responsible for the trans-national movement of quota and credits that are calculated under the UNFCCC.[331]

Based on an agreement concluded between the concerned countries or entities, the CDM allows the countries with emission-reduction obligations (Annex I Parties) under the UNFCCC to take part in emission-reduction projects operated in the developing and least developed countries (non-Annex I Parties).[332] The CDM projects produce CER credits that can be transferred to an Annex I Party, which can use CER units to fulfil its mitigation commitments under the Convention. As a consequence, the concerned Annex I Party to the Convention can fulfil its 'common responsibility' of preventing environmental degradation by fulfilling its 'differentiated responsibility' derived from the Convention – emission reduction into the atmosphere.[333] The CERs generated from the CDM projects are counted to meet the UNFCCC emission reduction obligations of the Annex I Parties provided the projects ensure the principle of 'additionality'[334] and generate 'measurable and long-term benefits' in climate change mitigation.[335] The 'additionality' concept means that a specific CDM project must ensure additional emission reduction in comparison with the emission reduction scenario that would have occurred in the absence of that specific project – which represents the base-line scenario.[336]

328 S. Seppänen et al., *Demand in a Fragmented Global Carbon Market: Outlook and Policy Options*, (online) Nordon, 2013, 12., available at https://www.diva-portal.org/smash/get/diva2:702582/FULLTEXT01.pdf (last accessed on August 10, 2020).
329 Ibid.
330 Ibid.
331 Arts. 3, 6 and 12 of the Kyoto Protocol 1997.
332 Art. 12 of the Kyoto Protocol 1997.
333 Each CER is equivalent to one ton of CO_2.
334 Art.12(5)(c) of the Kyoto Protocol 1997.
335 Art. 12(5)(b) of the Kyoto Protocol 1997.
336 E. Meijer and J. Werksman, 'Keeping it Clean – Safeguarding the Environmental Integrity of the Clean Development Mechanism', in D. Freestone and C. Streck

As 'additionality' determines the actual amount of emission reduction of a CDM project, it is important to determine 'additionality' in such a way that the CDM as a source of emission reduction cannot be undermined.[337]

Based on the fact that there are economic dissimilarities between the Parties to the UNFCCC, it is presumed that if a non-Annex I Party developing country can reduce its carbon emission compared to its *business-as-usual* level, and sell the CER units derived from the reduced emission of the CDM projects to the Annex I Party developed country, it will bring financial benefit to that non-Annex I Party country. At the same time, if an Annex I Party can fulfil its carbon reduction target by buying CERs from a non-Annex I Party country, it will be a cost-effective emission reduction for the Annex I Party country. Reason, reduction of carbon in its own territory is a costly venture for an Annex I Party developed country.[338] Thus, cost-effectiveness and flexibility can be considered as two vital reasons why the Kyoto Protocol allows the Annex I Parties to use the CDM to fulfil their emission reduction obligations.[339] Of course, the Parties will also have to respect the supplementary principle.

Consequently, the Annex I Parties to the Convention (e.g. any EU country) can invest in CDM projects in developing or least developed countries that might be a cost-effective tool for them to reduce their average annual carbon emission compared to their *business-as-usual* level. At the same time, it can also be of financial benefit to the concerned developing or least developed country as it might assist the country to eradicate poverty and facilitate local sustainable development.

Generally, the CDM projects are governed by bilateral agreements signed between private entity/entities of Annex I Party and non-Annex I Party countries. The concerned private entity has to be authorized by the concerned Annex I Party country, which is also a Party to the Kyoto Protocol. Though the general trend is that the CDM project developers are private entities coming from the Annex I Party countries, the CDM project developers may also come from a host country local company, a host country consortium, a multinational corporation or local, regional or national government.[340]

In the case study in Chapter 5 of this book, of the seven CDM projects (which also includes the CDM Programme of Activities) that are in operation in Bangladesh, three CDM projects and programmes are owned by privately

(eds.), *Legal Aspects of Implementing the Kyoto Protocol Mechanisms: Making Kyoto Work,* Oxford University Press, 2005, 193.

337 This view is not undisputed, though. See B. Müller, *Additionality in the Clean Development Mechanism: Why and What?,* Oxford Institute for Energy Studies, March, 2009, 14.

338 P. K. Gorecki, S. Lyons, and R. S.J. Tol, 'EU Climate Change Policy 2013–2020: Using the Clean Development Mechanism more Effectively in the Non-EU-ETS Sector', *Energy Policy,* Vol. 38(11), November 2010, 7466–7475.

339 Christina Voigt, 2006, 374.

340 Ibid, 361.

owned local companies,[341] one CDM programme is owned by a state-owned company,[342] two CDM projects and programmes are joint ventures with a developed country enterprise[343] and one CDM programme is owned by a foreign company.[344]

3.4.2 New mechanisms under the Paris Agreement

The Paris Agreement introduces new indirect financial mechanisms. In Art 6(1) of the Paris Agreement:

> [p]arties recognize that some Parties choose to pursue voluntary cooperation in the implementation of their nationally determined contributions to allow for higher ambition in their mitigation and adaptation actions and to promote sustainable development and environmental integrity.[345]

Thereafter it enumerates the parameters for a tradable unit, a cooperative mechanism like the Kyoto Protocol's CDM, and a non-market cooperative approach.[346] Art. 6(2) creates 'a tradable unit' and a new mitigation mechanism when it states:[347]

> [p]arties shall, where engaging on a voluntary basis in cooperative approaches that involve the use of *internationally transferred mitigation outcomes* towards nationally determined contributions, promote sustainable development and ensure environmental integrity and transparency, including in governance, and shall apply robust accounting to ensure, inter alia, the avoidance of double counting, consistent with guidance adopted by the Conference of the Parties serving as the meeting of the Parties to this Agreement.
>
> (Emphasis added)

This provision talks about 'internationally transferred mitigation outcomes', which are meant to be realized in the form of a tradable credit.[348] Parties can use these

341 Two bundle brick kiln CDM projects are owned by the Industrial and Infrastructure Development Finance Company (IIDFC), the 'Life Straw Family' CDM Programme of Activities (PoA) is owned by BRAC EPL.
342 'Efficient Lighting' is owned by the Infrastructure Development Company Limited (IDCOL), which is a state-owned public-private company.
343 CDM project Waste to Compost and the Solar Home Systems CDM PoA.
344 Improved Cooking Stove is owned by J.P. Morgan Energy Venture Corporation.
345 Art. 6(1) of the Paris Agreement 2015.
346 Cinnamon P. Carlarne and J. D. Colavecchio, 'Balancing Equity and Effectiveness: The Paris Agreement & the Future of International Climate Change Law', *NYU Environmental Law Journal* Vol. 27(2), 2019, 107–182, 165.
347 Art. 6(2) of the Paris Agreement 2015.
348 Cinnamon P. Carlarne and J. D. Colavecchio 2019, 165.

'internationally transferred mitigation outcomes' in order to achieve the commitments made under their respective nationally determined contributions. Such use of 'internationally transferred mitigation outcomes' shall be 'voluntary and authorized by participating Parties'.[349]

Art. 6(4) establishes another flexible mitigation mechanism with a view 'to contribut[ing] to the mitigation of greenhouse gas emissions and support[ing] sustainable development'. This mechanism is colloquially referred to as the Sustainable Development Mechanism (SDM).[350] The objectives of the SDM are enumerated as: promoting the mitigation of greenhouse gas emissions while fostering sustainable development; incentivizing and facilitating participation in the mitigation of greenhouse gas emissions by both the public and private sector; reducing the host Party's emission levels, while allowing other Parties to fulfil their nationally determined contributions; and delivering an overall mitigation in global emissions.[351]

The texts of Arts. 6(2) and 6(4) of the Paris Agreement can potentially bring about two outcomes. First, the establishment of units that can either be tradable or transferrable in any other form to mitigate Parties' self-determined mitigation goals.[352] Second, the establishment of a new cooperation mechanism which will either reflect the CDM introduced by Kyoto or be an extended version of the CDM.[353] However, one important difference between the aforementioned mechanisms and the CDM introduced by Kyoto is that mechanisms introduced under Art. 6 of the Paris Agreement are fully inclusive in nature. While only developing country Parties were entitled to host the CDM, the new mechanisms can be hosted by any Party to the Agreement.[354]

However, Parties are yet to develop fully operational models of these new mechanisms.[355] Although the Paris Rule Book has successfully made a set of rules for implementing various key provisions of the Paris Agreement, Parties have not yet agreed on various aspects of the proposed new mechanisms.[356]

In terms of application of the principle of equity on the basis of CDM experiences, Carlarne and Colavecchio (2019) reveal, 'it is difficult to create incentives for equitable distribution of projects and investment, especially outside of the rapidly developing economies, and to create incentives for projects that support long term sustainable development'.[357] Parties to the Agreement should consider these issues at the time of developing fully operational models of the new mechanisms.

349 Art. 6(3) of the Paris Agreement 2015.
350 Cinnamon P. Carlarne and J. D. Colavecchio 2019, 165.
351 Art. 6(4) of the Paris Agreement 2015.
352 Cinnamon P. Carlarne and J. D. Colavecchio 2019, 166.
353 Ibid.
354 Cinnamon P. Carlarne and JD Colavecchio 2019, 171.
355 Ibid, 165.
356 Ibid, 175–176.
357 Ibid, 171.

3.5 Comparison with other multinational environmental agreements

> In addition to international laws on climate change (including the UNFCCC, the Kyoto Protocol and the Paris Agreement), some other multilateral environmental agreements also include provision for the innovation and transfer of technologies. Examples of these multilateral environmental agreements include the International Treaty on Plant Genetic Resources for Food and Agriculture (ITPGRFA),[358] the UN Convention to Combat Desertification (UNCCCD),[359] the Basel Convention on the Control of Transboundary Movements of Hazardous Wastes and their Disposal (Basel Convention)[360] and the Convention on Biological Diversity (CBD),[361] etc. While all these agreements require technology transfer, the aim and scope of the technology transfer differs from agreement to agreement. Table 3.1 enumerates the technology transfer related provisions of the aforementioned multilateral environmental agreements.

Although the four legal instruments in Table 3.1 press for technology transfer, the mode, scope and nature of 'technology transfer' in those agreements are significantly different from those of climate regime. The differences arise in the objectives of technology transfer, sources of financing, coordination mechanism, capacity building mechanism, information/network building mechanisms and technology transfer modalities.[362]

3.5.1 Objectives of technology transfer

While technology transfer is a focal subject in the UNFCCC and the Paris Agreement, it is a far less focal subject in the UNCCD, Basel Convention and ITPGRFA. However, technology transfer remains a focal subject of the CBD.[363]

The objective of technology transfer under the UNFCCC is to enable the Parties 'to implement the provisions of the Convention', which is 'stabilization of greenhouse gas concentrations in the atmosphere at a level that would prevent dangerous anthropogenic interference with the climate system'.[364] A similar objective of technology transfer can be observed in Art. 10(1) of the

358 FAO Conference Res. 3/2001, Rome, 3 November 2001, in force 29 June 2004.

359 Convention to Combat Desertification in Those Countries Experiencing Serious Drought and/or Desertification, Particularly in Africa (Paris) 17 June 1994, in force 26 December 1996, 33 ILM 1328.

360 Convention on the Control of Transboundary Movement of Hazardous Wastes and Their Disposal (Basel Convention) 22 March 1989, in force 1992, 28 ILM 657.

361 Convention on Biological Diversity (Rio de Janeiro) 5 June 1992, in force 29 December 1993, 31 ILM 822.

362 See generally Zainal Abidin Sanusi, *Technology Transfer under Multilateral Environmental Agreements: Analyzing the Synergies*, UNU-IAS Working Paper No. 134, July 2005, 20–32.

363 Ibid, 20.

364 Art. 2 of the UNFCCC 1992.

Table 3.1 Technology transfer provisions under diverse multilateral environmental agreements

Name of the treaty/ convention/ protocol	*Provisions concerning the innovation and transfer of technologies*
International Treaty on Plant Genetic Resources for Food and Agriculture (ITPGRFA)	**Article 5** *Conservation, Exploration, Collection, Characterization, Evaluation and Documentation of Plant Genetic Resources for Food and Agriculture* 5 (1) Each Contracting Party shall, subject to national legislation, and in cooperation with other Contracting Parties where appropriate, promote an integrated approach to the exploration, conservation and sustainable use of plant genetic resources for food and agriculture and shall in particular, as appropriate: (e) Cooperate to promote the development of an efficient and sustainable system of ex situ conservation, giving due attention to the need for adequate documentation, characterization, regeneration and evaluation, and promote the development and transfer of appropriate technologies for this purpose with a view to improving the sustainable use of plant genetic resources for food and agriculture; **Article 8** *Technical Assistance* The Contracting Parties agree to promote the provision of technical assistance to Contracting Parties, especially those that are developing countries or countries with economies in transition, either bilaterally or through the appropriate international organizations, with the objective of facilitating the implementation of this Treaty. **Article 12** *Facilitated access to plant genetic resources for food and agriculture within the Multilateral System* 12.1 The Contracting Parties agree that facilitated access to plant genetic resources for food and agriculture under the Multilateral System, as defined in Article 11, shall be in accordance with the provisions of this Treaty. **Article 13** *Benefit-sharing in the Multilateral System* (b) Access to and transfer of technology (i) The Contracting Parties undertake to provide and/or facilitate access to technologies for the conservation, characterization, evaluation and use of plant genetic resources for food and agriculture which are under the Multilateral System. Recognizing that some technologies can only be transferred through genetic material, the Contracting Parties shall provide and/or facilitate access to such technologies and genetic material which is under the Multilateral System and to improved varieties and genetic material developed through the use of plant genetic resources for food and agriculture under the Multilateral System, in conformity with the provisions of Article 12. Access to these technologies, improved varieties and genetic material shall be provided and/or facilitated, while respecting applicable property rights and access laws, and in accordance with national capabilities.

(*Continued*)

Table 3.1 (Cont.)

Name of the treaty/ convention/ protocol	*Provisions concerning the innovation and transfer of technologies*
	(ii) Access to and transfer of technology to countries, especially to developing countries and countries with economies in transition, shall be carried out through a set of measures, such as the establishment and maintenance of, and participation in, crop-based thematic groups on utilization of plant genetic resources for food and agriculture, all types of partnership in research and development and in commercial joint ventures relating to the material received, human resource development, and effective access to research facilities.
	(iii) Access to and transfer of technology as referred to in (i) and (ii) above, including that protected by intellectual property rights, to developing countries that are Contracting Parties, in particular least developed countries, and countries with economies in transition, shall be provided and/or facilitated under fair and most favourable terms, in particular in the case of technologies for use in conservation as well as technologies for the benefit of farmers in developing countries, especially in least developed countries, and countries with economies in transition, including on concessional and preferential terms where mutually agreed, inter alia, through partnerships in research and development under the Multilateral System. Such access and transfer shall be provided on terms which recognize and are consistent with the adequate and effective protection of intellectual property rights.
	(c) Capacity-building Taking into account the needs of developing countries and countries with economies in transition, as expressed through the priority they accord to building capacity in plant genetic resources for food and agriculture in their plans and programme, when in place, in respect of those plant genetic resources for food and agriculture covered by the Multilateral System, the Contracting Parties agree to give priority to:
	(i) establishing and/or strengthening programme for scientific and technical education and training in conservation and sustainable use of plant genetic resources for food and agriculture,
	(ii) developing and strengthening facilities for conservation and sustainable use of plant genetic resources for food and agriculture, in particular in developing countries, and countries with economies in transition, and
	(iii) carrying out scientific research preferably, and where possible, in developing countries and countries with economies in transition, in cooperation with institutions of such countries, and developing capacity for such research in fields where they are needed.

(*Continued*)

Table 3.1 (Cont.)

Name of the treaty/ convention/ protocol	*Provisions concerning the innovation and transfer of technologies*
United Nations Convention to Combat Desertification in those Countries Experiencing Serious Drought and/or Desertification, particularly in Africa (UNCCD)	**Article 6** *Obligations of developed country Parties* In addition to their general obligations pursuant to Article 4, developed country Parties undertake to: ... (e) promote and facilitate access by affected country Parties, particularly affected developing country Parties, to appropriate technology, knowledge and know-how. **Article 12** *International cooperation* Affected country Parties, in collaboration with other Parties and the international community, should cooperate to ensure the promotion of an enabling international environment in the implementation of the Convention. Such cooperation should also cover fields of technology transfer as well as scientific research and development, information collection and dissemination and financial resources. **Article 16** *Information collection, analysis and exchange* The Parties agree, according to their respective capabilities, to integrate and coordinate the collection, analysis and exchange of relevant short term and long term data and information to ensure systematic observation of land degradation in affected areas and to understand better and assess the processes and effects of drought and desertification. This would help accomplish, inter alia, early warning and advance planning for periods of adverse climatic variation in a form suited for practical application by users at all levels, including especially local populations. To this end, they shall, as appropriate: a facilitate and strengthen the functioning of the global network of institutions and facilities for the collection, analysis and exchange of information, as well as for systematic observation at all levels, which shall, inter alia: ... (iii) use and disseminate modern technology for data collection, transmission and assessment on land degradation. **Article 17** *Research and development* 1 The Parties undertake, according to their respective capabilities, to promote technical and scientific cooperation in the fields of combatting desertification and mitigating the effects of drought through appropriate national, sub regional, regional and international institutions. To this end, they shall support research activities that:

(*Continued*)

Table 3.1 (Cont.)

Name of the treaty/ convention/ protocol	*Provisions concerning the innovation and transfer of technologies*
	a contribute to increased knowledge of the processes leading to desertification and drought and the impact of, and distinction between, causal factors, both natural and human, with a view to combatting desertification and mitigating the effects of drought, and achieving improved productivity as well as sustainable use and management of resources; b respond to well defined objectives, address the specific needs of local populations and lead to the identification and implementation of solutions that improve the living standards of people in affected areas; c protect, integrate, enhance and validate traditional and local knowledge, knowhow and practices, ensuring, subject to their respective national legislation and/or policies, that the owners of that knowledge will directly benefit on an equitable basis and on mutually agreed terms from any commercial utilization of it or from any technological development derived from that knowledge; d develop and strengthen national, sub regional and regional research capabilities in affected developing country Parties, particularly in Africa, including the development of local skills and the strengthening of appropriate capacities, especially in countries with a weak research base, giving particular attention to multidisciplinary and participative socio-economic research; e take into account, where relevant, the relationship between poverty, migration caused by environmental factors, and desertification; f promote the conduct of joint research programmes between national, sub regional, regional and international research organizations, in both the public and private sectors, for the development of improved, affordable and accessible technologies for sustainable development through effective participation of local populations and communities; and g enhance the availability of water resources in affected areas, by means of, inter alia, cloud-seeding. **Article 18** *Transfer, acquisition, adaptation and development of technology* 1 The Parties undertake, as mutually agreed and in accordance with their respective national legislation and/or policies, to promote, finance and/or facilitate the financing of the transfer, acquisition, adaptation and development of environmentally sound, economically viable and socially acceptable technologies relevant to combatting desertification and/or mitigating the effects of drought, with a view to contributing to the achievement of sustainable development in affected areas. Such cooperation shall be conducted bilaterally or multilaterally, as appropriate, making full use of the expertise of intergovernmental and non-governmental organizations. The Parties shall, in particular:

(*Continued*)

Table 3.1 (Cont.)

Name of the treaty/ convention/ protocol	*Provisions concerning the innovation and transfer of technologies*
	a fully utilize relevant existing national, sub regional, regional and international information systems and clearinghouses for the dissemination of information on available technologies, their sources, their environmental risks and the broad terms under which they may be acquired;
	b facilitate access, in particular by affected developing country Parties, on favourable terms, including on concessional and preferential terms, as mutually agreed, taking into account the need to protect intellectual property rights, to technologies most suitable to practical application for specific needs of local populations, paying special attention to the social, cultural, economic and environmental impact of such technology;
	c facilitate technology cooperation among affected country Parties through financial assistance or other appropriate means;
	d extend technology cooperation with affected developing country Parties, including, where relevant, joint ventures, especially to sectors which foster alternative livelihoods; and
	e take appropriate measures to create domestic market conditions and incentives, fiscal or otherwise, conducive to the development, transfer, acquisition and adaptation of suitable technology, knowledge, know-how and practices, including measures to ensure adequate and effective protection of intellectual property rights.
	2. The Parties shall, according to their respective capabilities, and subject to their respective national legislation and/or policies, protect, promote and use in particular relevant traditional and local technology, knowledge, know-how and practices and, to that end, they undertake to:
	a make inventories of such technology, knowledge, know-how and practices and their potential uses with the participation of local populations, and disseminate such information, where appropriate, in cooperation with relevant intergovernmental and non-governmental organizations;
	b ensure that such technology, knowledge, know-how and practices are adequately protected and that local populations benefit directly, on an equitable basis and as mutually agreed, from any commercial utilization of them or from any technological development derived therefrom;
	c encourage and actively support the improvement and dissemination of such technology, knowledge, know-how and practices or of the development of new technology based on them; and
	d facilitate, as appropriate, the adaptation of such technology, knowledge, knowhow and practices to wide use and integrate them with modern technology, as appropriate.

(*Continued*)

Table 3.1 (Cont.)

Name of the treaty/ convention/ protocol	*Provisions concerning the innovation and transfer of technologies*
	Article 19 *Capacity building, education and public awareness* 1 The Parties recognize the significance of capacity building – that is to say, institution building, training and development of relevant local and national capacities – in efforts to combat desertification and mitigate the effects of drought. They shall promote, as appropriate, capacity-building: a through the full participation at all levels of local people, particularly at the local level, especially women and youth, with the cooperation of non-governmental and local organizations; b by strengthening training and research capacity at the national level in the field of desertification and drought; c by establishing and/or strengthening support and extension services to disseminate relevant technology methods and techniques more effectively, and by training field agents and members of rural organizations in participatory approaches for the conservation and sustainable use of natural resources; d by fostering the use and dissemination of the knowledge, know-how and practices of local people in technical cooperation programmes, wherever possible; e by adapting, where necessary, relevant environmentally sound technology and traditional methods of agriculture and pastoralism to modern socio-economic conditions; f by providing appropriate training and technology in the use of alternative energy sources, particularly renewable energy resources, aimed particularly at reducing dependence on wood for fuel; g through cooperation, as mutually agreed, to strengthen the capacity of affected developing country Parties to develop and implement programmes in the field of collection, analysis and exchange of information pursuant to article 16; [...]
Basel Convention on the Control of Transboundary Movements of Hazardous Wastes and their Disposal (Basel Convention)	**Article 10** *International Co-operation* 1 The Parties shall co-operate with each other in order to improve and achieve environmentally sound management of hazardous wastes and other wastes. 2 To this end, the Parties shall:

(*Continued*)

Table 3.1 (Cont.)

Name of the treaty/ convention/ protocol	*Provisions concerning the innovation and transfer of technologies*
	a Upon request, make available information, whether on a bilateral or multilateral basis, with a view to promoting the environmentally sound management of hazardous wastes and other wastes, including harmonization of technical standards and practices for the adequate management of hazardous wastes and other wastes; b Co-operate in monitoring the effects of the management of hazardous wastes on human health and the environment; c Co-operate, subject to their national laws, regulations and policies, in the development and implementation of new environmentally sound low-waste technologies and the improvement of existing technologies with a view to eliminating, as far as practicable, the generation of hazardous wastes and other wastes and achieving more effective and efficient methods of ensuring their management in an environmentally sound manner, including the study of the economic, social and environmental effects of the adoption of such new or improved technologies; d Co-operate actively, subject to their national laws, regulations and policies, in the transfer of technology and management systems related to the environmentally sound management of hazardous wastes and other wastes. They shall also co-operate in developing the technical capacity among Parties, especially those which may need and request technical assistance in this field; e Co-operate in developing appropriate technical guidelines and/or codes of practice. **Article 14** *Financial Aspects* 1. The Parties agree that, according to the specific needs of different regions and subregions, regional or sub-regional centres for training and technology transfers regarding the management of hazardous wastes and other wastes and the minimization of their generation should be established. the Parties shall decide on the establishment of appropriate funding mechanisms of a voluntary nature.
Convention on Biological Diversity	**Article 16** *Access to and Transfer of Technology* 1 Each Contracting Party, recognizing that technology includes biotechnology, and that both access to and transfer of technology among Contracting Parties are essential elements for the attainment of the objectives of this Convention, undertakes subject to the provisions of this Article to provide and/or facilitate access for and transfer to other Contracting Parties of technologies that are relevant to the conservation and sustainable use of biological diversity or make use of genetic resources and do not cause significant damage to the environment.

(*Continued*)

Table 3.1 (Cont.)

Name of the treaty/ convention/ protocol	*Provisions concerning the innovation and transfer of technologies*
	2 Access to and transfer of technology referred to in paragraph 1 above to developing countries shall be provided and/or facilitated under fair and most favourable terms, including on concessional and preferential terms where mutually agreed, and, where necessary, in accordance with the financial mechanism established by Articles 20 and 21. In the case of technology subject to patents and other intellectual property rights, such access and transfer shall be provided on terms which recognize and are consistent with the adequate and effective protection of intellectual property rights. The application of this paragraph shall be consistent with paragraphs 3, 4 and 5 below. 3 Each Contracting Party shall take legislative, administrative or policy measures, as appropriate, with the aim that Contracting Parties, in particular those that are developing countries, which provide genetic resources are provided access to and transfer of technology which makes use of those resources, on mutually agreed terms, including technology protected by patents and other intellectual property rights, where necessary, through the provisions of Articles 20 and 21 and in accordance with international law and consistent with paragraphs 4 and 5 below. 4 Each Contracting Party shall take legislative, administrative or policy measures, as appropriate, with the aim that the private sector facilitates access to, joint development and transfer of technology referred to in paragraph 1 above for the benefit of both governmental institutions and the private sector of developing countries and in this regard shall abide by the obligations included in paragraphs 1, 2 and 3 above. 5 The Contracting Parties, recognizing that patents and other intellectual property rights may have an influence on the implementation of this Convention, shall cooperate in this regard subject to national legislation and international law in order to ensure that such rights are supportive of and do not run counter to its objectives. **Article 17** *Exchange of Information* 1 The Contracting Parties shall facilitate the exchange of information, from all publicly available sources, relevant to the conservation and sustainable use of biological diversity, taking into account the special needs of developing countries. 2 Such exchange of information shall include exchange of results of technical, scientific and socio-economic research, as well as information on training and surveying programmes, specialized knowledge, indigenous and traditional knowledge as such and in combination with the technologies referred to in Article 16, paragraph 1. It shall also, where feasible, include repatriation of information.

(*Continued*)

Table 3.1 (Cont.)

Name of the treaty/ convention/ protocol	*Provisions concerning the innovation and transfer of technologies*
	Article 18 *Technical and Scientific Cooperation* 1 The Contracting Parties shall promote international technical and scientific cooperation in the field of conservation and sustainable use of biological diversity, where necessary, through the appropriate international and national institutions. 2 Each Contracting Party shall promote technical and scientific cooperation with other Contracting Parties, in particular developing countries, in implementing this Convention, inter alia, through the development and implementation of national policies. In promoting such cooperation, special attention should be given to the development and strengthening of national capabilities, by means of human resources development and institution building. 3 The Conference of the Parties, at its first meeting, shall determine how to establish a clearing-house mechanism to promote and facilitate technical and scientific cooperation. 4 The Contracting Parties shall, in accordance with national legislation and policies, encourage and develop methods of cooperation for the development and use of technologies, including indigenous and traditional technologies, in pursuance of the objectives of this Convention. For this purpose, the Contracting Parties shall also promote cooperation in the training of personnel and exchange of experts. 5 The Contracting Parties shall, subject to mutual agreement, promote the establishment of joint research programmes and joint ventures for the development of technologies relevant to the objectives of this Convention. **Article 19** *Handling of Biotechnology and Distribution of its Benefits* 1 Each Contracting Party shall take legislative, administrative or policy measures, as appropriate, to provide for the effective participation in biotechnological research activities by those Contracting Parties, especially developing countries, which provide the genetic resources for such research, and where feasible in such Contracting Parties. 2 Each Contracting Party shall take all practicable measures to promote and advance priority access on a fair and equitable basis by Contracting Parties, especially developing countries, to the results and benefits arising from biotechnologies based upon genetic resources provided by those Contracting Parties. Such access shall be on mutually agreed terms.

(*Continued*)

Table 3.1 (Cont.)

Name of the treaty/ convention/ protocol	*Provisions concerning the innovation and transfer of technologies*
	3 The Parties shall consider the need for and modalities of a protocol setting out appropriate procedures, including, in particular, advance informed agreement, in the field of the safe transfer, handling and use of any living modified organism resulting from biotechnology that may have adverse effect on the conservation and sustainable use of biological diversity.
	4 Each Contracting Party shall, directly or by requiring any natural or legal person under its jurisdiction providing the organisms referred to in paragraph 3 above, provide any available information about the use and safety regulations required by that Contracting Party in handling such organisms, as well as any available information on the potential adverse impact of the specific organisms concerned to the Contracting Party into which those organisms are to be introduced.
	Article 20 *Financial Resources*
	4 The extent to which developing country Parties will effectively implement their commitments under this Convention will depend on the effective implementation by developed country Parties of their commitments under this Convention related to financial resources and transfer of technology and will take fully into account the fact that economic and social development and eradication of poverty are the first and overriding priorities of the developing country Parties.
	5 The Parties shall take full account of the specific needs and special situation of least developed countries in their actions with regard to funding and transfer of technology.
	Article 25 *Subsidiary Body on Scientific, Technical and Technological Advice*
	1 A subsidiary body for the provision of scientific, technical and technological advice is hereby established to provide the Conference of the Parties and, as appropriate, its other subsidiary bodies with timely advice relating to the implementation of this Convention. This body shall be open to participation by all Parties and shall be multidisciplinary. It shall comprise government representatives competent in the relevant field of expertise. It shall report regularly to the Conference of the Parties on all aspects of its work.
	2 Under the authority of and in accordance with guidelines laid down by the Conference of the Parties, and upon its request, this body shall:

(*Continued*)

Table 3.1 (Cont.)

Name of the treaty/ convention/ protocol	*Provisions concerning the innovation and transfer of technologies*
	a Provide scientific and technical assessments of the status of biological diversity;
	b Prepare scientific and technical assessments of the effects of types of measures taken in accordance with the provisions of this Convention;
	c Identify innovative, efficient and state-of-the-art technologies and know-how relating to the conservation and sustainable use of biological diversity and advise on the ways and means of promoting development and/or transferring such technologies;
	d Provide advice on scientific programmes and international cooperation in research and development related to conservation and sustainable use of biological diversity; and
	e Respond to scientific, technical, technological and methodological questions that the Conference of the Parties and its subsidiary bodies may put to the body.
	3 The functions, terms of reference, organization and operation of this body may be further elaborated by the Conference of the Parties.

Paris Agreement whereby 'Parties share a long-term vision on the importance of fully realizing technology development and transfer in order to improve resilience to climate change and to reduce greenhouse gas emissions'.

The objective of technology transfer under the CBD is 'conservation and sustainable use of biological diversity or make use of genetic resources and do not cause significant damage to the environment'.[365]

In Art. 18(1) of the UNCCD, Parties are required to 'promote, finance and/or facilitate the financing of the transfer, acquisition, adaptation and development of environmentally sound, economically viable and socially acceptable technologies' with a view to contributing 'to the achievement of sustainable development in affected areas'. It is important noting that the UNCCD concerns only those technologies, which are 'relevant to combatting desertification and/or mitigating the effects of drought'.[366]

Under the Basel Convention, the objective of Parties' technological cooperation is to 'improve and achieve environmentally sound management of hazardous wastes and other wastes'.[367] Finally, the objective of technology transfer under the ITPGRFA is to 'improv[e] the sustainable use of plant genetic resources for food and agriculture'.[368]

365 Art 16(1) of the CBD 1992.
366 Art. 18(1) of the UNCCD 1994.
367 Art. 10(1) of the Basel Convention 1989.
368 Art. 5(1)(1) of the IPTGRFA 2001.

3.5.2 Sources of finance

While the Basel Convention and the UNCCD have not outlined any specific commitment as to the transfer of financial resources, the CBD and ITPGRFA have adopted more precise provisions regarding their sources of financial resources.[369] In this regard, as described in Section 3.1 of this book, the UNFCCC and the Paris Agreement have specifically formed financial mechanisms for the purpose of fulfilling their objectives. The sources of finance for technology transfer under the climate regime include GCF, GEF and Marrakech Funds.[370] The main source of CBD international funding is GEF.[371] As land degradation is one of GEF's focal areas, GEF is also a main source of international funding for UNCCD.[372] However, the Basel Convention does not have access to international funds like GEF.[373] Funding for ITPGRFA is closely related to the Food and Agriculture Organization of the United Nations (FAO) funding.[374]

3.5.3 Coordination mechanisms

In terms of the coordination of technology innovation and transfer related mechanisms, the global climate regime is far more advanced than other conventions and treaties.[375] Although the CBD has an established mechanism, it is less advanced than that of the UNFCCC and the Paris Agreement.[376] The coordination mechanisms of the UNCCD are less established in comparison with the climate regime and the CBD. Although the Basel Convention has an established coordination mechanism, its framework is mainly focused on the regional level.[377] However, the ITPGRFA has a moderately advanced framework, where the 'Governing Body within the structure of Multilateral System' works as the main actor.[378]

3.5.4 Capacity building mechanisms

In terms of the capacity building of innovation and the transfer of environmentally sound technology, the global climate regime has 'extensive provisions on capacity building method', which has resulted in a developed framework. It has a 'structured execution method', which is based on the TNA.[379] It also covers diverse areas of capacity development.[380] Likewise the

369 Zainal Abidin Sanusi, 2005, 21.
370 See *supra* Chapter 3.2.
371 Zainal Abidin Sanusi, 2005, 22.
372 Ibid.
373 Ibid.
374 Ibid.
375 Cf. Zainal Abidin Sanusi, 2005, 24.
376 Ibid.
377 Ibid.
378 Ibid.
379 Ibid, 27.
380 Ibid.

global climate regime, the CBD also has extensive provisions for a capacity building mechanism and its framework 'emphasizes … integrating the capacity development agenda into national level'.[381] Compared to the climate regime and the CBD, the UNCCD has less extensive provisions regarding a capacity building mechanism, the development of which is based on 'both issue and geographical areas'.[382] The Basel Convention has vey general and nominal provisions on capacity building issues. Although the ITPGRFA contains extensive provisions regarding capacity building, it has not yet been fully developed outside the treaty.[383]

3.5.5 Network building mechanisms

The climate regime contains general provisions for encouraging exchange of information, which is structured and comprises of an advanced management and network system. In this regard, the Technology Transfer Clearing House (TT:Clear) works as a major source of information and network centre.[384] Like the climate regime, the CBD also contains general provisions for supporting access and sharing information. The CBD's major source of information and network centre is the Clearing House Mechanism.[385] The UNCCD also contains a general provision to encourage the exchange of information. However, the UNCCD's network building framework is poorly coordinated and Parties' access to the framework is somewhat difficult.[386] It does not have any widely recognized and accessible major source of information and network centre.[387] Although the Basel Convention contains general provisions for exchange of information on suitable waste management technology and its management system, it is difficult to gain access to that accumulated information.[388] At the Convention level, the Basel Convention does not have any widely recognized and accessible major source of information and network centre.[389] While the ITPGRFA contains an elaborate provision for a resource network and a framework for a global information system, it is 'still vague for operationalization'.[390] It has a multilateral system serving as an information centre. However, the scope of the accessibility framework of the information centre needs to be widened.[391]

381 Ibid.
382 Ibid.
383 Ibid.
384 Ibid, 29.
385 Ibid.
386 Ibid.
387 Ibid.
388 Ibid.
389 Ibid.
390 Ibid.
391 Ibid.

3.5.6 Modalities of technology transfer

In terms of modalities of technology transfer, both the climate regime and the CBD tend to prefer 'a combination of government/private sector and community driven pathways' with special emphasis on enhanced private sector involvement.[392] The UNCCD tends in the main to follow the government and community driven pathway with 'recent intensification of private sectors' involvement'.[393] The Basel Convention mostly follows government driven pathways.[394] While the ITPGRFA has 'no clear trend of pathways', based on the nature of the technology and of the need for capacity building, it is possible to deduce that both the government and private sectors are key players of technology transfer under the ITPGRFA.[395]

3.6 Private sector involvement

Broadly 'private sector engagement' or 'private sector involvement' can be understood as 'activities with the aim of engaging the private sector for development outcomes which involve the active participation of the private sector in the activity'.[396] In the context of battling climate change, 'private sector involvement' can arguably be denoted as 'private sector collaboration and partnerships' in climate change adaptation, mitigation, capacity building as well as innovation and transfer of environmentally sound technologies.[397]

The *Report of the Secretary-General's High-level Advisory Group on Climate Change Financing* (UN, 2010) considered that the declared vision of mobilizing climate finance to the non-Annex I Party developing and least developed countries in the order of US$ 100 billion per year was 'challenging', but 'feasible'.[398] In order to make the vision 'feasible', the *Report* suggested that the international source of future climate finance might require a variety of sources which could include public finance, development bank instruments, carbon markets and private capital.[399] Currently the accumulated amount of private sector climate finance is three times more than the accumulated amount of public sector finance.[400]

392 Ibid, 32.
393 Ibid.
394 Ibid.
395 Ibid.
396 Naeeda Crishna Morgado and Bérénice Lasfargues, *Engaging the Private Sector for Green Growth and Climate Action: An Overview of Development Co-Operation Efforts*, OECD Development Cooperation Working Paper 34, OECD, May 2017, 11.
397 Ibid, 11.
398 UN, *Report of the Secretary-General's High-level Advisory Group on Climate Change Financing*, 5 November, 2010, available at https://www.cbd.int/financial/interdevinno/un-climate-report.pdf (last accessed on April 25, 2020).
399 Ibid.
400 Paloma Szerman, 'Engaging Private Sector in Climate Finance: The Role of the Private Sector Facility of the Green Climate Fund', *Climate Change Law & Policy eJournal*, 2015, 14.

During the sessions of COP 19, the Annex II Parties expressed their view that the acceptance of the differentiated responsibilities of the Annex II Parties to provide financial and technological assistance in adaptation and mitigation activities to the non-Annex I Parties especially of the most climate change vulnerable developing and least developed country Parties should be realized through a joint initiative between public and private finance, and mostly through private finance mechanisms.[401] On this particular point, the non-Annex I Party developing countries are of the opinion that the finance for climate change adaptation and mitigation should come through a public funding mechanism, which in their view is preferable in realizing the principle of equity and CBDR.[402]

However, the Paris Agreement deems it necessary to involve both the public and the private sector, especially in realizing its proposed 'voluntary cooperation' mechanism.[403] One of the aims of introducing this 'voluntary cooperation' mechanism is to 'incentivize and facilitate participation in the mitigation of greenhouse gas emissions by public and private entities authorized by a Party'.[404] Furthermore, the Agreement requires enhanced 'public and private sector participation' in the implementation of Parties' nationally determined contributions.[405]

The Paris Rule Book elaborates on how private sector or alternative source of climate finance will be placed in the UNFCCC climate finance mechanism. In 'Methodologies for taking the necessary steps to facilitate the mobilization of support for adaptation in developing countries', the Paris Rule Book invites all Parties to increase private sector involvement in enhancing their 'enabling environments, policy frameworks, institutions and national public financial management system'.[406] Similarly, in 'Methodologies for reviewing the adequacy and effectiveness of adaptation and support', the Rule Book further invites Parties to involve the private sector.[407]

In relation to the innovation and transfer of environmentally sound technologies, the Paris Rule Book explicitly requires the promotion of the engagement of the private sector.[408] The Rule Book requires this to be done

401 Cf. T. Stern, 'The Shape of a New International Climate Agreement, speech given at the Conference 'Delivering Concrete Climate change action: Towards 2015', 22 October 2013, available at https://www.files.ethz.ch/isn/171926/The%20Shape%20of%20a%20New%20International%20Climate%20Agreement.pdf (last accessed on April 5, 2020).

402 A. Antypas and S. Neelakrantan, 'Not a Copout: Small but Meaningful Progress in Warsaw towards the 2015 Agreement', *Environmental Liability: Law, Policy and Practice,* Vol. 21(5), 2013, 172.

403 Art. 6(1) of the Paris Agreement 2015.

404 Art. 6(4)(b) of the Paris Agreement 2015.

405 Art. 6(8)(b) of the Paris Agreement 2015.

406 Decision 11/CMA.1, FCCC/PA/CMA/2018/3/Add.1, Para 22.

407 Ibid, Para 36.

408 Decision 15/CMA.1, Annex, Technology Framework ,Art. 10, Para 4 of the Paris Agreement, FCCC/PA/CMA/2018/3/Add.2, Para 7.

by: 1) building awareness regarding potential market opportunities in environmentally sound technology innovation; and 2) finding ways of motivating participation by the private sector.[409] In this regard, the Rule Book also focuses on building public and private sector partnerships in the development and transfer of the environmentally sound technologies.[410]

In order to guarantee an enabling environment and capacity building for technology development and transfer, the Paris Rule book advocates certain actions and activities, including, among others: 'assisting countries in developing and implementing policies for enabling environments to incentivize the private and public sector to fully realize the development and transfer' of environmentally sound technologies.[411] The required actions and activities also include 'assisting governments in playing a key role in fostering private sector involvement by designing and implementing policies, regulations and standards'.[412]

In addition, the Paris Rule Book considers enhancing the private sector's engagement and collaboration with other relevant stakeholders such as local communities and authorities, national planners and civil society organizations for the purpose of planning and implementing Technology Mechanism activities.[413] It also presses for enhanced voluntary 'engagement and collaboration with the private sector' for the purpose of leveraging expertise, experience and knowledge about effective enabling environments that assist implementation of the Paris Agreement.[414]

3.6.1 Private Sector Facility

COP 16 (held in 2010 in Cancun, Mexico) acknowledged that there are 'no individual sources that can simultaneously deliver the $100 billion target and meet the full range of end-use requirements'.[415] Accordingly the Cancun Summit welcomed funding from multiple sources including both the public and private sector.[416] In connection with sources of funding, in addition to establishing the GCF, the Cancun Summit also established a transitional committee in order to develop a strategy for the functioning of the GCF.[417] In 2011, the transitional committee recommended establishing a Private Sector Facility (PSF) which would be part of the GCF but different from the GCF's other financing tools.[418] The GCF Board accepted the recommendation and established the PSF.[419]

409 Ibid, Para 8(h)(i)–(ii).
410 Ibid, Para 8(i).
411 Ibid, Para 16(d).
412 Ibid, Para 16(e).
413 Ibid, Para 20(a).
414 Ibid, Para 20(b).
415 Paloma Szerman, 2015, 3.
416 Ibid.
417 Ibid.
418 Ibid.
419 Decision 3/CP.17, FCCC/CP/2011/9/Add.1, 15 March 2012, Paras. 41–44, cited in Paloma Szerman, 2015, 3.

The PSF is able to 'directly and indirectly finance private sector mitigation and adaptation activities at the national, regional and international levels'.[420] The operation of the Facility is intended to 'be consistent with a country-driven approach'.[421] It is intended to 'promote the participation of private sector actors in developing countries, in particular local actors, including small and medium-sized enterprises and local financial intermediaries'.[422] In line with the spirit of the principle of CBDR the PSF is committed to 'support[ing] activities to enable private sector involvement' in small island developing countries and least developed countries.[423]

In 2013, in its fourth meeting, the GCF Board adopted some key factors on which the PSF should focus achieving its objectives. These factors include increasing the investment's viability, reducing investment risk, funding capacity building efforts, assisting innovation and technological development and promoting the dissemination of information.[424]

In addition to the aforementioned key factors, the PSF should consider several additional issues. For instance, at the time of building local capacity, 'the PSF must be sensitive to the overall development models to which its funding contributes, and try to avoid to overload them'.[425] In this manner the PSF is expected to support local economies instead of just 'exporting economies via multinational corporations'.[426]

There are also suggestions about performance indicators. The measurements should not merely indicate the amount of greenhouse gases saved or the number of households having access to energy transformation. Instead of these measurements a holistic approach should be taken which needs to be 'adequate to capturing the multiple benefits of renewable energy transformations'.[427]

Moreover, in order not to act just as a 'capacity builder or information disseminator', and to make maximum use of its authority, the GCF and particularly the PSF are required to 'couple with ministers, utilities, regulators, financiers, and community representatives'. In this connection, the PSF needs to confirm its finances for local level manufacturers and national governments.[428]

Since knowledge sharing is an important component of capacity building, the PSF financing should also 'ensure funding to South-South learning experiences, promote access to knowledge through clean and patent-free technologies and be guided by a gender-sensitive approach'.[429]

420 Decision 3/CP.17, Para. 41.
421 Decision 3/CP.17, Para. 42.
422 Ibid, Para 43.
423 Ibid.
424 Green Climate Fund Board, Decision GCF/B.04/07, Business Model Framework: Private Sector Facility, 2013, 4–5, cited in Paloma Szerman, 2015, 10.
425 Paloma Szerman, 2015, 11.
426 Ibid.
427 Ibid,12.
428 Ibid.
429 Ibid.

3.7 Conclusion

One could argue that the success of the climate regime's technology transfer and financial cooperation mechanisms in many ways depends on the fulfilment by all Parties of their respective commitments. In this connection, Art. 4(1) of the UNFCCC has created an obligation of 'inventorying, reporting and cooperation'.[430] The Paris Agreement also establishes a 'transparency framework' in order to build 'mutual trust and confidence' and 'to promote effective implementation' of the provisions of the Agreement.[431] In line with the principle of CBDR, in implementing provisions of the Agreement, the 'transparency framework' should provide flexibility to the developing countries, who are in need of flexibilities[432] and to the least developed countries and small island developing states, which have special circumstances to be taken into consideration.[433] Under the 'transparency framework' of the Paris Agreement, 'developed country Parties shall, and other Parties that provide support should, provide information on financial, technology transfer and capacity-building support provided to developing country Parties under Articles 9, 10 and 11'.[434] Similarly, the framework requires developing country Parties to 'provide information on financial, technology transfer and capacity-building support needed and received under Articles 9, 10 and 11'.[435] Hence, the main objectives of the Convention and Agreement to combat climate change is aimed to attain through ensuring a transparency in developed country Parties' support to meet the financial , technological, and capacity building related needs of the developing country Parties.

430 Art. 4(1) of the UNFCCC 1992.
431 Art. 13(1) of the Paris Agreement 2015.
432 Art. 13(2) of the Paris Agreement 2015.
433 Art. 13(3) of the Paris Agreement 2015.
434 Art. 13(9) of the Paris Agreement 2015.
435 Art. 13(10) of the Paris Agreement 2015.

4 Technology transfer under the global trade regime

4.1 Introduction

International trade along with foreign direct investment, licensing and public knowledge are known as famous pathways for facilitating global technology transfer.[1] While all of the aforementioned channels do not promise the same level of technology transfer, to stimulate the process of transfer, countries should create a suitable environment for trading and licensing environmentally sound technologies as well as attracting investors to invest in research into innovation of environmentally sound technologies.

In order to create a suitable environment for technology transfer facilitating factors, countries should also be aware of the factors which impede technology transfer. Corvaglia (2014) categorizes the factors that impede technology transfer as 'technological, financial, institutional, information and social barriers', existing 'at every stage of the technology transfer sequence and often involving systemic socio-political circumstances'.[2] Lack or absence of 'access to essential information, skills and infrastructure' can frustrate the technology transfer process.[3] Lack or scarcity of financial resources can also impede the technology transfer process especially in developing countries.[4] Study shows that till now the main barrier for technology transfer in the renewable energy sector has been lack of investment caused by the high start-up cost.[5]

In addition to institutional barriers caused by limited institutional capacity, excessive bureaucratic procedures or lack or absence of legal and regulatory frameworks also play a negative role in the technology transfer process.[6]

1 Mahatab Uddin, *Climate Change and Requirement of Transfer of Environmentally Sound Technology,* Master's thesis, Department of Earth Science, Uppsala University, 2011, 4, available at https://www.diva-portal.org/smash/get/diva2:453274/FULLTEXT01.pdf (last accessed on July 31, 2020).

2 Maria Anna Corvaglia, 'South-South Technology Transfer Addressing Climate Change and Its (Missing) International Regulatory Framework', *Carbon and Climate Law Review*, Vol. 8(2), 2014, 125–137, 128.

3 Ibid.

4 Ibid,128.

5 Ibid, 129.

6 Ibid.

DOI: 10.4324/9781003056416-4

Likewise institutional barriers, political barriers that include 'interventions in domestic markets, corruption and weakness of civil society', etc. also have a negative impact on technology transfer.[7] In connection with political and institutional barriers, it is noteworthy that having an appropriate environmental regulatory framework in the recipient country is an important variable in promoting technology transfer.[8] Furthermore, as many multilateral environmental agreements contain technology related commitments, being a signatory country to multilateral environmental agreements also has a positive effect in facilitating technology transfer.[9] Finally, concerns about IPR raise their head in discussions about facilitators and barriers to technology transfer.[10]

Although many developing countries are 'deeply skeptical of the efficacy' of the IPR system, it is widely acknowledged that, in principle, the IPR system is 'designed to encourage innovation and facilitate trade in technology'.[11] The three main categories of intellectual property rights that can encourage disclosure of any new innovation or newly invented technology by preventing misappropriation of innovation are patent, copyright and trade secret (undisclosed information).[12] If any claimed invention satisfies novelty, inventive step (non-obviousness) and industrial application (useful) requirements, a patent is granted in favour of the inventor.[13] The protection is conferred for 20 years from the date of filing a patent application.[14] Copyright offers a longer period of protection from the unauthorized copying of expressed ideas and thoughts which includes software and original databases.[15] Trade secrets offer exclusive protection of commercially valuable information as long as 'reasonable steps' are taken to keep the information secret 'by the person lawfully in control of the information'.[16] However, the IPR related discussion in this chapter will mainly take into account the issues involved with patent protection for environmentally sound technologies.

While firms' willingness to transfer technology depends on the nature of the intellectual property system of the recipient country, discussion about the international transfer of environmentally sound technologies logically concerns that country's strength of IPR.[17] According to a Chatham House Report, 'a patent portfolio is a currency for attracting venture capital, entry into strategic

7 Ibid.
8 Ibid.
9 Ibid.
10 Ibid.
11 Keith E. Maskus and Ruth L. Okediji, 'Legal and Economic Perspectives on International Technology Transfer in Environmentally Sound Technology' in Mario Cimoli et al. (eds.), *Intellectual Property Rights: Legal and Economic Challenges for Development,* Oxford Scholarship Online, August 2014, 392.
12 Ibid, 397.
13 Art. 27(1) of the TRIPS Agreement 1994.
14 Art. 33 of the TRIPS Agreement 1994.
15 Cf Art. 9, Art.10 and Art. 12 of the TRIPS Agreement 1994.
16 Art. 39(2)(b) and (c) of the TRIPS Agreement 1994.
17 Varun Rai et al., 'International Low Carbon Technology Transfer: Do Intellectual Property Regimes Matter?', *Global Environmental Change,* Vol. 24(1), 2014, 60–74, 61.

alliances, protection against litigation, as well as opening opportunities for mergers and acquisitions'.[18] Arguments in favour of IPR further include that 'they facilitate investments in research and development, reduce licensing costs, add to the knowledge base, and enhance follow-on activity'.[19] In line with these points of view, developing countries need to strengthen their intellectual property system, because private firms will not be willing to license technologies without receiving 'adequate compensation' as well as 'credible protection from misappropriation' of their technologies.[20] However, the positive aspects of patents may not be applicable in the case of the transfer of environmentally sound technologies. This is because a patent can promote research and development, when there is a strong demand for new technological solutions, which is unlikely 'in the absence of policies to support high prices' for greenhouse gas emissions.[21]

Dissenting views also remain as to the 'ideal strength' of the IPR regime in developing countries.[22] Those who are in favour of a weaker IPR system in developing countries argue that if developing countries have a relatively weak IPR system they will be able to 'replicate and disperse more advanced technologies'.[23] They further argue that a strong IPR system in developing countries will make advanced technologies 'prohibitively expensive' for them.[24] Some opine that a strong IPR regime in developing countries 'may reduce the spread of technology if firms prioritize a stronghold on the technology value chain for fear of increasing market competition'.[25] However, the majority of studies opine that a strong IPR system 'will increase the level of innovation and technology transfer to developing and emerging countries'.[26]

Ockwell et. al (2010) think the differences in views of developed and developing countries as to the role of IPR in the transfer of environmentally sound technologies, are derived from the positions of these groups of countries regarding 'what the transfers are supposed to achieve'.[27] They think both groups of countries have an 'incomplete understanding of the process that contribute to achieving technological capacity development and technology diffusion'.[28] Hence, a report published in 2012 by UNFCCC rightly states:

18 Bernice Lee et al., *Who Owns Our Low Carbon Future? Intellectual Property and Energy Technologies*, Chatham House, 2009, available at https://www.chathamhouse.org/sites/default/ files/public/Research/Energy,% 20Environment%20and%20Development/r0909_lowcarbonfuture.pdf (last accessed on July 31, 2020).

19 Keith E. Maskus and Ruth L. Okediji, in Mario Cimoli et al. (eds.), Aug 2014, 392.

20 Ibid, 393.

21 Ibid.

22 Varun Rai et al., 2014, 61.

23 Ibid.

24 Ibid.

25 Ibid.

26 Ibid.

27 D. G. Ockwell et al., 'Intellectual Property Rights and Low Carbon Technology Transfer: Conflicting Discourses of Diffusion and Development', *Global Environmental Change*, Vol. 20(4), 2010, 729–738.

28 Ibid.

'[i]intellectual property rights were identified as an area for which more clarity would be needed on their role in the development and transfer of climate technologies based upon evidence on a case by case basis'.[29]

4.2 Transfer of environmentally sound technologies under TRIPS

The Agreement on Trade Related Aspects of Intellectual Property Rights (TRIPS) does not refer to the transfer of environmentally sound technology in its text, but it does refer to the necessity of technology transfer in general. The Preamble to TRIPS explicitly recognizes 'the underlying public policy objectives of national systems for the protection of intellectual property' which also include 'developmental and technological objectives'.[30] Besides, although TRIPS is not guided by the principle of equity and CBDR, it recognizes '*the special needs of the least-developed country Members* in respect of maximum flexibility in the domestic implementation of laws and regulations in order to enable them to create a sound and viable technological base' (emphasis added).[31]

Moreover, TRIPS' objective clause (i.e. Art. 7) states that 'the protection and enforcement' of IPR 'should contribute to the promotion of technological innovation and to the transfer and dissemination of technology'.[32] It further clarifies that the promotion of technological innovation and the transfer of technology need to be done in a way that is 'conducive to social and economic welfare'.[33] While the text of the TRIPS provisions does not specify the necessity and pressure for innovation and the transfer of environmentally sound technologies, these provisions can be helpful in explaining other TRIPS provisions, which might facilitate a favourable environment for innovation and the transfer of environmentally sound technologies.[34] Art. 7 has already been considered a guiding principle for explaining the global IPR regime by the Doha Declaration on TRIPS and Public Health 2000.[35]

However, in order to create a suitable IPR framework that can facilitate innovation and the transfer of environmentally sound technologies in developing and least developed countries, objective clause (i.e. Art. 7) of the TRIPS

29 UNFCCC, *Report on Activities and Performance of the Technology Executive Committee for 2012,* UN Doc. FCCC/SB/2012/2, 18 Oct. 2012, para 35(g), available at: https://unfccc.int/resource/docs/2012/sb/eng/02.pdf (last accessed on July 21, 2020).

30 Preamble to the TRIPS Agreement 1994.

31 Ibid.

32 Art. 7 of the TRIPS Agreement 1994.

33 Ibid.

34 Cf. Vienna Convention on the Law of Treaties, Art. 31(2), May 23, 1969, 1155 U.N.T.S. 331.

35 See generally WTO, *Declaration on the TRIPS Agreement and Public Health,* WT/MIN(01)/DEC/2, 20 Nov. 2001, para 5(a), available at: https://www.wto.org/english/thewto_e/minist_e/min01_e/mindecl_trips_e.htm (last accessed on July 31, 2020).

needs to be read in conjunction with TRIPS' principle clauses (i.e. Art. 8). Under Art. 8(1), at the time of formulating or amending their laws and regulations, countries are allowed to 'adopt measures necessary to protect public health and nutrition, and to promote the public interest in sectors of vital importance to their socio-economic and technological development'.[36] Although this principle clause does not refer to the issue of climate change or environmentally sound technologies, one could argue that the notion of 'public interest' should necessarily cover the battle against climate change. The issue can arguably be covered by the notion of 'public health', as the adverse effects of climate change can create a threat to public health in general.[37] Based on these arguments, countries may adopt or amend their national IPR frameworks in a manner that will create a favourable environment for innovation and the transfer of environmentally sound technologies.

Moreover, under Art. 8(2), countries are entitled to take 'appropriate measures' to prevent rights holders' abuse of IPR or rights holders participating in any practice 'which unreasonably restrain[s] trade or adversely affect[s] the international transfer of technology'.[38] In accordance with this provision, countries are allowed to remove barriers against the transfer of environmentally sound technologies through taking proper steps against the owners of IPR who display any tendency to abuse their rights over the relevant environmentally sound technology.

4.2.1 Patent standards

Developing countries can prevent excessive patenting by adopting strict patentability requirements. Since TRIPS has not set any minimum standard of creativity for granting a patent,[39] adopting a strict 'inventive step' or 'non-obviousness' requirement will not necessarily be inconsistent with TRIPS. If developing countries with better manufacturing capabilities adopt a strict patentability requirement, it may facilitate the transfer of the relevant technology to other developing countries in a smoother manner. However, developing countries also need to ensure that strong patentability requirements do not discourage small-scale inventive and adaptive efforts, especially those efforts that are made by local entrepreneurs.[40] In order to do this, these countries could introduce a strong utility model or petty patent, which offers 'short-term and narrow protection for adaptive inventions, with limited requirements for demonstrated novelty'.[41] There is evidence that utility models or petty patents have played a noteworthy role in productivity growth in countries like Brazil,

36 Art. 8(1) of the TRIPS Agreement 1994.
37 See generally Howard Frumkin et al., 'Climate Change: The Public Health Response', *American Journal of Public Health,* Vol. 98(3), 2008, 435–445.
38 Art. 8(2) of the TRIPS Agreement 1994.
39 See generally Art. 27 of the TRIPS Agreement 1994.
40 Keith E. Maskus et al. (eds.), August 2014, 392, 406.
41 Ibid.

Korea and Japan.[42] If a utility model or petty patent system could encourage local firms to innovate mitigation related environmentally sound technologies, it would arguably help developing countries to meet their local mitigation needs.[43]

4.2.2 Compulsory licensing

Art. 31 of TRIPS adopts provisions for a compulsory license or use of a patent without the authorization of the right holder. Under the compulsory license process, a non-patent holder can produce or import a patented technology without permission from the patent owner.[44] However, TRIPS guarantees that 'the right holder shall be paid adequate remuneration in the circumstances of each case, taking into account the economic value of the authorization'.[45] TRIPS also states that 'authorization of such use shall be considered on its individual merits'.[46] In this regard, Paragraph 5 of the Doha Declaration on TRIPS and Public Health makes it clear that countries have both the right to grant compulsory licenses and the 'freedom to determine the grounds upon which such licenses are granted'.[47] In practice, South Africa introduced a 'compulsory license' to manufacture essential drugs to fight national epidemics.[48] Similarly, Thailand employed the 'compulsory license' provisions for drugs which are essential to treat long-term, health-related problems.[49] Although the compulsory license provision of Art. 31 has so far only been used for essential medicines, in principle, the provision could also be applicable to patented environmentally sound technologies.[50]

However, the compulsory license provision of Art. 31 has also protected the primary interest of the original patent holder. In this regard, Art. 31(b) stipulates that prior to using the compulsory license, the proposed user needs to make 'efforts to obtain authorization from the right holder on reasonable commercial terms and conditions and that such efforts have not been successful

42 Ibid, 407.
43 Ibid.
44 Ibid.
45 Art. 31(h) of the TRIPS Agreement 1994.
46 Art. 31(a) of the TRIPS Agreement 1994.
47 WTO, *Declaration on the TRIPS Agreement and Public Health,* WT/MIN(01)/DEC/2, 20 Nov. 2001, Para 5(a), available at https://www.wto.org/english/thewto_e/minist_e/min01_e/mindecl_trips_e.htm (last accessed on August 10, 2020).
48 See generally Sophie Huddart et al., 'The Doha Declaration in Action: An Examination of Patent Law Flexibilities in the South African Acquired Immunodeficiency Syndrome Epidemic', *Journal of Health Specialities*, Vol. 5(1), 2017, 30–34.
49 Fabrice Mattei, 'A New Approach to Compulsory Licensing in Thailand', *Rouse* (31 May 2007), available at www.rouse.com/magazine/articles/news-and-articles/a-new-approach-to-compulsory-licensing-in-thailand? tag=life %20sciences (last accessed on August 10, 2020).
50 Keith E. Maskus and Ruth L. Okediji, in Mario Cimoli et al. (eds.), Aug 2014, 407.

within a reasonable period of time'. However, member states may receive a waiver from this requirement 'in the case of a national emergency or other circumstances of extreme urgency or in cases of public noncommercial use'. Since TRIPS does not define which circumstances can be considered a 'national emergency', in principle member states are at liberty to define their own national emergency situation.[51] Some scholars think that the possible consequences of climate change might create 'a situation of extreme emergency', which may give member states waiver from the requirement of seeking a voluntary license from the patent right holders before using a compulsory license.[52]

Art. 31 has also set out several procedural conditions for granting a compulsory licence. For instance, the scope and duration of using a patent without the authorization of the right holder shall remain 'limited to the purpose for which it was authorized'.[53] Furthermore, such use shall be non-exclusive[54] and non-assignable.[55]

Moreover, Art. 31(f) of TRIPS states that the issuance of a compulsory license shall be 'predominantly for the supply of the domestic market of the member authorizing such use'. It means if any country allows a compulsory license for any patented environmentally sound technology, that specific technology cannot be exported to other countries. This might pose difficulties for those member states that do not have manufacturing capabilities. Those countries will neither be able to authorize any domestic firm to manufacture the required environmentally sound technology nor be able to import them from other member states.[56] However, an amendment of Art. 31(f) that was made in 2005 allowed 'a permanent waiver of the domestic market requirement for pharmaceuticals'.[57] A similar kind of waiver for environmentally sound technologies could be helpful in promoting the transfer of those technologies in developing and least developed countries.[58]

However, as per Art. 31(k) of TRIPS, members will not be required to meet the various conditions for granting compulsory licenses, if such licenses are granted in order 'to remedy a practice determined after judicial or administrative process to be anti-competitive'. It means that to grant a compulsory license for any environmentally sound technology that is required, developing countries will not have to meet the various conditions if the administrative or judicial process of the country concerned can determine the existence of any anti-competitive practice. Hence, developing and least developed countries

51 Cf. ibid.
52 Ibid.
53 Art. 31(c) of the TRIPS Agreement 1994.
54 Art. 31(d) of the TRIPS Agreement 1994.
55 Art. 31(e) of the TRIPS Agreement 1994.
56 Keith E. Maskus et al. (eds.), August 2014, 407.
57 Ibid, 408.
58 Ibid.

should adopt proper policies and regulations that might create a possibility for them to utilize the scope and opportunities of the provision.[59]

4.2.3 Exclusions from patentability

Art. 27 of TRIPS permits member states to exclude any claimed invention from patent rights 'within their territory of the commercial exploitation' if it is essential 'to protect *ordre public* or morality, including to protect human, animal or plant life or health or to avoid serious prejudice to the environment'.[60] The patentability of some environmentally sound technologies might fall under this exemption.[61] This is because although an environmentally sound technology improves one feature of the environment, it may worsen another feature.[62] For instance, a technology that can limit over-fishing in one area may have a negative impact on other coastal ecological balances.[63] However, exclusion from patentability on environmental grounds can be 'politically difficult and seemingly inconsistent with the terms of the TRIPS Agreement'.[64] Moreover, it is also uncertain whether or not limiting such patentability would enhance access to environmentally sound technologies. However, at the time of assessing patentability, Art. 27 permits national patent offices 'to balance, in the context of national mitigation or adaptation strategies, the anticipated impact of the technology on environmental goals'.[65]

4.3 Transfer of environmentally sound technologies under TRIMS

TRIMS acknowledges that 'certain investment measures can cause trade-restrictive and distorting effects'.[66] In accordance with Art. 2 of TRIMs, any investment related measure which is inconsistent with the principle of national treatment (Art. III, The General Agreement on Tariffs and Trade (GATT)) and with the prohibition of a quantitative restriction (Art. XI, GATT) is forbidden for WTO members.[67] TRIMS stipulates that local content requirements and trade-balancing requirements or export restrictions are inconsistent with these WTO principles.[68] But, banning the 'local content requirement' is arguably not

59 Ibid.
60 Art. 27(2) of the TRIPS Agreement 1994.
61 Keith E. Maskus and Ruth L. Okediji, in Mario Cimoli et al. (eds.), Aug 2014, 408.
62 Ibid.
63 Ibid.
64 Ibid.
65 Ibid.
66 Preamble to the TRIMs Agreement 1994.
67 Art. 2(1) of the TRIMs Agreement 1994.
68 M. L. Sterlini, 'The Agreement on Trade-Related Investment Measures' in Arthur E. Appleton and Michael J. Plummer (eds.), *The World Trade Organization: Legal, Economic and Political Analysis*, Vol. 1, Springer, 2005, 440.

an appropriate method of facilitating innovation and the transfer of environmentally sound technologies. This is because the 'local content requirement' in a foreign investment evidently fosters the rate of innovation and transfer of technologies.[69] With this in mind, one could argue that the TRIMS provision banning the 'local content requirement' should be waived for investment in the environmentally sound technology sectors. Such a waiver might particularly facilitate technology transfer by building cooperation between developed and developing countries. Besides, although it may conflict with the 'national treatment' principle, TRIMS might consider including 'technology transfer' as an essential requirement for investing in the innovation and production of environmentally sound technologies.

To include the 'local content requirement' or 'technology transfer requirement' in TRIMS, thus avoiding conflict with the 'national treatment' principle, the international trade regime may arguably consider relying on the CBDR principle of the international climate regime. As we have observed a kind of 'differential treatment' as a result of IPR flexibility in relation to 'public health' or compulsory licensing for essential medicines under TRIPS, arguably similar differential treatment for environmentally sound technologies could be adopted by TRIMS.

One could justify the suggested inclusion of 'local content' or 'technology transfer' requirements or any other preferential treatment facilitating the transfer of environmentally sound technologies in developing and least developed countries, based on a 'global emergency' criterion. It is possible to denote the situation as a 'global emergency', as global climate change is a 'common concern of humankind'.

4.4 Conclusion

Since innovation and the transfer of environmentally sound technologies is essential to combat climate change globally, countries may consider adopting and implementing the aforementioned flexibility of TRIPS which will facilitate innovation and the transfer of required technologies. Besides, the international trade regime governing TRIMs may consider adopting the flexibilities suggested above for the purpose of facilitating the innovation and transfer of environmentallly sound technologies. Since the principle of CBDR is an essential tool in attaining sustainable development – a common goal for both the climate regime and the trade regime[70] – in order to adopt provisions to remove trade barriers on environmental goods and services, the international trade regime could consider relying on this principle.

69 M. A. Corvaglia, 2014, 137.

70 Art. 3(4) of the UNFCCC 1992; see also Preamble to the Marrakech Agreement establishing the World Trade Organization 1994.

5 Case study

5.1 Introduction

Prior to describing the CDM projects or CDM Programme of Activities in Bangladesh and their role in the transfer of environmentally sound technologies and in facilitating local sustainable development, it is important and relevant to describe the criteria applied by the Designated National Authority of Bangladesh to assess the potential sustainable development impact of the proposed CDM projects.

Although environmental objectives such as reduction in the emission of greenhouse gases, reduction in pollution of the environment and environmental management based on resource efficiency have received comparable importance in all host countries, the assessment criteria of the sustainable development impact of the CDM projects differ from country to country. This is due to the fact that the standard set by the Designated National Authorities is largely dictated by the national development goal of the country concerned.[1] The national development goal of a country is drawn up on the basis of its specific needs and circumstances.[2]

5.2 Sustainable development criteria for the CDM projects in Bangladesh

As per the official document determining the sustainable development criteria of the CDM projects in Bangladesh, the main development objectives of the country are development of the economy and social development.[3] The economic and social development objectives of the country include 'poverty alleviation through creation of jobs', 'reducing vulnerability to environmental

1 Ritika Tewari, *Mapping of Criteria Set by DNAs to Assess Sustainable Development Benefits of CDM Projects, Contribution to the Research Programme of the CDM Policy Dialogue,* The Energy and Resources Institute (TERI), India, July 2012, 4.
2 Ibid.
3 Ministry of Environment and Forest and Climate Change (MOEF), *Sustainable Development Criteria for CDM Projects,* Department of Environment (DOE), Government of the People's Republic of Bangladesh, August 2004, 3.

DOI: 10.4324/9781003056416-5

stresses', 'improving quality of life', 'improving health and sanitation system for the society', 'augmenting reserves of foreign exchange and improving balance of payment'.[4] The national development goal of poverty alleviation through creation of jobs in Bangladesh reflects the principle of intra-generational equity.

The development objectives for the transport sector in Bangladesh have been specified as 'improving traffic management', 'reducing traffic jam through mass transit system' and 'lowering pollution from traffic system'. For the industrial sector the development objectives have been set as 'fuel switching from imported fuels to domestic natural gas'. For the energy sector the development objectives have been set as 'adoption of efficient and cost-effective technologies for power generation', and 'progress in transmission and distribution of electricity'. Hence, in order to receive approval from the Designated National Authority, any proposed CDM project in Bangladesh needs to comply with the development objectives of the relevant sector.[5]

The evaluation of the sustainable development impact of a potential CDM project in Bangladesh is based on three basic questions. The first question is: *Does the CDM project aggravate any existing environmental problem?* If the answer is affirmative, the project is rejected and not eligible to be taken for further assessment. If answer to the first question is negative, the project becomes eligible to be assessed by the second question of the assessment process: *Does the CDM project violate any development objectives of the country?* If the answer to this question is affirmative, the project becomes rejected and isn't taken any further. If answer to the second question is negative, the project becomes eligible to be examined by the third question of the assessment process: *Does the project strongly address any development or environmental goal?* [6]

Passing the first and second step of the assessment process means that the proposed CDM project is environmentally sound and it does not contradict Bangladesh's broader development goals. However, passing the first two steps of the assessment process does not necessarily mean the project has a positive sustainable development impact.

To determine the level of sustainable development impact of a proposed CDM project, the answer to the third question of the assessment process needs to be affirmative. Hence, if a proposed CDM project addresses any of Bangladesh's development or environmental goals in a direct fashion it becomes eligible to be launched.[7]

However, merely addressing environment and development related issues is not enough to pass the third step of the sustainable development impact assessment process. The description of the way the proposed project will address any of Bangladesh's environmental or development objectives has to be done in a manner that guarantees two more issues. First, it needs to show that

4 Ibid, 3.
5 Ibid, 3.
6 Ibid, 4.
7 Ibid.

the project will have a 'positive impact' on achieving the aforementioned national development objective. Secondly, the claimed 'positive impact' has to be shown to be 'significant'.[8]

If the government or public sector proposes a CDM project, it might be accepted after passing the second step in the process. This is because it is presumed that public sector CDM projects are initiated in close consultation with the Designated National Authorities and are designed pursuant to the national development and environment goals. However, if a CDM project is proposed by a private sector actor and does not pass the aforementioned third step, meaning that it does not provide any proof of making a 'significant' positive impact towards achieving any of the national development or environment goals, the project is required to go through an advanced screening tool. This tool is comprised of an appropriate set of sustainable development criteria.[9]

The survey conducted by Tewari (2012) observed that the assessment of the sustainable development impact of the CDM projects conducted by different Designated National Authorities is largely based on the three basic pillars of sustainable development: the social impact, the economic impact and the environmental impact of the projects on the locality.[10] Similarly, in establishing the advanced sustainable development impact assessment tool for CDM projects proposed by the private sector that do not pass the third step of the simple sustainable development impact assessment tool, the Designated National Authority of Bangladesh mainly takes into account the potential impact of the CDM projects on the local environment, economy and society.

In assessing the impact of a project on society, the Designated National Authority of Bangladesh principally considers the role of the potential CDM project in reducing poverty.[11] Although the study conducted by Tewari (2012) states that many Designated National Authorities consider the 'technological development' or 'transfer of environmentally sound technologies' issues to be part of the economic impact of a project, the Designated National Authority of Bangladesh considers the issue of 'technological development' to be the single determiner of the sustainable development impact assessment tool.[12] In view of this position on technology transfer, one could argue that the advanced sustainable development impact assessment tool for CDM projects proposed by the private sector in Bangladesh puts more emphasis on technology transfer than do those of many other non-Annex I Parties to the Convention.

The Designated National Authority of Bangladesh also includes the 'capacity building' impact of the proposed CDM projects as a separate criterion of the sustainable development impact assessment tool. This means, when the Designated National Authority of Bangladesh assesses the future sustainable

8 Ibid.
9 Ibid.
10 Cf. Ritika Tewari, 2012, 6.
11 MOEF, August 2004, 3.
12 Ibid.

development impact of a CDM project proposed by the private sector, it considers whether the CDM project might have a positive role in 'capacity building' by establishing more similar projects in the country.[13] Capacity building refers to the transfer of knowledge, experiences, skills and practices concerning any specific technology or group of technologies.[14] One could argue that the inclusion of 'capacity building' as an essential component of Bangladesh's advance sustainable development impact assessment tool reflects and promotes the principle of intra-generational equity.

Consequently, the Designated National Authority of Bangladesh considers five kinds of impact of CDM project proposed by the private sector in determining its potential sustainable development impact. These five criteria are: 'environmental development' impact; 'economic development' impact; 'social development' impact or impact on 'poverty reduction'; 'technological development' impact; and 'capacity building' impact. While the environmental, social and economic aspects are known as the 'three pillars' of sustainable development,[15] the other two criteria – the technological and capacity building aspects – are also known as important tools in the promotion of sustainable development.[16]

As technology transfer is a known tool in the promotion of sustainable development and capacity building is a known element of technology transfer,[17] one can presume that both the 'technological development' and 'capacity building' criterion of the advanced sustainable development impact assessment tool of Bangladesh are intended to supplement the social, economic and environmental development criteria of the assessment tool. Moreover, 'technology transfer' is a tool of intra-generational resource distribution leading to a means of realizing the principle of CBDR.[18] Similarly, 'capacity building' is a tool of intra-generational resource distribution leading to a means of realizing the principle of equity.[19] In view of this, it is possible to remark that the abovementioned 'technological development' and 'capacity building' requirements guarantee that the principles of equity and CBDR have a guiding role in Bangladesh's advanced sustainable development impact assessment tool.[20]

Moreover, one could argue that the underlying spirit of the principle of equity further guides the advanced sustainable development impact assessment tool for CDM projects proposed by the private sector in Bangladesh. This is because the standards applied by the advanced sustainable development impact assessment tool specifically include 'poverty reduction' (as a scale of social development) as a core part of the assessment tool.[21]

13 Ibid, 5.
14 For details about 'capacity building' see *supra* Chapter 3.3.1.1.
15 See *supra* Chapter 1.2.
16 Chapter 34 of Agenda 21.
17 Ibid.
18 Cf. *supra* Chapter 2.7.2.
19 *Supra* Chapter 2.6.
20 Cf. *supra* Chapter 2.7.2, see also *supra* Chapter 3.3.1.1.

Bangladesh's simple sustainable development impact assessment tool for CDM projects considers all the environmental, social and economic benefits simultaneously and so arguably follows the 'integration' or 'reconciliation' approach of sustainable development.[22] Complying with the 'principle of integration' of sustainable development, the simple sustainable development impact assessment tool gives priority to the 'environmental aspect' (environmental benefit) over the 'development aspects' (social and economic benefits) of any proposed CDM project. This is evident from the three questions of the assessment tool described above.[23]

Since the spirit of the 'principle of integration' of sustainable development is followed by the 'liberal' explanation of 'environmental integrity' of CDM projects,[24] one could argue that Bangladesh's simple sustainable development assessment tool reflects the 'liberal' explanation of the 'environmental integrity' of CDM projects.[25]

The said preference for 'environmental aspects' over 'development aspects' in the simple sustainable development assessment tool has arguably an extensive effect in manifesting equity based on the realization of the principle of CBDR.[26] As a Party to the UNFCCC, Bangladesh has 'common but differentiated responsibilities' to take 'climate change considerations into account, to the extent feasible' to prevent environmental degradation.[27] Through its sustainable development assessment tool for CDM projects, Bangladesh arguably complies with its 'common but differentiated responsibilities' derived from the Convention by taking account of the 'environmental aspects' of the proposed projects, in particular.[28] One could therefore argue that Bangladesh's observation of the principle of CBDR by prioritizing the 'environmental aspects' of proposed CDM projects also leads to a manifestation of the principle of equity in the promotion of sustainable development in the country.[29]

21 See *supra* Chapter 2.6, Chapter 2.7 and Chapter 2.7.2.
22 Cf. *supra* Chapter 2.4, which provides details about the 'principle of integration' of sustainable development.
23 The three questions are: *Does the CDM project aggravate any existing environmental problem?, Does the CDM project violate any development objectives of the country?* and *Does the project strongly address any development or environmental goal?*
24 Cf. *supra* Chapter 2.4.
25 Cf. *supra* Chapter 2.4.
26 Cf. *supra* Chapter 2.6.
27 See Art. 4(f) of the UNFCCC 1992, see also Arts. 4(c) and 4(d) of the UNFCCC 1992.
28 Through complying with its common responsibility for preventing environmental degradation.
29 Cf. *supra* Chapter 2.2, 2.5, 2.6 and 2.7.

5.3 Sustainable development through the transfer of environmentally sound technologies in Bangladesh

The seven registered CDM projects and Programme of Activities[30] of Bangladesh can be divided into three broad categories: 1) Energy Efficiency; 2) Renewable Energy; and 3) Waste Recycling. Five CDM projects and the Programme of Activities belong to the Energy Efficiency category, one CDM Programme of Activities belongs to the Renewable Energy category and one CDM project belongs to the Waste Recycling category.

The Energy Efficiency category includes two brick-kiln bundle CDM projects (hereinafter also referred to as the 'brick-kiln' CDM projects), the Supplying Energy Efficient Bulb Programme of Activities (hereinafter also referred to as the 'efficient lighting' CDM programme),the Supplying Improved Cooking Stoves CDM Programme of Activities (hereinafter also referred to as the 'improved cooking stoves' CDM programme) and the Supplying Water Straw CDM Programme of Activities (hereinafter also referred to as the 'life straw family' CDM programme).

The Renewable Energy category includes the Installation of Solar Home Systems Solar Home Systems CDM Programme of Activities (hereinafter also referred to as 'solar home systems' CDM programme).

The 'waste recycling' category includes the Waste to Compost CDM project (hereinafter also referred to as 'waste to compost' CDM project). Descriptions of the CDM projects and CDM Programme of Activities of Bangladesh and their role in promoting sustainable development by promoting the transfer of environmentally sound technologies are given later in this chapter.

This chapter's technology transfer assessment will mainly be based on (or was based on) the technology transfer criteria given by Cools (2007). In her dissertation about the assessment of technology, Cools has specified four vital criteria for technology transfer: 1) foreign origin; 2) grade of novelty; 3) performance development; and 4) capacity building.[31]

The Cools' first criterion, 'foreign origin', refers to the fact that the technology must come from abroad and be employed in the CDM hosting country. The second criterion, 'grade of novelty', is determined by the fact that the technology must be new to the market, or to that specific host country, or to the relevant industrial sector of the host country. The third criterion, 'performance development', refers to the requirement that the technology should possess an improved quality environmental performance to reduce greenhouse gas emissions into the atmosphere or that it will generate more CERs in comparison with the credits generated by existing technologies. The fourth

30 The CDM Programme of Activities is comprised of a group of individual projects that follow the same methodology with the same Project Design Document (PDD) and reference number.

31 S. L. Y. Cools, 'Assessing Technology Transfer in the Clean Development Mechanism', dissertation for the Master of Philosophy in Environmental and Development Economics degree, University of Oslo, 2007, 33–38.

criterion, 'capacity building', refers to the requirement that the transferred technology should be accompanied by the tacit knowledge associated with that technology. The purpose of the fourth criterion is to ensure that the 'transferred technology' will boost the skill of the host country in manufacturing, operating and mastering new technologies.[32]

In addition to the technology transfer criteria given by Cools, assessment in this chapter will also follow (or has followed) the criteria given by Das (2011). According to Das, if a CDM project that requires technology 'imports equipment only' to the host country, it should not be considered to be a technology transfer. However, when such a kind of transfer of equipment is accompanied by a 'contribution towards technological learning and capability building' in the host country, it will constitute a transfer of technology.[33] As a definition of the term 'contribution', a CDM project is considered to be contributing to technology transfer if any of the following three scenarios are true: 1) a host country entity develops a technology, specifically for a CDM project, in collaboration with some foreign entity and the transfer is first and foremost a transfer of knowledge on technology development; 2) a technology and/or equipment import is accompanied by in-house technological efforts by the host country project participant to adapt or improve upon the imported technology/equipment; and 3) a technology and/or technologies accompanied by training by foreign entities in the operation and maintenance of the imported technology and/or technology.[34] Moreover, the assessments will also consider (or have considered) the technology transfer definition found in the IPCC Special Report and Agenda 21.[35]

5.3.1 Brickkilns

The brick-producing industry is very energy-intensive and a source of a huge amount of greenhouse gas emissions (estimated as producing 3.0 million tons of CO_2 emissions per year).[36] While the annual growth rate of the construction sector is 8–10 per cent (2–3 per cent higher than GDP), the annual growth rate of the brick-producing industry is more than 5 per cent.[37] This estimated

32 Ibid.
33 K. Das, *Technology Transfer under the Clean Development Mechanism: An Empirical Study of 1000 CDM Projects,* Working Paper 014, The Governance of Clean Development Working Paper Series, School of International Development, University of East Anglia, UK, July 2011, 4–6.
34 Ibid, 5.
35 *Supra* Chapter 1.3.
36 Small-scale CDM Programme of Activities Design Document Form (CDM SSC-PoA-DD) - Version 03, *Improving Kiln Efficiency in the Brick Making Industry in Bangladesh* (Reference No. 5125), Version 15, Date 18/04/2011, 4, available at https://cdm.unfccc.int/Projects/DB/DNV-CUK1313585039.34/view (last accessed on March 22, 2021).
37 World Bank, *Introducing Energy-efficient Clean Technologies in the Brick Sector of Bangladesh,* The World Bank and Energy Sector Management Assistance Program (ESMAP), June 2011, 78.

growth of the brick sector of the country may lead to an enhanced amount of annual greenhouse gas emissions from the sector, which may be a potential obstacle for the 'green economy' development path of Bangladesh adopted by the Government of Bangladesh.[38]

The traditional brick-producing industry in Bangladesh is seasonal.[39] Bricks are only produced in the dry season.[40] The technology traditionally used in the sector is old and out-dated, and the labour efficiency is very low.[41] The method of management is informal and the ownership pattern is dominated by small and medium-size enterprises (SMEs) with little or no large-scale cooperation.[42] Almost all workers are employed as temporary workers.[43] Thus, there is a huge need for the introduction of new technology in the brick-manufacturing sector that might promote the efficiency of the sector and facilitate sustainable development in the country.

Given these circumstances, the Infrastructural Development Finance Company Ltd. (IIDFC)[44] (as a bundling agent) has initiated two brick-kiln bundling CDM projects in Bangladesh.[45] These projects have employed Hybrid Hoffman Kiln (HHK) technology in the brick-manufacturing industries in the country.[46] The special characteristic of these two CDM projects is an integrated environmental management plan. The integrated environmental management plan means the monitoring and regulating of the environmental impact of the projects is not limited to the predetermined checklist, but environmental safeguard issues are considered to be a dynamic obligation of the project. The dynamic environmental obligation requires Parties to modify their management plan in any situation that could possibly have a negative impact on the local environment.[47]

To mitigate any possible negative impact of the project on the local environment, the projects have divided their mitigation measures into two parts: the construction phase and the operational phase. Such mitigation measures include

38 Cf. MOEF, *Bangladesh: Technology Needs Assessment and Technology Action Plans for Climate Change Mitigation,* Government of the People's Republic of Bangladesh, December 2011, ii.
39 *Improving Kiln Efficiency in the Brick Making Industry in Bangladesh,* Version 15, 7.
40 Ibid.
41 Ibid.
42 Ibid.
43 Ibid.
44 Industrial and Infrastructural Development Finance Company Limited (IIDFC) is a leading financial institution promoted by ten commercial banks from both the public and private sector, three insurance companies and the Investment Corporation of Bangladesh (ICB), available at https://cdm.unfccc.int/Projects/projsearch.html (last accessed on March 22 2021).
45 UNFCCC Reference Nos. 5125, and 6085.
46 IIDFC, *Improving Kiln Efficiency in the Brick Making Industry in Bangladesh: Hybrid HoffmnKlin (HHK) Project: Environment Management Framework (EMF),* Dhaka, 2009, 1.
47 Ibid, 10.

a list of the possible negative impact of different sectors making the operator responsible for taking precautions and proper measures to avoid them.[48]

In the Project Design Document of one of the two bundle CDM projects, it has been estimated that each Hybrid Hoffman Kiln would produce around 15 million bricks per year, whereas each old kiln could only produce 2 million bricks per year.[49] Thus, each new kiln is expected to be 7.5 times more efficient in comparison with traditional brick-kiln projects.[50] This production efficiency, resulting from the energy efficiency of the Hybrid Hoffman Kiln, is expected to reduce greenhouse gas emissions by a large amount, and to generate huge CERs derived from the reduced amount of greenhouse gas emissions.

The bundling agent of the CDM projects has provided loans for some Hybrid Hoffman Kiln operators. Though the World Bank, acting as a trustee of various carbon funds, is involved in the project as initial purchaser (on behalf of the Annex I Parties) of the CERs, the Bank has not invested in any physical infrastructure of the project.[51]

The technology of the Hybrid Hoffman Kiln is new to Bangladesh, introduced through the brick-kiln bundle projects. The technology was developed in China, although it was first invented in Germany in the middle of the nineteenth century. For the purpose of establishing the projects, the 'brick-kiln' CDM projects directly transferred equipment for the Hybrid Hoffman Kiln from China.[52] As the technology was new to Bangladesh, transfer of operational know-how was also essential to establish the projects. Based on above reasoning, the 'brick-kiln' CDM projects have a direct role in transferring environmentally sound technologies to Bangladesh. The transfer includes both 'hard technology' (i.e. equipment) and 'soft technology' (i.e. know-how).

The transfer of both equipment and knowledge through the 'brick-kiln' CDM projects has taken place through the development of local equipment suppliers and/or engineering consultant firms that offered 'capacity building' in the form of training for local staff members of the firms operating the projects. The 'brick-kiln' CDM projects also promote technology transfer by building technical capacity through the involvement of local private partners, staff of the local private partners and local firms that were not partners. The technologies transferred through the CDM projects were new to Bangladesh at the time of preparing the Project Design Document. The transferred technology offers an improved quality environmental performance as it reduces greenhouse gas emissions into the atmosphere. Such transfer of technology involves 'capacity building' in Bangladesh as, at the time of applying the advanced Hybrid

48 Ibid, 10.
49 *Improving Kiln Efficiency in the Brick Making Industry in Bangladesh,* Version 15, April 18, 2011, 10.
50 Ibid.
51 Ibid, 21.
52 *Improving Kiln Efficiency in the Brick Making Industry in Bangladesh,* Version 15, April 18, 2011, 5.

Hoffman Kiln technology, the local project owners had to adapt and modify some features of it in order to adjust to the local climate and geography.[53]

Since the technology employed in the 'brick-kiln' CDM projects was brought from China and the technology was new in Bangladesh at the time of designing the project, it certainly complies with the first two criteria of technology transfer set by Cools: 'foreign origin' and 'grade of novelty'. While the transferred Hybrid Hoffman Kiln offers improved quality environmental performance, the CDM projects also fulfil the 'performance development' criterion of Cools. By modifying and adapting features of the technology to meet the requirements of the local climate, the 'brick-kiln' CDM projects meet the fourth criterion of Cools- 'capacity building'. So, measured against the benchmark set by Cools, it can certainly be said that the 'brick-kiln' CDM projects of Bangladesh promote the transfer of environmentally sound technologies in full manner. Moreover, by promoting technological 'capacity building' the 'brick-kiln' CDM projects also promote the 'inter-generational equity' component of sustainable development.[54]

By making a 'contribution towards technological learning and capability building', the 'brick-kiln' CDM projects comply with Das' second and third criteria. The second criterion is met as the Hybrid Hoffman Kiln technology imported to Bangladesh is also associated with in-house technological efforts by the local project participants to adapt or improve the technology. The third criterion is met, because the local project operators receive assistance from foreign entities to operate and maintain the Hybrid Hoffman Kiln technology. Therefore it can be claimed that the technology transferred under the 'brick-kiln' CDM projects also makes a 'contribution towards technological learning and capability building' in Bangladesh.[55]

Based on the above explanations, it is also true that the technology transfer that takes place in Bangladesh through the 'brick-kiln' CDM projects fulfils the technology transfer definition of the IPCC (Metz, Davidson, Martens, Van Rooijen Van Wie Mcgrory, 2000) which requires the transfer of 'the process of learning' to 'understand' and 'utilize' the transferred technology. While it is not possible to claim that the transfer also includes the ability to replicate the technology, it could be said that the technology imported through the 'brick-kiln' CDM projects includes 'the capacity to choose it, adapt it to local conditions, and integrate it with indigenous technologies'. In view of this the technology transfer through this CDM project also complies with the technology transfer definition found under the Special Report of the IPCC (Metz et al., 2000).

On the same grounds, it arguably complies with the requirements of 'transfer of necessary technological know-how as well as building up of

53 While in original design the dryer for produced brick was underground, it was modified as over ground to adapt with climate of Bangladesh.

54 Cf. *supra* Chapter 2.6.1.

55 Cf. *supra* Chapter 5.3.

economic, technical, and managerial capabilities for the efficient use and further development of transferred technology' of the technology transfer definition of Agenda 21.[56]

5.3.2 Waste to compost

In Bangladesh, there is no statutory law obligation covering landfill gas recovery or the reduction of organic waste. Though the Bangladesh Environment Conservation Act 1995 and the Bangladesh Environment Conservation Rules 1997[57] provided definitions and instructions on how to handle waste, limit emissions and make an environmental impact assessment, none of the two laws mentioned landfill gas extraction.[58] Hence, the landfill organic waste of the country is not usually converted into compost. As a result, the organic waste is free to release methane gases into the atmosphere.

There are some inevitable initial barriers to establishing compost plants in Bangladesh. As such no commercial large-scale composting projects have been established in the country. Given these circumstances, the guarantee of financial return by establishing a CDM project could facilitate establishing composting plants in Bangladesh.[59]

Therefore, the WWR Bio Fertilizer Ltd., a joint venture of the Waste Concern[60] in association with its Dutch partner[61] has initiated the world's first compost plant CDM project in Bangladesh.[62] The project collects vegetable waste from Dhaka City Corporation and takes that waste to the compost site in its own transport.[63]

56 Cf. *supra* Chapter 1.3.
57 Environmental Conservation Rules 1997, available at https://www.elaw.org/system/files/Bangladesh+–+Environmental+Conservation+Rules,+1997.pdf (last accessed on August 3, 2020).
58 Project Design Document Form (CDM-PDD), *Composting of Organic Waste in Dhaka*, Version 17, 9 December 2005, 18.
59 Ibid, 7.
60 Waste Concern, based in Bangladesh, is a Social Business Enterprise (SBE) set up with the objective of contributing to waste recycling, environmental improvement, renewable energy, employment generation for the urban poor and sustainable development. See www.wasteconcern.com (last accessed on July 30, 2020).
61 WWR Bio Fertilizer Ltd. is a waste process project with Dutch and Bengali partners in Dhaka, which is financed by the Netherlands Development Finance Company (FMO), Triodos Innovation Fund, World Wide Recycling/Waste Concern and Dutch-Bangla Bank. Total costs of the project amount to 12 million EUR, FMO is a shareholder and lender in this deal. The project received an honourable mention at the 2008 World Business and Development Awards. See more on FMO, available at https://www.fmo.nl/k/n114/news/view/1129/179/Worlds-First-Clean-Compost-Plant-opened-in-Bangladesh.html (last accessed on September 30, 2019).
62 UNFCCC Reference No. 0169.
63 WWR Bio Fertilizer Ltd., 'Fact Sheet', available at www.wasteconcern.org/latest News/leaflet%20 final.pdf (last accessed on September 30, 2019).

In the 'waste to compost' CDM project the organic waste is aerobically degraded so that non-fossil CO_2 turns into compost and becomes a reusable product. Generally, in anaerobic conversion, the landfill waste creates landfill gases like methane, which is emitted into the atmosphere if the landfill is not properly covered. Such emissions generally occur because of the usual practice of organic waste management in Bangladesh.[64] The 'waste to compost' CDM project prevents methane emissions into the atmosphere by converting organic waste into compost. The amount of prevented methane emissions, which otherwise would occur, is calculated as CERs.[65]

The 'waste to compost' CDM project also assists Bangladesh's agricultural sector as it replaces the use of chemical fertilizers that cause greenhouse gas emissions into the atmosphere. Moreover, the outcome of the project (i.e. compost) increases production in cornfields, which helps reduction of greenhouse gases from the atmosphere by fixing carbon (i.e. carbon sinks). These additional carbon reductions by the 'waste to compost' CDM project are not included in calculating CERs. Consequently, it creates more 'environmental benefit' from a global perspective.[66]

Though the technologies used in the composting plant are proven technologies, at the time of designing the CDM, the necessary technologies were not available in Bangladesh.[67] Thus, the project involved transferring 'hard' technologies from abroad. Moreover, as most of the employees of the project were recruited from the host country, Bangladesh, and the employees did not have the know-how required to operate the project, the necessary know-how also had to be transferred to Bangladesh.[68] It meant, in addition to the transfer of equipment, the 'waste to compost' CDM project required foreign expertise and training. For this purpose, consultants and staff from abroad had to go to Bangladesh and work for the CDM project.

Thus, the 'waste to compost' CDM project is arguably involved in the transfer of both equipment and know-how by importing equipment from abroad and building technical capacity through guaranteeing the involvement of local partners, staff and firms. This CDM project has also promoted the transfer of both equipment and knowledge by building partnerships between foreign technology supplier firms and local project operators. It has given rise to the transfer of know-how/knowledge by providing training for local staff

64 Ibid.
65 Ibid.
66 Ibid.
67 One ton of net input will result in approximately 300 kg of compost. The planned total gross input of 700 tonnes per day (200,000 tonnes per year) results in approximately 160 tonnes of compost per day (50,000 ton per year) plus 140 tonnes of non-organic per day. These figures are continuously monitored (see monitoring plan), see Project Design Document, version 2, in effect as of (1 July, 2004), *Composting of Organic Waste in Dhaka*, Version 17, 9 December 2005, 5.
68 Composting of Organic Waste in Dhaka, Version 17, 9 December 2005, 5.

members of the local project-implementing firm in the use of the transferred foreign technology.

The foreign technologies that have been transferred as essential equipment for operating the project were new in Bangladesh at the time of designing the project. The transferred technology also contained features of improved quality environmental performance. The transfer of technology that occurred because of this CDM project helped to establish similar projects in other locations in Bangladesh where it would be possible for local companies to use these technologies without seeking foreign expertise.[69] Hence, it can be argued that the 'waste to compost' CDM project plays a positive role in building capacity in Bangladesh in respect of adaptation and application of the transferred technologies to the local environment. Consequently, by facilitating technological 'capacity building' the 'waste to compost' CDM project has participated in promoting sustainable development in Bangladesh through upholding 'intergenerational equity' in the country.[70] The project has also facilitated the principle of equity by ensuring the participation of all the stakeholders involved including the local stakeholders.[71]

The 'waste to compost' CDM project complies with the first requirement of Cools 'technology transfer' criteria 'foreign origin'. This requirement is fulfilled because the Worldwide Recycling BV, Netherlands and the Envotherm, Denmark manufactured the transferred technologies. Since the technology was totally new in Bangladesh at the time of the planning stage of the CDM, it also meets Cools' second criterion, 'grade of novelty'. The project complies with Cools' third criterion, 'performance development', because it increases production efficiency. Finally, since the project also transferred capacity of expansion of the project without seeking assistance from foreign expertise, it clearly meets Cools' fourth criterion, 'capacity building'. As it complies with all four of Cools' technology transfer criteria, the 'waste to compost' CDM project clearly participated in the transfer of environmentally sound technologies to Bangladesh.

To assess the 'contribution towards technological learning and capability building', the 'waste to compost' CDM project complies with the first and third criterion of Das. The first criterion is met because the required technological establishment of the 'waste to compost' CDM project was developed in collaboration with the Worldwide Recycling BV, Netherlands. The third criterion is met because the local project operator receives assistance from foreign entities to operate and maintain the waste to compost plant. Consequently, it is clear that the technology transferred through the 'waste to compost' CDM project makes a 'contribution towards technological learning and capability building' in Bangladesh.

69 As no foreign assistance was required to take at the time of expansion of the current project.
70 Cf. *supra* Chapter 2.6.1.
71 Ibid.

Given the above details, it is evident that the technology transfer through the 'waste to compost' CDM project includes the transfer of 'the process of learning to understand, utilize, and replicate the technology, including the capacity to choose it, adapt it to local conditions, and integrate it with indigenous technologies'. As such, it also fulfils the technology transfer definition of the IPCC (Metz et al., 2000). Similarly, one could argue that the 'waste to compost' CDM project promotes the 'transfer of necessary technological know-how as well as building up of economic, technical, and managerial capabilities for the efficient use and further development of transferred technology', which is also a fulfilment of the technology transfer definition of Agenda 21.[72]

5.3.3 Solar home systems

The Small-scale CDM Programme of Activities entitled Installation of Solar Home Systems in Bangladesh ('solar home systems')[73] is designed to install solar home systems with a capacity ranging from 20 to 200 watt-peak (Wp) in households and other places in Bangladesh that do not have access to electricity from the grid. The households this project aims to help would generally use kerosene for lighting and batteries to run television and other electronic apparatus at the time of designing the CDM programme. Small electronic appliances like mobiles, etc. were charged at local stores as those use diesel-run generators to supply power. The objective of the 'solar home systems' CDM programme was to save greenhouse gas emissions created from burning fossil fuels (e.g. kerosene, diesel, etc.) and earn saleable CER units.[74]

The coordinating or managing entity of the 'solar home systems' CDM programme is the Infrastructure Development Company Limited which provides financial assistance to the Component Project Activity implementers.[75] The Infrastructure Development Company Limited implements Component Project Activities by means of its 29 partner organizations.[76] As an example of 'solar home systems' CDM Programme of Activities, the examples in this section will mainly include the Component Project Activity implemented by Grameen Shakti, a sister concern of the Grameen Bank (co-recipient of Nobel Peace Prize in 2006).

The Component Project Activity implemented by Grameen Shakti primarily consisted of 194,869 units of solar home systems with capacities of 30 Wp and 40 Wp in rural areas of Bangladesh, where no electricity connection was available.[77] The primary aim was to install these units within eight years

72 See *supra* Chapter 1.3.

73 The UNFCCC Reference no. 2765.

74 Small-scale CDM Programme of Activities Design Document Form (CDM-SSC-CPA-DD), *Installation of Solar Home Systems in Bangladesh (30Wp and 40Wp)*, Version 02, November 6, 2007, 2

75 Ibid.

76 Ibid.

77 30 Wp and 40 Wp SHS are a suitable mode of supplying power for small electrical loads such as compact fluorescent lamps. Although only available for a limited

(between 2007 and 2015).The technical elements required for the 'solar home systems' CDM programme included: 1) solar module (30, 40 Wp); 2) battery; 3) charge controller; 4) fluorescent tube lights with special electronic ballasts; 5) mounting structure; 6) installation kits; and 7) cables and connecting devices.[78]

The technology used in the 'solar home systems' CDM programme is new to the people of Bangladesh who live in rural or remote areas. Most of those people are not financially capable of acquiring such technology. It was therefore essential to find a strategy to make the system both popular and affordable to the people living in these areas.[79] The strategy was to introduce a micro-financing model. In order for the micro financing model to be applied, the partner organization offered soft loans to its users.[80]

To make the technology familiar and popular different programmes and initiatives were taken by the relevant partner organizations. These programmes included demonstrations, fairs, meetings and introducing the concept at the local level. In addition to these, the partner organization Grameen Shakti also offered free operation and maintenance services for three years after installation and promised these services with minimum charges after completion of the three year warranty.[81]

At the time the 'solar home systems' CDM Component Project Activity was established by Grameen Shakti, only 32 per cent of the total population of Bangladesh had access to grid electricity[82] and others were dependent on kerosene or diesel-run lamps. Consequently, the solar home systems technology was new to those people, who had no idea how to use and maintain it. This 'technical barrier' reduced the popularity of the solar home systems projects. Because of the low market share of solar home systems technology, it was not easy to find technicians in this sector. Thus, the major challenge in implementing the project was to provide after sales service for the operation and maintenance of the project by creating a network of technical service providers across the country. This added extra costs to the normal cost of the project so the CERs that could potentially be generated by the projects acted as the 'saviours' of the project. This is because a proportion of the revenue of the CERs was considered to be instrumental in covering the extra cost of providing countrywide training in maintaining and operating the project and building a network of technology centres.[83]

The Design Documents for this Programme of Activities as well as the Component Project Activity implemented by Grameen Shakti have not

number of hours in a day, the supply is reliable. Further, the solar home system is easy to maintain with adequate training.

78 *Installation of Solar Home Systems in Bangladesh (30Wp and 40Wp),* Version 02, November 6, 2007, 2.

79 Ibid.

80 Ibid, 29.

81 Ibid.

82 Ibid, 27.

83 Ibid, 7.

claimed to have transferred new technologies in any specific manner. This is because the solar home system technologies had been introduced in Bangladesh commercially before this CDM Programme of Activities was designed.[84]

However, the Coordinating/Managing Entity(CME) of the CDM Programme of Activities claims that it promotes the transfer of both equipment and knowledge, since the equipment has been transferred by importing it from abroad and knowledge has been transferred through the establishment of local suppliers/engineering consultant firms that have helped through their 'capacity building'. Such development has taken place by providing training to the staff members of the local suppliers/engineering consultant firms/companies.[85]

Although the technologies transferred through the 'solar home systems' CDM programme are manufactured outside Bangladesh and the transfer was made to fulfil the needs of the CDM Programme of Activities, they were actually not 'new' in Bangladesh at the time of designing the CDM programme.

Grameen Shakti, a partner organization of the CDM programme, claims that the transfer of both equipment and knowledge from abroad takes place via this programme. Grameen Shakti claims that the 'solar home systems' CDM programme also facilitates building technical capacity by observing the project implementing process implemented by the foreign experts. It also claims that the CDM programme helps by transferring know-how through signing maintenance and/or operations agreements with the foreign equipment supplier. It further claims that the equipment and know-how is transferred from abroad through partnerships between the foreign technology supplier and Grameen Shakti.[86]

Grameen Shakti has launched a network of technology centres which provide local community training in how to operate and maintain the solar home systems. Arguably by launching such a network the project has taken part in technology diffusion from one region to another within the country.[87] More importantly, the network of technology centres has promoted 'capacity building' among local communities in applying the transferred technology. Such a role in 'capacity building' has also arguably promoted intra-generational equity in the locality.[88] Furthermore, the 'solar home systems' CDM programme has also played a role in the development of technology, which is an indirect component of technology transfer.[89]

84 Ibid, 8.
85 Ibid, 7.
86 *Installation of Solar Home Systems in Bangladesh (30Wp and 40Wp),* Version 02, November 6, 2007, 7.
87 Ibid, 7, see also S. Dahlke, *Solar Home Systems for Rural Electrification in Developing Countries, An Industry Analysis and Social Venture Plan,* available at http://www.csbsju.edu/Documents/CSB% 20Sustainability /Solar%20Paper. pdf (last accessed on September 30, 2015).
88 Cf. *supra* Chapter 2.6.
89 Ibid, 7.

However, since some technologies employed in 'solar home systems' CDM programme are brought from abroad, it arguably meets Cools' first requirement of technology transfer, 'foreign originality'. However, as the technology was already commercially available in Bangladesh at the time of designing the projects, the 'solar home systems' CDM programme does not meet the second criterion of Cools, 'grade of novelty'.

The technology imported via the 'solar home systems' CDM programme has improved quality environmental performance in reducing greenhouse gas emissions into the atmosphere compared to the sources of energy that would be employed in absence of this CDM programme. For this reason, it could be said that the CDM programme complies with Cools' 'performance development' condition.

Since the CDM programme played a positive role in building local capacity by providing training, creating technology networks and inspiring further research and development of the technology, it arguably meets Cools' fourth condition, 'capacity building'. Therefore, since the 'solar home systems' CDM programme meets three out of the four criteria of the technology transfer benchmark set by Cools, this CDM programme can be said to have been partially responsible for transferring environmentally sound technologies in Bangladesh.

The 'solar home systems' CDM complies with second condition of Das. This condition is met because the solar home systems technology imported to Bangladesh is associated with the in-house technological efforts of the local project participants to adapt or improve the technology. As such, one could claim that the technology transferred through the 'solar home systems' CDM programme makes a positive 'contribution towards technological learning and capability building' in Bangladesh. For this reason, arguably, like the 'brick-kiln', and the 'waste to compost' CDM projects, the 'solar home systems' CDM programme has also taken part in promoting intra-generational equity in Bangladesh by promoting technological 'capacity building'.[90]

Based on the above discussion, it could be argued that the partial technology transfer through the 'solar home systems' CDM programme includes the transfer of 'the process of learning' to 'understand' and 'utilize', but it does not fully transfer the process of how to 'replicate the technology'. As per the statements of the project implementing partner organizations, the partial transfers of technology under this CDM programme may also arguably include 'the capacity to choose it, adapt it to local conditions, and integrate it with indigenous technologies'. From these perspectives, this CDM programme partially fulfils the technology transfer definition of the IPCC (Metz et al., 2000). Similarly one could claim that the 'solar home systems' CDM programme partially promotes the 'transfer of necessary technological know-how as well as building up of economic, technical, and managerial capabilities for the efficient

90 Cf. *supra* Chapter 2.6.

use and further development of transferred technology'. This can be claimed as a 'partial fulfilment' of the technology transfer definition of Agenda 21.[91]

5.3.4 Improved cooking stoves

The objective of the Small-scale CDM Programme of Activities entitled 'Improved Cooking Stoves' was to distribute energy efficient cooking stoves in Bangladesh.[92] The goal of the CDM programme was to distribute two kinds of improved cooking stoves: domestic biomass-burning stoves, and non-domestic biomass-burning stoves.[93]

The coordinating/managing entity of the 'improved cooking stoves' CDM programme is J.P. Morgan Ventures Energy Corporation (JPMVEC). J.P. Morgan coordinates the efforts of various partner organizations in distributing improved cooking stoves across Bangladesh. Grameen Shakti, the German Technical Cooperation (GTZ) and Rahim Afroz, etc. are major partner organizations for the 'improved cooking stoves' CDM programme.[94]

The improved cooking stoves distributed under this CDM programme save energy by transferring heat from the fuel to the cooking pot more efficiently than would traditional stoves used in rural Bangladesh. The traditional cooking stoves are made up of 'three-stone' cooking stoves. The traditional cooking stove is comprised of a mud-built cylinder with three elevated points (by three stones) upon which the cooking tools are placed. One of the spaces between the elevated points is used to insert fuel and smoke comes out of the other two spaces. These stoves can be made either under or above the ground. The excessive depths of these traditional stoves reduce the efficiency of the fuel because air prevents the smooth transfer of heat to the cooking pot. This thermal inefficiency of the traditional cooking stove was solved by the 'improved cooking stoves' CDM programme. The CDM programme introduced a modified and improved version of the traditional cooking stove. Apart from providing increased thermal efficiency, the advantage of the improved cooking stove is that it matches the traditional cooking habits of the rural people of Bangladesh.[95]

The original methodology for developing the improved cooking stove is not new in Bangladesh. Though the original method is based on common scientific knowledge, the methodology is continuously being developed through further research. Hence, this CDM programme contributes by transferring environmentally sound technologies to Bangladesh in two ways: by encouraging

91 See *supra* Chapter 1.3.
92 The UNFCCC Reference no. 4791.
93 Small-scale CDM Programme of Activities Design Document Form (CDM SSC-PoA-DD) - Version 01, *Improved Cooking Stoves in Bangladesh*, Version 07.1, 28/06/2011, 2.
94 Ibid, 3.
95 Ibid, 2.

local research and development, and by creating of the possibility to transfer more efficient similar technologies from abroad.

The Programme of Activities Design Document of the 'improved cooking stoves' CDM programme explicitly states, 'During the life of the project, research and development work may result in more efficient Improved Cooking System models, which shall be absorbed' by this CDM programme.[96] In order to come up with a more efficient cooking system, the partner organizations are encouraged to invest in research and development of this technology. They are also encouraged to transfer the know-how of designing more efficient improved cooking stove from other countries where it has been proved to be more 'efficient'.[97]

The 'improved cooking stoves' CDM programme promotes the transfer of knowledge by building the technical capacity of native equipment suppliers and/or consultants' firms to improve local stoves. The technical capacity has been built by involving local private and public partners and staff of the project-implementing firms, by observing the way external experts implement the project and by building partnerships between foreign technology suppliers and local partner organizations.

The technology or know-how employed in the 'improved cooking stoves' CDM programme was not new in Bangladesh at the time of designing the CDM programme. The technology employed was not much more energy efficient or better performing than the similar technology already available in Bangladesh. However, some partner organizations[98] have engaged themselves in research to develop performance as well as build capacity in the application of the improved cooking stoves.

Thus, Cools' standard of technology transfer is applied to the 'improved cooking stoves' CDM programme, it is clear that the projects do not comply with Cools' 'foreign origin' and 'grade of novelty' criteria. In comparison to the source of energy that would be employed in the absence of the 'improved cooking stoves' CDM programme, it complies with Cools' 'performance development' requirement. Since some partner organizations have invested in research to develop the performance of the technology used, one could argue that this CDM programme also complies with Cools' 'capacity building' criterion. Thus, the 'improved cooking stoves' CDM programme meets two out of the four conditions of technology transfer defined by Cools and consequently has partially promoted the transfer of environmentally sound technologies in Bangladesh.

In determining whether or not the 'improved cooking stoves' CDM programme makes a 'contribution towards technological learning and capability building', it is clear that it complies with the second criterion of Das. The criterion is met as the know-how imported by this CDM programme has given

96 Ibid, 7.
97 Ibid, 7.
98 E.g. German Technical Cooperation (GIZ).

rise to in-house technological efforts by the local project partners to adapt or improve the technology.[99] Thus, the 'partial' technology transfer that occurred as a result of the 'improved cooking stoves' CDM programme made a positive 'contribution towards technological learning and capability building' in Bangladesh.

Based on the above facts, it can be said that the 'partial' technology transfer under this CDM programme involves the transfer of 'the process of learning to understand, utilize, and replicate the technology'– essential requirements of technology transfer definition given by the IPCC (Metz et al., 2000). Similarly, one could argue that the 'improved cooking stoves' CDM programme promotes the 'transfer of necessary technological know-how as well as building up of economic, technical, and managerial capabilities' – an essential condition of technology transfer according to the definition of Agenda 21.[100]

While small-scale promotion of technology transfer may have a small impact on promoting sustainable development, the 'improved cooking stoves' CDM programme has played a certain role in the promotion of sustainable development in Bangladesh by promoting 'inter-generational equity' through facilitating technological 'capacity building'.

5.3.5 Efficient lighting

The objective of the small-scale CDM Programme of Activities entitled 'Efficient Lighting Initiative of Bangladesh' was to replace household incandescent lamps (ICLs) with energy efficient compact fluorescent lamps (CFLs) that offer the same or a higher output.[101] Since the CFLs consume one-fourth of the energy consumed by ICLs, replacement of the ICLs with CFLs was expected to result in reduced use of electricity generated from fossil fuel power plants. Thus, savings of electricity through this CDM programme were expected to reduce the consumption of fossil fuel in power generating plant and thereby reducing the emission of greenhouse gases into the atmosphere.[102] Furthermore, the reduced greenhouse gas emissions were expected to generate saleable CER units.

The Design Document of the 'efficient lighting' CDM programme did not include any claim regarding its role in the transfer of environmentally sound technologies in Bangladesh. As an alternative, it promised to promote technological sustainability. Though CFLs were already commercially available in Bangladesh at the time of designing the CDM programme, they did not function well due to the lower quality of the technology applied by the manufacturers. Moreover, the CFLs available on the market were more costly than

99 The project implemented by German Technical Cooperation (GIZ).
100 Cf. *supra* Chapter 1.3.
101 The UNFCCC Reference no. 4793.
102 Small-scale CDM Programme of Activities Design Document Form (CDM SSC-PoA-DD) – Version 01, *Efficient Lighting Initiative of Bangladesh (ELIB), Version 07,* Date: 22/04/2011, 2.

the ICLs. For this reason, the CFLs that were available were not reaching the households in Bangladesh. In order to make the CFLs more popular, the objective of the 'efficient lighting' CDM programme was to import CFLs that contain better technology and maintain a better standard.[103]

If Cools' standard of technology transfer is applied to this CDM programme, it arguably complies with Cools' first criterion, 'foreign origin'. This is because the technology was imported from abroad to Bangladesh. Since the technology was commercially available in Bangladesh at the time of designing the CDM programme, it does not comply with the 'grade of novelty' criterion. As the objective of the CDM programme was to introduce better quality technology in comparison to the technologies available on the market at that time, one could argue that it meets Cools' 'performance development' criterion. Finally, it is evident the 'efficient lighting' CDM programme does not comply with Cools' 'capacity building' requirement. This is because the 'efficient lighting' CDM programme neither transfers any know-how/knowledge nor promotes any research activities. Given these facts, one may logically deduce that as the 'efficient lighting' CDM programme only complies with Cools' 'foreign origin' criterion it plays a very small or nominal role in transferring environmentally sound technologies to Bangladesh.

With regard to making a 'contribution towards technological learning and capability building', it is evident that the 'efficient lighting' CDM programme does not comply with any of the three conditions defined by Das. Similarly, this CDM programme does not fulfil the technology transfer criteria defined under Agenda 21, and the IPCC (Metz et al., 2000).

5.3.6 Life straw family

The objective of the Small-scale CDM Programme of Activities entitled the 'Energy Efficiency Program in Rural Bangladesh' was to distribute more than 1.0 million low emission water purification units[104] to around 4.71 million people in Bangladesh.[105] Since the low emission water purification technology purifies microbiologically contaminated water, this CDM programme was aimed at reducing the demands of conventional water treatment by purifying water using non-renewable biomass.[106] As per the description in the Design

103 Ibid.

104 The low emission water purification units are based on point-of-use water filter technology. This technology is capable of transforming microbiologically contaminated water into safe drinking water. It is capable of filtering from 18,000 litres (For Family Life Straw 1.0) up to 30,000 litres (For Family Life Straw 2.0) EPA quality water. (The United States Environmental Protection Agency (EPA) has fixed the amounts of specific contaminants for tap water supplied by US public water systems. Such amount of water is enough to meet the needs of a family with five members for three to five years).

105 The UNFCCC Reference no. 9276.

106 Small-scale CDM Programme of Activities Design Document Form (CDM SSC-PoA-DD), Version 02.0, *Energy Efficiency Program in Rural Bangladesh,* Version 01, Date: 14/08/2012, 1.

Document of the CDM programme, the information about distribution of units will be stored in a database based on which the amount of carbon emission reduction will be calculated.[107] The Coordinating/Managing Entity of this CDM programme is BRAC Impact Investment Limited.[108]

The objective of this CDM programme was to apply a kind of low greenhouse gas emitting technology that complies with the 'protective' criterion set by the World Health Organization (WHO).[109] It also complies with the comparable national standard.[110] The low greenhouse gas emitting water purifying technology employed in this CDM programme is called Life Straw® Family 2.0. The Life Straw® Family 2.0 is a table top unit that does not need electricity to be operated. Considering a standard of 5.5 'litres use of water per person per day' and 4.7 persons per family, it has been estimated that the Life Straw Family will be required to be replaced every two years on average. Consequently, there will be no need for monthly/weekly intervention. A lower 'litres use of water per person per day' result in giving the Life Straw Family a year more longevity. Thus, the aim of the project is to repair or replace the Life Straw Family every two/three years using the money earned by selling CERs.[111]

As it imports the Life Straw Family from Switzerland, the CDM programme has taken part in the transfer of equipment ('hard technology') to Bangladesh. Since the technology is new in Bangladesh the capacity to maintain the technology ('soft technology') has also been transferred to the country.

The 'life straw family' CDM programme promotes the transfer of both equipment and knowledge by signing a maintenance and/or operations agreement with foreign equipment suppliers. Technology transfer also takes place by building partnerships between foreign technology suppliers and local partner organizations.

The CDM programme promotes the transfer of knowledge by providing training for local staff members who work with the project implementing companies about foreign technology, and by building some technical capacity by guaranteeing the involvement of local partners, and the staff of the local project implementing firms. The technology is new in Bangladesh and it provides improved quality environmental performance by reducing greenhouse gas emissions into the atmosphere.[112] The role of the 'life straw family' CDM programme in promoting technological 'capacity building' arguably also facilitates 'intra-generational equity' in the locality.[113]

If Cools' standard of technology transfer is applied to the 'life straw family' CDM programme, it complies with the first condition of Cools' benchmark,

107 Ibid, 1.
108 Ibid, 3.
109 Ibid.
110 Energy Efficiency Program in Rural Bangladesh, Version 01, 2012, 3.
111 Ibid, 4.
112 Ibid.
113 Cf. *supra* Chapter 2.6.

'foreign origin'. This condition is met because a Swiss company Vestergaard produces the technology employed in this CDM programme. The CDM programme also complies with the second condition of Cools, 'grade of novelty' because the technology was not available in Bangladesh at the time the programme was designed.

The technology applied under the 'life straw family' CDM programme reduces greenhouse gas emissions by replacing the use of fossil fuel or biomass as fuel to boil water. Therefore, the technology employed in this CDM programme complies with Cools' third condition, 'performance development'.

The 'life straw family' CDM programme helps to build local capacity by arranging training in the use of the imported technology. Consequently, it meets Cools' fourth condition , 'capacity building'. Therefore, since this CDM programme complies with all four of Cools' requirements, it is evident it facilitates the transfer of environmentally sound technologies in a complete manner.

In assessing its 'contribution towards technological learning and capability building', the 'life straw family' CDM programme complies with the third criterion of Das as the local partner organization of the CDM programme receives assistance from the foreign technology supplier entities in operating and maintaining the technologies deployed. It can therefore be argued that the technology transferred by the 'life straw family' CDM programme makes a positive 'contribution towards technological learning and capability building' in Bangladesh.

It can also be said that the technology transfer under the 'life straw family' CDM programme includes the transfer of 'the process of learning' to 'understand' and to 'utilize' the technology. However, the CDM programme does not transfer the process of replicating the technology. The transfer of technology through the 'life straw family' CDM programme does not necessarily include 'the capacity to choose it, adapt it to local conditions' and 'integrate it with indigenous technologies'. As such, one may remark that the transfer of environmentally sound technologies by the 'life straw family' CDM programme only 'partially' complies with the technology transfer definition of the IPCC (Metz et al., 2000). Similarly, the transfer of environmentally sound technologies by the 'life straw family' CDM programme only partially complies with the technology transfer definition of Agenda 21.[114]

5.4 Summing-up

This study finds that among the seven CDM projects (which also includes the CDM Programme of Activities) in Bangladesh four CDM projects and programmes promote the transfer of both equipment and knowledge,[115] one

114 Cf. *supra* Chapter 1.3.

115 Two 'brick-kiln' CDM projects, the 'waste to compost' CDM project, the 'life straw family' CDM PoA, and the 'solar home systems' CDM PoA.

CDM programme[116] promotes the transfer of equipment only and one CDM programme[117] promotes the transfer of relevant knowledge and know-how.

The study conducted on the Project Design Documents and the Programme of Activities Design Documents reveals that six CDM projects in Bangladesh meet Cools' first requirement of the technology transfer benchmark, 'foreign originality'.[118] Likewise, four CDM projects and programmes[119] comply with Cools' second requirement, 'grade of novelty'.[120] All seven CDM projects and programmes[121] fully comply with Cools' third requirement, 'performance development'.[122] Finally, all seven CDM projects and programmes[123] meet Cools' fourth requirement, 'capacity building'.[124]

Based on these statistics, four out of seven of the existing CDM projects and Programme of Activities[125] in Bangladesh meet all four requirements set by Cools. Thus, it is possible to remark that these four CDM projects and programmes fully promote the transfer of environmentally sound technologies. By fully complying with three requirements of Cools' index, two CDM programmes[126] partially promote the transfer of environmentally sound technologies. Finally, by fulfilling two of Cools' conditions, one CDM programme 'nominally' promotes the transfer of environmentally sound technologies in Bangladesh.[127] Such 'nominal' technology transfer is better termed 'just import' the technology.

Six out of the seven CDM projects and programmes make a positive 'contribution' to 'technological learning and capability building' as defined by Das. In view of that, these six CDM projects and programmes also comply with the

116 I.e. the 'efficient lighting' CDM PoA.
117 I.e. the 'improved cooking stoves' CDM PoA.
118 Two 'brick-kiln' CDM projects, the 'waste to compost' CDM project, the 'life straw family' CDM PoA, the 'solar home systems' CDM PoA and the 'efficient lighting' CDM PoA.
119 Two 'brick-kiln' CDM projects, the' waste to compost' CDM project, the 'Life Straw Family' CDM PoA.
120 The technology must be new to the market, or to that specific host country, or to the relevant industrial sector in the host country.
121 Two 'brick-kiln' CDM projects, the 'waste to compost' CDM project, the 'life straw family' CDM PoA, the 'efficient lighting' CDM PoA and the 'improved cooking stoves' CDM PoA.
122 The technology should possess improved quality environmental performance to reduce greenhouse gas emissions into the atmosphere.
123 Two 'brick-kiln' CDM projects, the 'waste to compost' CDM project, the 'solar home systems' CDM PoA, and the 'life straw family' CDM PoA, the 'efficient lighting' CDM PoA and the 'improved cooking stoves' CDM PoA.
124 Transfer also tacit/know-how, which will boost the skill of the host countries in manufacturing, operating and mastering new technologies.
125 Two 'brick-kiln' CDM projects, the 'life-straw family' CDM PoA and the 'waste to compost' CDM project.
126 The 'solar home systems' CDM PoA, and the 'improved cooking stoves' CDM PoA.
127 The 'efficient lighting' CDM PoA.

technology transfer definition of Agenda 21 and the IPCC (Metz et al., 2000).[128]

Therefore, among all the CDM projects and programmes of Bangladesh, 57.14 per cent promote the transfer of environmentally sound technologies in a full manner, whereas 28.57 per cent promote technology transfer partially and 14.28 per cent have a 'nominal role' in transferring environmentally sound technologies in the country. It is noteworthy that 85.71 per cent of all CDM projects and programmes hosted by Bangladesh have either fully or partially taken part in building technological capacity in the country. Such promotion of 'capacity building' is expected to engender a suitable technological environment that in the long run might accelerate the speed of technology transfer in the country. This is also important in realizing intra-generational equity, which leads to the realization of sustainable development.[129]

This academic investigation observes that 85.71 per cent of the CDM projects and programmes hosted by Bangladesh employ environmentally sound technologies, which originated abroad. Of the CDM projects and programmes in Bangladesh 57.14 per cent employ environmentally sound technologies, which were 'novel' or 'new' in Bangladesh at the time of preparing the official Project Design Documents. Interestingly, this study finds that 100 per cent of CDM projects and programmes hosted by Bangladesh employ environmentally sound technologies, which are involved in 'performance development' to a greater or lesser extent by improving production efficiency.

With regard to the role of the CDM projects in making a 'contribution towards technological learning and capability building' as defined by Das, this investigative study finds that 85.71 per cent of CDM projects and programmes in Bangladesh make a large or small-scale contribution 'towards technological learning and capability'. Likewise, 85.71 per cent of CDM projects and programmes in Bangladesh fully or partially conform to the technology transfer conditions specified by Agenda 21 and the IPCC (Metz et al., 2000).

However, the result of this investigative research suggests that the introduction of environmentally sound technologies through CDM projects and programmes in Bangladesh has a positive impact on local sustainable development. The sustainable development impact of the CDM projects and programmes include environmental, social and economic benefits. The environmental benefit of a project relates to the impact of a project on local air quality, water quality, land quality and biodiversity, while the social benefit involves the impact on health security, access to education and welfare activities, etc. Assessment of the economic benefit of a project was based on the impact of the project on job creation, generating a source of earning, achieving energy efficiency and ensuring a balance of payment.

128 Except 'efficient lighting' CDM PoA.
129 Cf. *supra* Chapter 2.6.

The findings of this investigative study suggest that except for one CDM Programme of Activities,[130] all the CDM projects and programmes operating in Bangladesh directly or indirectly assist in improving local air quality. Two CDM projects and programmes improve soil/land quality.[131] Two CDM programmes have a direct or indirect role in improving local water quality.[132] Five CDM projects and programmes, which includes two bundle CDM projects[133] and three CDM programmes,[134] have a positive impact on the conservation of local biodiversity.

The investigation also suggests that six out of the seven CDM projects and programmes have a direct or indirect impact on the reduction of health risks.[135]All seven CDM projects and programmes either directly or indirectly promote educational activities or build awareness among the local population. Six CDM projects and programmes have a direct or indirect role in promotion of social welfare activities.[136]

Finally, all seven CDM projects and programmes in Bangladesh have a positive impact on economic benefits through job creation and sources of earning. Apart from the 'waste to compost' CDM project all the CDM projects and programmes have a direct role in increasing energy efficiency. The 'waste to compost' CDM project also has an indirect role in improving energy efficiency by reducing the use of chemical fertilizers, which are manufactured in factories run on non-renewable energy.

Hence, although 57.14 per cent of CDM projects and programmes in Bangladesh have a positive role in transferring environmentally sound technologies in a full manner in the country, 71.42 per cent of all CDM projects and programmes in the country play a positive role in promoting sustainable development. An important finding is that one CDM programme of Bangladesh only partially promotes the transfer of environmentally sound technologies, but it facilitates sustainable development in a complete manner.[137]

130 The 'efficient lighting' CDM PoA.
131 The 'waste to compost' CDM project, and the 'improved cooking stoves' CDM PoA.
132 The 'life straw family' CDM PoA and the 'solar home systems' CDM PoA.
133 Two 'brick-kiln' CDM projects.
134 The 'life straw family' CDM PoA and the 'solar home systems' CDM PoA.
135 All CDM projects and CDM PoAs except the 'efficient lighting' CDM PoA.
136 Ibid.
137 The 'improved cooking stoves' CDM PoA.

6 Concluding remarks

This study observes that the principles of equity and CBDR under the UNFCCC play a positive role (to a greater or lesser extent) in promoting sustainable development by transferring environmentally sound technologies to the developing and least developed countries. These guiding principles of the UNFCCC are realized through direct or indirect financial mechanisms established under the UNFCCC, the Kyoto Protocol and the Paris Agreement.[1]

Although the UNFCCC financial mechanisms through its different branches and activities play a positive role in facilitating the transfer of environmentally sound technologies to non-Annex I Party least developed countries, the success rate in transferring technology to least developed countries is not sufficient in comparison to the volume of urgent need for technology. While the principle of equity along with the principle of CBDR play a positive role in transferring environmentally sound technologies to the least developed countries, there remains an enormous opportunity to enhance the positive role of those principles.

6.1 Remarks on direct financial mechanisms

Different financial mechanisms of the UNFCCC, as described in Chapter 3 of this book, have different characteristics. While the objective of all direct UNFCCC funds is to provide financial assistance for the non-Annex I Party developing and least developed countries, the LDCF only gives financial assistance to the non-Annex I Party least developed countries. Furthermore, the AF only provides funding for those non-Annex I Party developing and least developed countries that are Parties to the Kyoto Protocol. However, the recently formed GCF Trust Fund is accessible by any non-Annex I Party developing and least developed country.[2]

1 For direct financial mechanism see *supra* Chapter 3.2, and for indirect financial mechanism (e.g. CDM) see *supra* Chapter 3.4.

2 Cf. *supra* Chapter 3.2.3. See also Alpha Oumar Kaloga with contribution by David Eckstein, *Rationalization of the Financial Mechanism of the UNFCCC: Options for Adaptation Finance,* Briefing paper, German Watch, February, 2015, 13.

DOI: 10.4324/9781003056416-6

Since the GEF Trust Fund is especially entitled to provide funding for mitigation activities, it only facilitates the transfer of mitigation related technologies to non-Annex I Party developing and least developed countries.[3] The LDCF, the SCCF and the AF provide funding for adaptation related activities as these facilitate the transfer of adaptation related environmentally sound technologies. The objective of funding from the LDCF includes supporting capacity building, national planning and concrete action. The funding from the AF is restricted to concrete adaptation projects. One could therefore argue that the AF promotes the transfer of adaptation related technologies as well as sustainable development in the non-Annex I Party least developed countries by funding concrete adaptation projects. Similarly, the LDCF promotes sustainable development in the non-Annex I Party least developed countries by transferring adaptation related technologies through providing funding for concrete projects as well as for capacity building related projects.[4]

Since non-Annex I Party least developed countries are mostly in need of adaptation related technologies,[5] both the LDCF and the AF can effectively facilitate the transfer of environmentally sound technologies and promote sustainable development in those countries.[6] In addition, since these countries are in enormous need of capacity building, the LDCF plays an additional role in facilitating capacity building in this group of countries.[7]

Financial cooperation from the SCCF is available for adaptation related projects and for the transfer of environmentally sound technologies, which includes both adaptation and mitigation related technologies. Hence, this Fund can facilitate the transfer of both adaptation and mitigation related environmentally sound technologies to developing and least developed countries by providing funding for adaptation and mitigation related projects or by providing funding for the projects/programmes that are solely aimed at the transfer of adaptation and/or mitigation related technologies.[8]

Since financial assistance from the GCF is available for both adaptation and mitigation purposes, it can play a significant role in promoting sustainable development by transferring both adaptation and mitigation related environmentally sound technologies to developing and least developed countries.[9]

In terms of mode of access to the fund, the AF was the first fund established under the international climate regime that provides an option of 'direct access' to its fund,[10] while the GEF allows an individual state the modality of 'direct access' only in the case of national communications and national portfolio

3 Ibid, 13.
4 Cf. *supra* Chapter 3.2.2.
5 Cf. *supra* Chapter 3.3.1.5.
6 Cf. *supra* Chapter 3.2.2.
7 Ibid.
8 Ibid.
9 Cf. *supra* Chapter 3.2.3.
10 Adaptation Fund, *Direct Access,*https://www.adaptation-fund.org/about/direct-access/ (last accessed on September 3, 2019).

formation.[11] The GCF allows 'direct access' to its funding system through national funding entities.[12]

An important feature of the GCF is the creation of a private sector facility. This implies that the projects and programmes initiated by private sector investment are expected to become more common in GCF in comparison with other direct funding mechanisms. However, private sector investment needs to follow a 'country-driven approach' to become eligible to receive funding from the GCF.[13]

The private sector has no 'direct access' to any of the UNFCCC funds for climate finance. However, the private sector may have access to the GCF under the option of a PSF, at a later stage of any project/programme financed by the GCF.[14] The role of the private sector under the GEF is only as a source of co-financing.[15]

It is important noting that although the international climate regime has established above-stated direct funding mechanisms, the realization of financial cooperation under these mechanisms is mostly dependent on the relevant Parties' (especially Annex II Parties to the Convention) commitment to contributing. At the same time, role of these direct financial mechanisms in transferring environmentally sound technologies specially in least developed countries depends on the nature of the projects implemented through receiving funds from these mechanisms. For this reason, least developed countries need to design projects in a manner which will make sure transfer of those technologies which they need most to tackle climate change issues.

6.2 Remarks on indirect financial mechanisms

It is likely that the CDM or its successor project-based mechanisms (introduced by the Paris Agreement) will remain as an essential part of the future international climate policy framework, as it has proved successful in engaging the private sector in greenhouse gas mitigation activities, and the capital flow from carbon credits can leverage a large amount of investment in low-emission technology in developing countries.[16] EU and US policy-makers have also indicated that they expect the private sector and offsetting, rather than direct government payments, to be the main mechanisms for funding for climate change mitigation.[17]

11 GEF, *Types of Project,*https://www.thegef.org/about/funding/project-types (last accessed on September 3, 2019).

12 A recent Decision of the GCF governing body has also reconfirmed the option of 'direct access' modality. See GCF/B.08/45, 3 December 2014; Decision B.08/09, 3 December 2014.

13 GCF, *Governing Instrument for the Green Climate Fund,* 2011, 2.

14 GCF/B.08/38. 6 October 2014.

15 For details about the private sector financing policy of the GEF, see GEF/C.46/09, May 6, 2014.

16 Ellis et al., 'CDM: Taking Stock and Looking Forward', *Energy Policy,* Vol. 35(1), 15–28.

17 Alister Doyle and Gerard Wynn, 'UN Climate Talks Advance, Poor Urge more CO2 Cuts', *Reuters,* 2009 (released 12 June, 2009), available at http://in.reuters.

Though new climate finance of 100 billion US$ per year was pledged by developed countries to assist the adaptation and mitigation mechanism in developing countries, a major share of this amount is likely to come from the private sector through market mechanisms.[18] Since market mechanisms or similar kind of indirect financial mechanisms encourage the involvement of private entities to combat climate change, any proposal to reform CDM structures and/ launch similar mechanisms introduced under the Paris Agreement should take into account the potential involvement of more financial sources to provide funding for the development and transfer of environmentally sound technologies.

At the global level, although CDM projects have succeeded in involving the private sector in global greenhouse gas emission reduction procedures and in facilitating the transfer of environmentally sound technologies in many non-Annex I Party countries, the mechanism still has room for improvement. Past experiences of the global operation of CDM have brought to light several weaknesses that need to be addressed and resolved when launching similar mechanisms under the Paris Agreement.

During the first phase of the CDM, it was observed that most of the CDM projects were hosted by a few advanced developing countries (e.g. China, India, Brazil) as a result of the advanced infrastructural situation of these states. The future CDM mechanism (or similar mechanisms established under Art. 6 of the Paris Agreement) needs to think about shifting the focus from advanced developing to less developing or least developed nations. This is essential to ensure equity based on the principle of CBDR. The decision of the EU to buy CER units only from the projects hosted by the least developed countries is a step towards shifting CDM projects from advanced developing nations to the least developed nations. A similar approach may also be adopted by other developed nations or by the Conference of the Parties to the UNFCCC.

Since the indirect financial mechanism like CDM is based on the market mechanism and financial gain is associated with these projects, sometimes it is evident that the most efficient environmentally sound technologies are not employed in a project in order to gain more economic benefit. This may lead to transferring less efficient technologies to the host country. Host country sustainable development criteria for CDM projects (or other projects under similar mechanisms established under Art. 6 of the Paris Agreement) should individually address this issue.[19]

com/article/2009/06/12/us-climate-idINTRE55B2Y020090612 (last accessed on July 15, 2015).

18 Sampo Seppänen et al., Demand in a Fragmented Global Carbon Market: Outlook and Policy Options, Nordic Council of Ministers, Nordon, 2013, available at https://www.diva-portal.org/smash/get/diva2:702582/FULLTEXT01.pdf (last accessed on August 10, 2020), 12.

19 Cf. UNEP-DTU, available at www.cdmpipeline.org/cdm-projects-type.htm#1 (last accessed on July 16, 2015).

With regard to the transfer of environmentally sound technology, it has been observed that generally investors want to invest in those CDM projects that increase the energy efficiency of the existing energy sources.[20] Consequently, as most of the existing electricity generating plants in the developing and least developed countries are run on fossil fuel, the investors in CDM projects invest in those existing projects, with the result that the host countries are dependent on high carbon strategies for a longer duration.[21] It is important that this issue is addressed properly in newly introduced similar mechanisms.

While the shape and modalities of the future indirect financial mechanisms are not yet clear, it is important to make sure that the future similar mechanisms take account of the special circumstances and project hosting capacities of the least developed countries. It has also been evident from the case studies conducted in Bangladesh that the CDM projects hosted in the country assisted more in building technological capacity than direct technology transfer. This implies that the least developed countries can improve their technological capacity by hosting an increasing number of similar projects. Thus, it is essential to make sure that the future indirect financial mechanisms are framed in a manner that will make hosting projects easier for the least developed countries.

This is possible through implementation of the principle of CBDR in framing future indirect financial mechanisms. Applying this principle can facilitate the scope of the transfer of environmentally sound technologies by both expanding the market for CERs for the least developed countries and by encouraging those countries to host more projects. The principle of CBDR can also promote the environmental integrity and sustainable development impact of projects. By applying a differential approach of the principle of CBDR on the eligibility of a country to host a project, it is possible to prevent some advanced non-Annex I Party countries from hosting CDM projects (or other projects under similar mechanisms established under Art. 6 of the Paris Agreement) for the sake of promoting these activities in some less advanced non-Annex I Party countries. Such an approach has already been evidenced in the EU Decision about buying CERs for the 2013–2020 period.[22]

It is also possible to apply the principle of CBDR to test the 'additionality' of the proposed CDM projects (or other projects under similar mechanisms

20 ENTTRANS, 'Promoting Sustainable Energy Technology Transfers through the CDM: Converting from a Theoretical Concept to Practical Action', 2007, 88, available at https://jin.ngo/images/jin/publications/ENTTRANS_final_report.pdf (last accessed on August 18, 2020).

21 De Sepibus Joëlle, *The Environmental Integrity of the CDM Mechanism – a Legal Analysis of Its Institutional and Procedural Shortcomings,* NCCR Working Paper No. 2009/24, 2009 18, available at www.nccr-trade.org/images/stories/research/header_ip6/environmental%20integrity%20CDM.pdf (last accessed on July 18, 2015). trade.org/images/stories/research/header_ip6/environmental%20integrity%20CDM.pdf (last accessed on July 18, 2015).

22 Directive 2008/101/EC.

established under Art. 6 of the Paris Agreement) by providing a positive list of projects that may be deemed to be 'additional' automatically. Conversely, it is also possible to exclude controversial projects by making a 'negative list' of projects that will be deemed 'non-additional'. To avoid the procedural difficulties of hosting projects in the least developed countries, it is possible to simplify the 'additionality' test of specific projects in order for them to be hosted by those countries.[23]

Conferring authority on the least developed countries to provide flexibility in assessing 'additionality' for some types of CDM projects (or other projects under similar mechanisms established under Art. 6 of the Paris Agreement) which are important for the transfer of environmentally sound technologies or the promotion of the sustainable development of the country concerned can be another form of implementation of the principle of CBDR. Such a form of realization of the principle can be important in the least developed countries. For instance, while Bangladesh has a huge need of production of electricity, providing a flexible 'additionality' assessment method may encourage stakeholders to invest in CDM projects (or other projects under similar mechanisms established under Art. 6 of the Paris Agreement) in the power generation sector.

Differentiation based on the project may also promote access to the required mitigation technologies for the least developed countries. For instance, a positive list with regard to the 'additionality' test of those CDM projects (or other projects under similar mechanisms established under Art. 6 of the Paris Agreement) that will employ the required mitigation technologies (identified by the TNA) not already available in a least developed country might facilitate the transfer of those technologies to the country concerned.

Another form of differentiation through introducing a 'cap' based on the type of project or on the capabilities of the host country may also promote the volume of projects hosted in the least developed countries. From the CER supply side perspective, it is recommended that Parties to the UNFCCC should agree to introduce a 'cap' for each host country on the amount of CER units they can generate. As a result, no single country or no group of countries with favourable conditions will be able to enjoy the majority of the facilities derived from CDM (or similar mechanisms established under Art. 6 of the Paris Agreement); rather the countries with less strong financial and technological capabilities, especially the least developed countries, will be able to benefit from the mechanism.

As with the supply side, introduction of a 'cap' on the CER demand side may also work as a positive step in promoting the amount of CDM projects (or other projects under similar mechanisms established under Art. 6 of the Paris Agreement) in the least developed countries. All Parties to the Convention or Agreement may promise that the countries buying CERs will not buy more than a particular number from a particular host country.[24] Such a kind of 'cap'

23 See generally H. V. Asselt et al., 'Differentiation under the CDM: Options and Challenges', in M. Mehling et al. (eds.), *Implementing the Clean Development Mechanism: Legal and Institutional Challenges*, Lexicon, 2009.

from the demand side perspective may assist in the proper distribution of the facilities derived from hosting CDM projects (or other projects under similar mechanisms established under Art. 6 of the Paris Agreement). Moreover, it would also be possible to introduce a positive 'cap' requiring countries buying CER units to buy a certain amount of them from a specific group of countries, as decided under the EU ETS scheme where CER units can only be bought from the least developed counties.

While a 'cap' or 'quota' for specific host countries could promote the proper regional distribution of the projects, a similar 'cap' for some specific projects may promote the sectors that might have a better technology transfer and sustainable development impact in the least developed countries. For this reason, future CDM projects (or other projects under similar mechanisms established under Art. 6 of the Paris Agreement) may consider introducing a 'cap' based on both the capability of the host country and the type of project.

Differentiation in capacity building and financial cooperation has been realized through the Nairobi Framework, whereby the UNFCCC, United Nations Development Programme (UNDP), United Nations Environment Programme (UNEP), World Bank and African Development Bank jointly work to strengthen the capability of sub-Saharan Africa in hosting CDM projects.[25] Such a kind of differentiated approach, for instance, financial cooperation in the validation, verification and certification of CDM (or similar mechanisms established under Art. 6 of the Paris Agreement) projects of all least developed countries (or those least developed countries, which are most vulnerable to adverse impacts of climate change) can be a fruitful measure in increasing CDM projects (or other projects under similar mechanisms established under Art. 6 of the Paris Agreement) as such facilitating technology transfer and sustainable development in those countries.[26]

Differentiation based on a levy on CDM (or similar mechanisms established under Art. 6 of the Paris Agreement) related activities might also have a positive impact and encourage stakeholders in the least developed countries to host more projects. While some differentiation already exists for the least developed countries (e.g. exemption of the least developed countries from the adaptation levy of 2 per cent of the CER units issued,[27] the administrative levy on CERs issued), the future CDM (or similar mechanisms established under Art. 6 of the Paris Agreement) may think of introducing more flexibility on levies for the least developed countries.[28]

24 Ibid.

25 The initiative was welcomed by the Conference of the Parties to the UNFCCC serving as Meeting of the Parties to the Kyoto Protocol (COP/MOP) in Decisions 1/CMP.2 and 6/CMP.2.

26 Cf. *Analysis of Possible Means to Reach Emission Reduction Targets and of Relevant Methodological Issues*, Technical paper, UN Doc. FCCC/TP/2008/2, 6 August 2008, 18.

27 Decision 17/CP.7, Para 15(a).

28 Decision 2/CMP.3, Para 31.

To ensure the promotion of sustainable development through CDM projects (or other projects under similar mechanisms established under Art. 6 of the Paris Agreement), it is also possible to implement the principle of CBDR by setting a threshold level of sustainable development.[29] At present the right to determine the sustainable development criteria of a CDM project is vested in the host country. The authority of the host country in determining sustainable development is justifiable since every country may have different priority issues to promote sustainable development, based on the socio-economic and geographical condition of the country. But setting a threshold level on some basic issues to determine the sustainable development impact and environmental integrity of CDM projects (or other projects under similar mechanisms established under Art. 6 of the Paris Agreement) might ensure that all these projects guarantee a minimum level of sustainable development and environmental integrity.

However, based on the study of the CDM projects and programmes in Bangladesh one could argue that since many inhabitants of the least developed countries live below the poverty line, the inclusion of micro-financing may be appropriate to facilitate the smooth operation of CDM (or similar mechanisms established under Art. 6 of the Paris Agreement) projects in the least developed countries.[30] At the time of implementing the 'solar home systems' CDM Programme in Bangladesh, it was realized that without having access to some financial assistance, the poor rural people were not in a position to avail themselves of the comparatively costly solar home system. Thus Grameen Shakti (as a subsidiary of Grameen Bank) introduced the concept of micro-financing with their CDM projects.[31] Under the micro-financial mechanism the household was required to pay only 10 per cent of the total cost as down payment, and the rest of the amount was scheduled to be paid in 42 equally divided monthly instalments.[32] A similar model of 'micro-credit' based CDM projects (or other projects under similar mechanisms established under Art. 6 of the Paris Agreement) may be successful in other least developed countries.

A final remark on the UNFCCC indirect financial mechanism - CDM concerns the long delay in obtaining Executive Board (EB) approval for projects and not having a strong enough system of governance.[33] The study finds

29 See generally H. V. Asselt et al. in M. Mehling et al. (eds.), Lexicon, 2009

30 Micro-credit is part of micro-finance which offers a broad range of financial services to poor people. It is thought that the modern system of micro-credit originated in 1983 in Bangladesh with the establishment of the Grameen Bank founded by Prof. Muhammad Yunus. For details about micro-credit, see Tazul Islam, *Microcredit and Poverty Alleviation*, Ashgate Publishing, Ltd., 2012.

31 The Grameen Bank is a micro-finance organization and community development bank in Bangladesh. This Nobel Peace Prize-winning organization was founded in 1983. It offers small loans (known as micro-credit or 'Grameen credit') to the poor without taking any collateral. For more about the Grameen Bank, see www.grameen.com (last accessed on September 30, 2015).

32 UN Doc. FCCC/TP/2008/2, 6.

33 Cf. C. Streck and J. Lin, 'Making Markets Work: A Review of CDM Performance and the Need for Reform', *European Journal of International Law*, Vol. 19(2), 2008, 409–442.

that the current lengthy cycle of the CDM projects results in stakeholders being reluctant to initiate CDM projects.[34] Given this situation, a differentiated approach that simplifies and expedites different stages of the project cycle, and minimizes transaction costs would assist the least developed countries and their private stakeholders to host more CDM projects. These issues should also be taken into account at the time of finalizing modalities for the indirect financial mechanisms established under the Paris Agreement.

6.3 Remarks on private sector involvement

It is observed that the majority of private sector involvement takes place in climate change mitigation activities that involve the clean energy sector and green financial products and services.[35] Statistics show that in 2013, around 80 per cent of climate related development support went to mitigation projects, while only 11 per cent went to adaptation projects and 12 per cent went to projects that cover both adaptation and mitigation.[36] A study conducted by the OECD shows that in the year 2013–2014, more than 90 per cent of mobilized private finance was planned to be deployed to mitigation projects.[37] Arguably the reason private sector finances focus more on mitigation lies in the 'difficulties in measuring and tracking adaptation finance'.[38] While globally agreed metrics exist for measuring mitigation activities (e.g. MtCO2e),[39] no consensus or globally agreed metric exists for measuring adaptation activities.[40]Since both adaptation and mitigation are essential to combat climate change, future private sector involvement should necessarily increase its focus on adaptation activities. In this regard, non-Annex I Party developing and specially least developed countries may think of utilizing PSF to engage private sectors in adaptation related activities.

The study also suggests that most of the development partners' efforts to involve the private sector take place in the energy sector.[41] This happens as a result of investment in renewable energy projects by bilateral development finance institutions and development banks' private sector operations.[42] After renewable energy projects, the private sector mostly get involved in green

34 Ibid.
35 Naeeda Crishna Morgado and Bérénice Lasfargues, *Engaging the Private Sector for Green Growth and Climate Action: An Overview of Development Co-Operation Efforts*, Development Cooperation Working Paper 34, OECD, May, 2017, 25.
36 Ibid.
37 OECD, Climate finance in 2013–14 and the US$ 100 billion goal, a report by the OECD in collaboration with Climate Policy Initiative, OECD Publishing, Paris, 2015, 29, available at http://dx.doi.org/10.1787/ 97892642 49424-en (last accessed on September 2, 2020).
38 Naeeda Crishna Morgado and Bérénice Lasfargues, 2017, 25.
39 Metric tons of carbon dioxide equivalent.
40 Naeeda Crishna Morgado and Bérénice Lasfargues, 2017,26.
41 Ibid.
42 Ibid.

banking or multi-sector projects such as urban development.[43] With regard to financing green banking, most of the development partners' efforts include development of green credit lines for the purpose of supporting renewable energy and energy efficient projects in developing countries.[44] However, natural resource related sectors, like agriculture and forestry, are less targeted by global efforts to involve the private sector.[45] This situation should be changed and private sector involvement in agriculture and forestry should be increased. This is because agriculture accounts for about 24 per cent of annual global greenhouse gas emissions.[46]

Finally, study shows that more than 70 per cent of private sector involvement in activities to combat climate change take place in middle income countries (that includes upper middle income and lower middle income countries).[47] On the other hand, only about 25 per cent of total private sector involvement in similar activities takes place in the least developed countries.[48] This is arguably inconsistent with the principles of equity and CBDR as well as the sustainable development principle of the global climate regime.[49] Hence, in line with the promotion and observance of the principle of equity and CBDR,[50] private sector involvement in activities dealing with climate change should focus more on least developed countries. In this regard, a positive collaboration between international trade regime and international climate regime can be built to create a favorable environment for enhanced private sector investment to tackle climate change and facilitate sustainable development in the least developed countries.

43 Ibid.
44 Ibid.
45 Ibid.
46 IPCC, Climate Change 2014: Mitigation of Climate Change. Contribution of Working Group III to the Fifth Assessment Report of the Intergovernmental Panel on Climate Change [O. Edenhofer, R. Pichs-Madruga, Y. Sokona, E. Farahani, S. Kadner, K. Seyboth, A. Adler, I. Baum, S. Brunner, P. Eickemeier, B. Kriemann, J. Savolainen, S. Schlomer, C. von Stechow, T. Zwickel, J.C. Minx, (eds.)]. 2014, 8.
47 Naeeda Crishna Morgado and Bérénice Lasfargues, *Engaging the Private Sector for Green Growth and Climate Action: An Overview of Development Co-Operation Efforts*, OECD, May, 2017, 26.
48 Ibid, 27.
49 Cf. *supra* Chapter 2.5, 2.6 and 2.7.
50 See *supra* Chapter 2.6 and 2.7.

Bibliography

Books

Baslar, Kemal, *The Concept of the Common Heritage of Mankind in International Law* (Martinus Nijhoff Publishers, 1998).

Birnie, P., Boyle, A., and Redgwell, C., *International Law and the Environment* (Oxford University Press, 2009, 3rd ed.).

Blakeney, M., *Legal Aspects of the Transfer of Technology to Developing Countries* (ESC Publishing Ltd., 1989).

Boyle, Alan E. and Freestone, David (eds.), *International Law and Sustainable Development: Past Achievements and Future Challenges* (Oxford University Press, 2001).

Bugge, Hans Christian and Voigt, Christina (eds.), *Sustainable Development in International and National Law: What Did the Brundtland Report Do to Legal Thinking and Legal Development, and Where Can We Go from Here?* (Europa Law Publishing, 2008).

Christiansen, L., Olhoff, A., and Trærup, S. (eds.), *Technologies for Adaptation: Perspectives and Practical Experiences*, UNEP Risø, 2011.

Cordonier Segger, M.-C. and Khalfan, A. (eds.), *Sustainable Development Law: Principles, Practices, and Prospects* (Oxford University Press, 2004).

Cullet, Philippe, *Differential Treatment in International Environmental Law* (Ashgate, 2003).

Dworkin, R., Taking *Rights Seriously* (Harvard University Press, 1977).

Elkington, J., *Cannibals with Forks: The Triple Bottom Line of 21st Century Business* (Capstone, 1997).

Ehnert, Ina, *Sustainable Human Resource Management: A Conceptual and Exploratory Analysis from a Paradox Perspective* (Physica-Verlag, 2009).

French, D., *International Law and Policy of Sustainable Development* (Manchester University Press, 2005).

Hart, H. L. A., The *Concept of Law* (Clarendon Press, 1961).

Heidering, Antoinette, *International Law, Sustainable Development and Water Management* (Eduron Publishers, 2004).

Hu¨lsmann, M., *Management im Orientierungsdilemma: Unternehmen zwischen Effizienzund Nachhaltigkeit* (German Universitats-Verlag, 2003).

Islam, Tazul, *Microcredit and Poverty Alleviation* (Ashgate Publishing, Ltd., 2012).

Keeley, Brian, *Income Inequality: The Gap between Rich and Poor*, OECD Publishing, 2015.

King, Ken, *The Incremental Costs of Global Environmental Benefits* (GEF, 1993).

Macrory, Richard, *Reflections on 30 Years of EU Environmental Law: A High Level of Protection* (Europa Law Publishing, 2006).

Meadows, D. H., Meadows, D. L., Randers, J. and Behrens III, W. W., *The Limits to Growth* (Universe Books, 1972).

Nolon, John R. and Salkin, Patricia E., *Climate Change and Sustainable Development Law in a Nutshell* (West Academic Publishing, 2010).

Revesz, Richard L., Sands, Philippe, and Stewart, Richard B., *Environmental Law, the Economy and Sustainable Development: The United States, the European Union and the International Community* (Cambridge University Press, 2008).

Rogers, Peter P., *An Introduction to Sustainable Development* (Routledge, 2008).

Rosenberg, N., *Inside the Black Box: Technology and Economics* (Cambridge University Press, 1982).

Sands, Philippe, *Principles of International Environmental Law* (Cambridge University Press, 2003, 2nd ed.).

Sen, Amartya, *Poverty and Famines: An Essay on Entitlement and Deprivation* (Oxford University Press, 1981).

Sen, Amartya, *Resources, Values and Development* (Harvard University Press, 1984).

Voigt, Christina, *Sustainable Development as a Principle of International Law: Resolving Conflicts between Climate Measure and WTO Law* (Martinus Nijhoff Publishers, 2009).

Weiss, Brown, *In Fairness to Future Generations* (Transnational Publishers, Inc., 1989).

Yamin, Farhana and Depledge, Joanne, *The International Climate Change Regime: A Guide to Rules, Institutions and Procedures* (Cambridge University Press, 2004).

Book chapters

Agius, E., 'Obligations of Justice Towards Future Generations: A Revolution on Social and Legal Thought' in E. Agius and S. Busuttil (eds.), *Future Generations and International Law* (Routledge, 1998) 10.

Aslam, M. A., 'Equal Per Capita Entitlements: A Key to Global Participation on Climate Change?' in K. Baumert with Odile Blanchard, Silvia Llosa, and James F. Perkaus (eds.), *Building on the Kyoto Protocol: Options for Protecting the Climate* (World Resources Institute, 2002) 175–202.

Asselt, Harro Van, Haug, Constanze, Bakker, Stefan, and Gupta, Joyeeta, 'Differentiation under the CDM: Options and Challenges' in M. Mehling, K. Upstone-Hooper, and A. Merrill (eds.), *Implementing the Clean Development Mechanism: Legal and Institutional Challenges*, (Lexicon, 2009) 27–48.

Bugge, Hans Christian, '1987–2007: "Our Common Future" Revised' in Hans Christian Bugge and Christina Voigt (eds.), *Sustainable Development in International and National Law* (Europa Law Publishing, 2008) 7.

Kolari, Tuula, 'The Principle of Common but Differentiated Responsibilities as Contributing to Sustainable Development through Multilateral Environmental Agreements' in Hans Christian Bugge and Christina Voigt (eds.), *Sustainable Development in International and National Law* (Europa Law Publishing, 2008) 252.

Kranzberg, M., 'The Technical Elements in International Technology Transfer: Historical Perspectives' in J. R. McIntyre and D. S. Papp (eds.), *The Political Economy of International Technology Transfer* (Quorum Books, 1986) 33.

Lowe, V., 'Sustainable Development and Unsustainable Arguments' in A. Boyle and D. Freestone (eds.), *International Law and Sustainable Development: Past Achievements and Future Challenges* (Oxford University Press, 1999) 32.

Lowe, V., 'The Politics of Law-Making: Are the Method and Charter of Norm Creating Changing?' in M. Byers (ed.), *The Role of Law in International Politics: Essays in International Relations and International Law* (Oxford University Press, 2000) 214–215.

Maskus, Keith E. and Okediji, Ruth L., 'Legal and Economic Perspectives on International Technology Transfer in Environmentally Sound Technology' in Mario Cimoli, Giovanni Dosi, Keith E. Maskus, Ruth L. Okediji, and Jerome H. Reichman (eds.), *Intellectual Property Rights: Legal and Economic Challenges for Development* (Oxford Scholarship Online, 2014) 392.

Meijer, E. and Werksman, J., 'Keeping it Clean – Safeguarding the Environmental Integrity of the Clean Development Mechanism' in D. Freestone and C. Streck (eds.), *Legal Aspects of Implementing the Kyoto Protocol Mechanisms: Making Kyoto Work* (Oxford University Press, 2005) 193.

Rajamani, Lavanya, 'The Doctrinal Basis for and Boundaries of Differential Treatment in International Environmental Law' in Lavanya Rajamani (ed.), *Differential Treatment in International Environmental Law* (Oxford University Press, 2006) 162.

Rowlands, I. H., 'Atmosphere and Outer Space' in D. Bodansky, J. Brunee, and E. Hey (eds.), *The Oxford Handbook of International Law* (Oxford University Press, 2007, 2nd ed.) 316.

Segger, Marie-Claire Cordonier, 'Sustainable Development in International Law' in H. C. Bugge and C. Voigt (eds.), *Sustainable Development in International and National Law* (Europa Law Publishing, 2008) 92.

Shelton, D., 'Equity' in D. Bodansky, J. Brunee, and E. Hey (eds.), *The Oxford Handbook of International Law* (Oxford University Press, 2007, 2nd ed.) 658.

Sterlini, M. L., 'The Agreement on Trade-Related Investment Measures' in Arthur E. Appleton. and Michael J.Plummer (eds.), *The World Trade Organization: Legal, Economic and Political Analysis, Vol.* 1 (Springer, 2005) 440.

Stillwell, M., 'Trade and Environment in the Context of Sustainable Development' in Marcus W.Gehring and Marie-Claire Cordonier Segger, *Sustainable Development in World Trade Law* (Kluwer International, 2005) 45.

Trinidade, A. C. and Attard, D. J, 'The Implication of the "Common Concern of Mankind" concept' in Toru Iwama (ed.), *Policies and Laws on Global Warming: International and Comparative Analysis* (Environmental Research Centre, 1991) 7.

Yamineva, Yulia and Kulovesi, Kati, 'The New Framework for Climate Finance Under the United Nations Framework Convention on Climate Change: A Breakthrough or an Empty Promise?' in J. Erkki Hollo, Kati Kulovesi, and Michael Mehling (eds.), *ClimateChangeand theLaw* (Springer, 2013) 196.

Journal articles

Antypas, A. and Neelakrantan, S., 'Not a Copout: Small but Meaningful Progress in Warsaw towards the 2015 Agreement', *Environmental Liability: Law, Policy and Practice*, Vol. 21(5), 2013, 172.

Aviles, Luis A., 'Sustainable Development and Environmental Legal Protection in the European Union: A Model for Mexican Courts to follow?', *Mexican Law Review*, Vol. VI (2), June2014, 266.

Babatunde, E. O., 'In the Light of Different National Circumstances: Equity under the Paris Agreement', *Cambridge Law Review*, Vol. IV(II), 2019, 130.

Beder, Sharon, 'Costing the Earth: Equity, Sustainable Development and Environmental Economics', *New Zealand Journal of Environmental Law*, Vol. 4, 2000, 229.

Beg, N. *et al.*, 'Linkages between Climate Change and Sustainable Development', *Climate Policy*, Vol. 2(2–3), 2002, 129–144.

Bodansky, D., 'Customary (and Not So Customary) International Environmental Law', *Indiana Journal of Global Legal Studies*, Vol. 3, 1995, 105.

Bodansky, D., 'Reflections on the Paris Conference', *Opinio Juris*, December 15, 2015, available at http://opiniojuris.org/2015/12/15/reflections-on-the-paris-conference (last accessed on August 14, 2020).

Carlarne, Cinnamon P. and Colavecchio, J. D., 'Balancing Equity and Effectiveness: The Paris Agreement & the Future of International Climate Change Law', *NYU Environmental Law Journal*, Vol. 27(2), 2019, 165.

Chandani, A., 'Distributive Justice and Sustainability as a Viable Foundation for the Future Climate Regime', *Carbon & Climate Law Review* Vol. 1(2), 2007, 152, 154.

Ciplet, D. J., Roberts, T., and Khan, M., 'The Politics of International Climate Adaptation Funding: Justice and Division in the Green House', *Global Environmental Politics*, Vol. 1, 2013, 49–68.

Cordonier Segger, M.-C., Khalfan, A., Gehring, M., and Toering, M., 'Prospects for Principles of International Sustainable Development Law after the WSSD: Common but Differentiated Responsibilities, Precaution and Participation', *Review of European Community & International Environmental Law*, Vol. 12(1), 2003, 56.

Corvaglia, Maria Anna, 'South-South Technology Transfer Addressing Climate Change and Its (Missing) International Regulatory Framework', *Carbon and Climate Law Review* Vol. 8(2), 2014, 128.

Cullet, P., 'Equity and Flexibility Mechanisms in the Climate Change Regime: Conceptual and Practical Issues', *Review of European Community & International Environmental Law*, Vol. 8(2), 1999, 168.

Daly, H. E., 'Boundless Bull', *Gannett Center Journal*, Vol. 4(3), 1990, 113–118.

Deleuil, T., 'The Common but Differentiated Responsibilities Principle : Changes in Continuity after the Durban Conference of the Parties', *Review of European Community & International Environmental Law* 21(3), 271–281.

Dovers, S. and Handmer, J., 'Contradictions in Sustainability', *Environmental Conservation*, Vol. 20(3), 1993, 217–222.

Ellis, J. E., Winklerb, H., Corfee-Morlota, J., and Gagnon-Lebrunc, F., 'CDM: Taking Stock and Looking Forward', *Energy Policy*, Vol. 35(1), 2007, 15–28.

Filho, W. L., 'Dealing with Misconceptions on the Concept of Sustainability', *International Journal of Sustainability in Higher Education*, Vol. 1(1), 2000, 9–19.

Frumkin, Howard, Hess, Jeremy, Luber, George, Malilay, Josephine, and McGeehin, Michael, 'Climate Change: The Public Health Response', *American Journal of Public Health*, Vol. 98(3), 2008, 435–445.

Gorecki, P. K., Lyons, S. and Tol, R. S. J., 'EU Climate Change Policy 2013–2020: Using the Clean Development Mechanism more Effectively in the Non-EU-ETS Sector', *Energy Policy*, Vol. 38(11), November2010, 7466–7475.

Harris, P. G., 'Common but Differentiated Responsibility: The Kyoto Protocol and United States Policy', *New York University Environmental Law Journal*, Vol. 7(1); 1999, 22.

Huddart, Sophie, Nash, Madlen, Abdelrasoul, Aya, Bacearnicova, Inna, Bourque, Kyla, and Mishra, Lipi, 'The Doha Declaration in Action: An Examination of Patent Law Flexibilities in the South African Acquired Immunodeficiency Syndrome Epidemic', *Journal of Health Specialities*, Vol. 5(1), 2017, 30–34.

Kates, Robert W., Parris, T. M., and Leiserowitz, A. A., 'What is Sustainable Development? Goals, Indicators, Values, and Practices', *Environment, Science, and Policy for Sustainable Development*, Vol. 47(3), 2005, 11.

Kettunen, M. and Brink, P. T., 'Nature, Green Economy and Sustainable Development: The Outcomes of UN Rio+20 Conference on Sustainable Development', *Nature Conservation*, Vol. 2, 2012, 1–6.

Khan, Mizan R. and Roberts, J. Timmons, 'Adaptation and International Climate Policy', *WIREs Climate Change*, Vol. 4(3), 2013, 172.

Le, Hanh and Delbosc, Anais, 'Japan's Bilateral Offset Crediting Mechanism: A Bilateral Solution to a Global Issue?', *Climate Brief*, 11, January2012, 3.

Lehtonen, M., 'The Environmental-Social Interface of Sustainable Development: Capabilities, Social Capital, Institutions', *Ecological Economics*, Vol. 49(2), 2004, 199–214.

Macey, Adrian, 'The Road to Durban and Beyond: The Progress of International Climate Change Negotiations', *Policy Quarterly*, Vol. 8(2), 2012, 27.

Maljean-Dubois, Sandrine, 'The Paris Agreement: A New Step in the Gradual Evolution of Differential Treatment in the Climate Regime?', *Review of European, Comparative & International Environmental Law*, Vol. 25(2), 2016, 153.

Marong, A. B. M. Christina, 'From Rio to Johannesburg: Reflections on the Role of International Legal Norms in Sustainable Development', *Georgetown International Environmental Law Review*, Vol. XVI(1), 2003, 45.

Mebratu, D., 'Sustainability and Sustainable Development: Historical and Conceptual Review', *Environmental Impact Assessment Review*, Vol. 18, 1998, 493–520.

Ockwell, D., Haum, R., Mallett, A. and Watson, J., 'Intellectual Property Rights and Low Carbon Technology Transfer: Conflicting Discourses of Diffusion and Development', *Global Environmental Change*, Vol. 20(4), 2010, 729–738.

Ott, H. E., Sterk, W., and Watanabe, R., 'The Bali Road Map: New Horizons for Global Climate Policy', *Climate Policy*, Vol. 8(1), 2008, 91–95.

Rai, V., Schultz, K., and Funkhouser, E., 'International Low Carbon Technology Transfer: Do Intellectual Property Regimes Matter?', *Global Environmental Change*, Vol. 24(1), 2014, 61.

Rajamani, Lavanya, 'The Principle of Common but Differentiated Responsibilities and the Balance of Commitments under the Climate Regime', *Review of European Community & International Environmental Law*, Vol. 9(2), 2002, 121.

Rajamani, Lavanya and Bodansky, Daniel, 'The Paris Rule Book: Balancing International Perceptiveness with National Discretion', *International and Comparative Law Quarterly*, Vol. 68(4), October2019, 1025.

Remarks by C. C. Joyner, 'Common but Differentiated Responsibility', *American Society of International Law Proceedings*, 96, 2002, 358.

Robinson, J., 'Squaring the Circle? Some Thoughts on the Idea of Sustainable Development', *Ecological Economics*, 48(4), 2004, 369–384.

Rodi, M., 'Bridging the Divided in Global Climate Policy – Strategies for Enhanced Participation and Integration', *Carbon & Climate Law Review*, Vol. 1(2), 2007, 164, 166.

Sands, Philippe, 'International Law in the Field of Sustainable Development', *British Yearbook of International Law*, Vol. 65, 1994, 343–344.

Sohn, L. B., 'The Stockholm Declaration on the Human Environment', *The Harvard International Law Journal*, Vol. 14(3), 1973, 480.

Spence, C., Kulovesi, K., Gutiérrez, M., and Muñoz, M., 'Great Expectations: Understanding Bali and the Climate Change Negotiation Process', *Review of European Community & International Environmental Law*, Vol. 17(2), 2008, 142–153.

Streck, C. and Lin, J., 'Making Markets Work: A Review of CDM Performance and the Need for Reform', *European Journal of International Law*, Vol. 19(2), 2008, 409–442.

Sutter, Christoph, and Parreno, Juan Carlos, 'Does the Current Clean Development Mechanism (CDM) Deliver Its Sustainable Development Claim? An Analysis of Officially Registered CDM Projects', *Climatic Change*, Vol. 84(1), 2007, 75–90.

Szerman, Paloma, 'Engaging Private Sector in Climate Finance: The Role of the Private Sector Facility of the Green Climate Fund', *Climate Change Law & Policy eJournal*, 2015, 14.

Tickell, Oliver, 'COP 19: Poor Countries Left in the Dark on Climate Finance', *Ecologist*, November 14, 2013, available at https://theecologist.org/2013/nov/14/cop19-poor-countries-dark-climate-finance (last accessed on April 15, 2020).

Voigt, Christina and Ferreira, Felipe, 'Differentiation in the Paris Agreement', *Climate Law*, Vol. 6(1–2), 2016, 63.

Voigt, Christina and Ferreira, Felipe, '"Dynamic Differentiation": The Principles of CBDR-RC, Progression and Highest Possible Ambition in the Paris Agreement', *Transnational Environmental Law*, Vol. 5(2), 2016, 285–303.

Winkler, H. and Rajamani, L., 'CBDR&RC in a Regime Applicable to All', *Climate Policy*, Vol. 14(1), 2014, 104.

Reports, guidelines, policy briefs, working papers and technical papers

Analysis of Possible Means to Reach Emission Reduction Targets and of Relevant Methodological Issues, Technical paper, FCCC/TP/2008/2, August 6, 2008.

Atteridge, Aaron, *Private Sector Finance and Climate Change Adaptation, How Can Voluntary Private Finance Support Adaptation in Developing Countries?*Stockholm Environment Institute, 2009.

Blanco, Gabriel and Coninck, Heleen de, *The Technology Mechanism under the UNFCCC: Ways Forward*, Policy brief, Climate & Development Knowledge Network, October2012.

Blanco, Gabriel, Coninck, Heleen de, and Würtenberger, Laura, *The Technology Mechanism under the UNFCCC: Ways Forward*, Policy brief, Climate and Development Knowledge Network, October2012, available at https://cdkn.org/wp-content/uploads/2014/07/policy_brief_-_the_technology_mechanism_under_the_unfccc_-_ways_forward.pdf (last accessed on August 18, 2020).

Brown, J. and Jacobs, M., *Leveraging Private Investment: The Role of Public Sector Climate Finance*, Overseas Development Institute (ODI), 2011.

Brown, Valerie A. and Switzer, Margaret, A., *Engendering the Debate: A Discussion Paper for Consideration by the ESD Working Groups*, Office of the Status of Women, Canberra, June1991.

Centre for International Sustainable Development Law (CISDL), *The Principle of Common but Differentiated Responsibilities: Origins and Scope*, World Summit on Sustainable Development 2002, Johannesburg, August 26, CISDL legal brief, available at http://cisdl.org/public/docs/news/brief_common.pdf (last accessed on September 30, 2015).

Compilation and Synthesis of Fifth National Communications. Note by the Secretariat. Addendum. Financial Resources, Technology Transfer, Vulnerability, Adaptation and Other Issues relating to the Implementation of the Convention by Parties Included in Annex I to the Convention, UN Doc. FCCC/SBI/2011/INF.1/Add.2, 20 May 2011.

Das, K., *Technology Transfer under the Clean Development Mechanism: An Empirical Study of 1000 CDM Projects*, Working Paper 014, The Governance of Clean Development Working Paper Series, School of International Development, University of East Anglia, UK, July2011.

Drexhage, John and Murphy, Deborah, *Sustainable Development: From Brundtland to Rio 2012*, UN, 2010.

ENTTRANS, 'Promoting Sustainable Energy Technology Transfers through the CDM: Converting from a Theoretical Concept to Practical Action', 2007, available at https://jin.ngo/images/jin/publications/ENTTRANS_final_report.pdf (last accessed on August 18, 2020).

Falk, J., *Social Equity and the Urban Environment, Report to the Commonwealth Environment Protection Agency*, Commonwealth Environment Protection Authority, 1993.

Guidelines for the Preparation of National Communications by Parties Included in Annex I to the Convention, UN Doc. FCCC/CP/1999/7, 16 February2000 (Guidelines for Annex I National Communications).

Haites, Erik, *Development Perspectives for a Post-Copenhagen Climate Financing Architecture*, OECD, 2010.

Hepburn, J. and Ahmad, I., 'The Principle of Common but Differentiated Responsibilities: A Legal Working Paper' in Recent Developments in International Law Related to Sustainable Development Series, CISDL, 2005.

Hepburn, J. and Khalfan, A., *The Principle of Equity and the Eradication of Poverty*, Draft Working Paper, CISDL, March 2005.

Industrial and Infrastructural Development Finance Company Limited (IIDFC), *Improving Kiln Efficiency in the Brick Making Industry in Bangladesh: Hybrid Hoffmn Klin (HHK) Project: Environment Management Framework (EMF)*, IIDFC, 2009.

International Union for Conservation of Nature and Natural Resources (IUCN), *World Conservation Strategy: Living Resource Conservation for Sustainable Development*, IUCN, 1980.

Inter-Governmental Panel on Climate Change (IPCC), *Climate Change: Synthesis Report.* Contribution of Working Groups I, II and III to the Fourth Assessment Report of the Intergovernmental Panel on Climate Change [Core Writing Team, Pachauri, R. K. and Reisinger, A. (eds.)]. IPCC, 2007.

Inter-Governmental Panel on Climate Change (IPCC), *Climate Change: Mitigation of Climate Change.* Contribution of Working Group III to the Fifth Assessment Report of the Intergovernmental Panel on Climate Change [Edenhofer, O., Pichs-Madruga, R., Sokona, Y., Farahani, E., Kadner, S., Seyboth, K., Adler, A., Baum, I., Brunner, S., Eickemeier, P., Kriemann, B., Savolainen, J., Schlomer, S., Stechow, C. von, Zwickel, T., Minx, J.C. (eds.)], Cambridge University Press, 2014.

International Law Association's International Law on Sustainable Development Committee, *International Law on Sustainable Development*, Third Report, Rio de Janeiro Conference, 2008.

Joëlle, De Sepibus, *The Environmental Integrity of the CDM Mechanism – a Legal Analysis of Its Institutional and Procedural Shortcomings*, NCCR Working Paper No. 2009/24, 2009, available at: www.nccr-trade.org/images/stories/research/header_ip6/environmental%20integrity%20CDM.pdf (last accessed on July 18, 2015).

Kaloga, Alpha O., with contribution by Eckstein, David, *Rationalization of the Financial Mechanism of the UNFCCC: Options for Adaptation Finance*, Briefing paper, German Watch, 2015.

Lee, Bernice, Iliev, Ilian, and Preston, Felix, *Who Owns Our Low Carbon Future? Intellectual Property and Energy Technologies*, Chatham House, 2009, available at https://www.chathamhouse.org/sites/default/files/public/Research/Energy,%20Environment%20and%20Development/r0909_lowcarbonfuture.pdf (last accessed on August 18, 2020).
Metz, B., Davidson, O., Martens, J.-W., Van Rooijen, S., and Van Wie Mcgrory, L. (eds.), *Methodological and Technological Issues in Technology Transfer*, Special Report of the Intergovernmental Panel on Climate Change, Cambridge University Press, 2000.
Ministry of Environment and Forestry (MOEF), *Sustainable Development Criteria for CDM Projects*, Department of Environment (DOE), Government of the People's Republic of Bangladesh, August2004, 3.
Ministry of Environment and Forest and Climate Change (MOEF), *Bangladesh: Technology Needs Assessment and Technology Action Plans for Climate Change Mitigation*, Department of Environment (DOE), Government of the People's Republic of Bangladesh, December2011.
Morgado, Naeeda Crishna and Lasfargues, Bérénice *Engaging the Private Sector for Green Growth and Climate Action: An Overview of Development Co-Operation Efforts*, OECD Development Cooperation Working Paper 34, OECD, May 2017.
Müller, B., *Additionality in the Clean Development Mechanism: Why and What?*, Oxford Institute for Energy Studies, March2009.
Müller, B., *The Reformed Financial Mechanism of the UNFCCC: Part II The Question of Oversight Post Copenhagen Synthesis Report*, Oxford Institute for Energy Studies, 2010.
Organisation for Economic Co-operation and Development (OECD), *Climate Finance in 2013–14 and the USD 100 Billion Goal*, A report by the OECD in collaboration with Climate Policy Initiative, OECD Publishing, 2015, http://dx.doi.org/10.1787/9789264249424-en (last accessed on April 25, 2020).
Oxfam, *Climate 'Fiscal Cliff' Looms for Developing Countries if Leaders Come to Doha with No New Money*, available at https://www.oxfam.org/en/press-releases/climate-fiscal-cliff-loomsdeveloping-countries-if-leaders-come-doha-no-new-money (last accessed on April 15, 2020).
Oxfam, 'Rich Countries Must End Obsession with Private Climate Finance', November 20, 2013, available at https://www.oxfam.org/en/press-releases/rich-countries-must-end-obsession-private-climate-finance (last accessed on March 22, 2021).
Ozorio, A. M., *Environment and Development: The Founex Report on Development and Environment*, Carnegie Endowment for International Peace, 1972.
Pauw, P., Brandi, C., Richerzhagen, C., Bauer, S. and Schmole, H., *Different Perspectives on Differentiated Responsibilities: A State-of-the-Art Review of the Notion of Common but Differentiated Responsibilities in International Negotiations*, Discussion Paper 6/2014, German Development Institute/Deutsches Institut für Entwicklungspolitik (DIE), 2014.
Pichs, R., Swart, R., Leary, N., and Ormond, F. (eds), *Development, Sustainability, and Equity*, IPCC and WMO, 2000.
Rudyk, Ilja, Volpe, Alessia and Boshell, Francisco, *Development and Deployment of Climate Change Mitigation Technologies: Evidence to Support Policy Making*, European Patent Office (EPO) and International Renewable Energy Agency, 2017, available at http://documents.epo.org/projects/babylon/eponet.nsf/0/C6AD54B736F9B9E5C125814E0040E951/$FILE/Development_and_deployment_of_climate_change_mitigation_technologies-Policy_Brief_en.pdf (last accessed on August 12, 2020), 6.
Sanusi, Zainal Abidin, *Technology Transfer under Multilateral Environmental Agreements: Analyzing the Synergies*, UNU-IAS Working Paper No. 134, July2005.

Schwarte, Christoph and Massawa, Emily, *Equity Issues in the Climate Change Negotiations*, European Capacity Building Initiative (ECBI) Policy Report, August2009.

Seppänen, S.*et al., Demand in a Fragmented Global Carbon Market: Outlook and Policy Options*, Nordic Council of Ministers, Nordon, 2013, available at https://www.diva-portal.org/smash/get/diva2:702582/FULLTEXT01.pdf (last accessed on August 10, 2020).

Technology Executive Committee (TEC), *Enhancing Implementation of Technology Needs Assessments: Guidance for Preparing a Technology Action Plan*, UNEP-DTU, 2016.

Tewari, Ritika, *Mapping of Criteria Set by DNAs to Assess Sustainable Development Benefits of CDM Projects, Contribution to the Research Programme of the CDM Policy Dialogue*, The Energy and Resources Institute (TERI), India, July2012.

Trujillo, N. C. and Nakhooda, S., *The Effectiveness of Climate Finance: A Review of the Adaptation*, Working Paper 373, U.K. Aid, March2013.

United Nations (UN) Commission on Sustainable Development; UN Department for Policy Coordination and Sustainable Development. Division for Sustainable Development, *Report of the Expert Group Meeting on Identification of Principle of International Law for Sustainable Development*. Geneva, September 26–28, 1995.

United Nations (UN), *Report of the Secretary-General's High-level Advisory Group on Climate Change Financing*, November 5, 2010, available at https://www.cbd.int/financial/interdevinno/un-climate-report.pdf (last accessed on April 25, 2020).

United Nations Development Programme (UNDP), *Handbook for Conducting Technology Needs Assessment for Climate Change*, UNDP, November2010.

United Nations Development Programme (UNDP), *Human Development Report*, UNDP, New York, 1998.

United Nations Framework Convention on Climate Change (UNFCCC), *United Nations Framework Convention on Climate Change (UNFCCC): Handbook*, UNFCCC, 2006.

United Nations Framework Convention on Climate Change (UNFCCC), *Guidelines for Completing the Project Design Document (CDM-PDD), and the Proposed New Baseline and Monitoring Methodologies (CDM-NM)*, UNFCCC, Bonn, Version 07, 2008, 92.

United Nations Framework Convention on Climate Change (UNFCCC), *Financing Climate Change Action – Investment and Financial Flows for a Strengthened Response to Climate Change*, June2009.

United Nations World Commission on Environment and Development (WCED) (ed.), *Report of the World Commission on Environment and Development: Our Common Future*, Oxford University Press, 1987.

World Bank, *State and Trends of the Carbon Market 2009*, World Bank, 2009.

World Bank, *Introducing Energy-efficient Clean Technologies in the Brick Sector of Bangladesh*, World Bank and Energy Sector Management Assistance Program (ESMAP), June2011.

Thesis/Dissertations

Amin, M. R., 'Technology Transfer for Sustainable Development through Clean Development Mechanism (CDM): The Bangladesh Perspectives', Thesis submitted for the purpose of Doctor of Philosophy, Murdoch University, Australia, 2005.

Cools, S. L. Y., 'Assessing Technology Transfer in the Clean Development Mechanism', Dissertation for the Master of Philosophy in Environmental and Development Economics degree, University of Oslo, 2007.

Uddin, Mahatab, 'Climate Change and Requirement of Transfer of Environmentally Sound Technology ', Master's thesis, Department of Earth Science, Uppsala University, 2011, available at https://www.diva-portal.org/smash/get/diva2:453274/FULLTEXT01.pdf (last accessed on July 31, 2020).

Voigt, C., 'Sustainable Development as a Principle of Integration in International Law: Resolving Conflicts between WTO Law and Climate Change Mitigation Measures', Doctoral thesis, University of Oslo, 2006, 219.

Conference paper

Munasinghe, M., 'Development, Equity and Sustainability (DES) in the Context of Climate Change', Paper prepared for the IPCC Expert Meeting on Development, Equity and Sustainability, Colombo, Sri Lanka, April 27–29, 1999.

Newspapers/Periodicals

Bullard, Robert, 'The Politics of Race and Pollution: An Interview with Robert Bullard', *Multinational Monitor*, June, 1992,21–25.

Doyle, Alister and Wynn, Gerard, 'UN Climate Talks Advance, Poor Urge more CO2 Cuts', *Reuters* (released 12 June, 2009), available at http://in.reuters.com/article/2009/06/12/us-climate-idINTRE55B2Y020090612 (last accessed on July 15, 2015).

Gomez-Echeverri, Luis and Müller, Benito, 'The Financial Mechanism of the UNFCCC: A Brief History', ECBI Policy Brief, April 2009.

Lucia, Vito De, 'Environmental Law & Policy: Common but Differentiated Responsibility', *The Encyclopedia of Earth*, January 27, 2007, available at www.eoearth.org/view/article/151320/ (last accessed on September 30, 2015).

Mattei, Fabrice, 'A New Approach to Compulsory Licensing in Thailand', *Rouse* (May 31, 2007), available at www.rouse.com/magazine/articles/news-and-articles/a-new-approach-to-compulsory-licensing-in-thailand? tag=life %20sciences (last accessed on August 14, 2020).

Vidal, J., 'Rio+20: Earth Summit Dawns with Stormier Clouds than in1992', *The Guardian*, June 19, 2012.

Conference of the Parties (COP) Decisions

Decision 5/CP.6, FCCC/CP/2001/5, 25 September 2001.
Decision 2/CP.7, FCCC/CP/2001/13/Add.1, 21 January 2002.
Decision 3/CP.7, FCCC/CP/2001/13/Add.1, 21 January 2002.
Decision 4/CP.7, FCCC/CP/2001/13/Add.1, 21 January 2002.
Decision 5/CP.7, FCCC/CP/2001/13/Add.1, 21 January 2002.
Decision 7/CP.7, FCCC/CP/2001/13/Add.1, 21 January 2002.
Decision 17/CP.7, FCCC/CP/2001/13/Add.2, 21 January 2002.
Decision 27/CP.7, FCCC/CP/2001/13/Add.4, 21 January 2002.
Decision 5/CP.9, FCCC/CP/2003/6/Add.1, 22 April 2004.
Decision 1/CP.13, FCCC/CP/2007/6/Add.1, 14 March 2008.
Decision 3/CP.13, FCCC/CP/2007/6/Add.1. 14 March 2008.
Decision 2/CP.14. FCCC/CP/2008/7/Add.1, 18 March 2009.
Decision 2/CP.15, FCCC/CP/2009/11/Add.1, 30 March 2010.
Decision 1/CP.16, FCCC/CP/2010/7/Add.1, 15 March 2011.

Decision 1/CP.17, FCCC/CP/2011/9/Add.1, 15 March 2012.
Decision 2/CP.17, FCCC/CP/2011/9/Add.1, 15 March 2012.
Decision 3 /CP.17, FCCC/CP/2011/9/Add.1, 15 March 2012.
Decision 3/CP.17, FCCC/CP/2011/9/Add.1, 15 March 2012.
Decision 1/CP.18, FCCC/CP/2012/8/Add.1, 28 February 2013.
Decision 3/CP.18, FCCC/CP/2012/8/Add.1, 28 February 2013.
Decision 7/CP.18, FCCC/CP/2012/8/Add.1, 28 February 2013.
Decision 9/CP. 18, FCCC/CP/2012/8/Add.1, 28 February 2013.
Decision 1/CP.19, FCCC/CP/2013/10/Add.1, 31 January 2014.
Decision 2 /CP.19, FCCC/CP/2013/10/Add.1, 31 January 2014.
Decision 4/CP.19, FCCC/CP/2013/10/Add.1, 31 January 2014.
Decision 25/CP.19, FCCC/CP/2013/10/Add.3, 31 January 2014.
Decision 1/CP.20, FCCC/CP/2014/10/Add.1, 2 February 2015.
Decision 1/CP.21, FCCC/CP/2015/10/Add.1, 29 January 2016.

Conference of the Parties serving as the meeting of the Parties to the Kyoto Protocol (CMP) Decisions

Decision 1/CMP.2, FCCC/KP/CMP/2006/10/Add.1, 2 March 2007.
Decision 6/CMP.2, FCCC/KP/CMP/2006/10/Add.1, 2 March 2007.
Decision 1/CMP.3, FCCC/KP/CMP/2007/9/Add.1, 14 March 2008.
Decision 2/CMP.3, FCCC/KP/CMP/2007/9/Add.1, 14 March 2008.
Decision 1/CMP.6, FCCC/KP/CMP/2010/12/Add.1, 15 March 2011.
Decision 2/CMP.10, FCCC/KP/CMP/2014/9/Add.1, 2 February 2015.

Conference of the Parties serving as the meeting of the Parties to the Paris Agreement (CMA) Decisions

Decision 11/CMA.1, FCCC/PA/CMA/2018/3/Add.1, 19 March 2019.
Decision 15/CMA.1, FCCC/PA/CMA/2018/3/Add.2, 19 March 2019.
Decision 2/CMA.2, FCCC/PA/CMA/2019/6/Add.1, 16 March 2020.
Decision 6/CMA.2, FCCC/PA/CMA/2019/6/Add.1, 16 March 2020.
Decision 7/CMA.2, FCCC/PA/CMA/2019/6/Add.1, 16 March 2020.

GCF documents

Green Climate Fund (GCF), *Governing Instrument for the Green Climate Fund*, 2011, available at https://www.greenclimate.fund/sites/default/files/document/governing-instrument.pdf (last accessed on August 14, 2020).
GCF/B.04/07, 12 June 2013.
GCF/ B.08/09, 3 December 2014.
GCF/B.08/45, 3 December 2014.
GCF/B.08/38. 6 October 2014.

UN documents

FAO Conference Res. 3/2001, Rome, 3 November 2001, in force 29 June 2004, available at www.planttreaty.org (last accessed on 12 August 2020).
Report of the Conference of the Parties on Its First Session, Berlin 28 March to 7 April 1995 Decision 1/CP.1. The Berlin Mandate: Review of Adequacy of Art.4 Paragraph 2 (a) and

(b), of the Convention, Including Proposals Related to a Protocol and Decision on Follow-up, UN Doc. FCCC/CP/1995/7/Add.1, 6 June 1995.

Secretary-General remarks to the 'Moving to Implementation: Findings from the UNDG Dialogues on post-2015 Implementation', New York, September 25, 2014.

U.N. Doc. A/7291, Annex, 1968.

U.N. Doc. A/CONF.48/PC. 12, Annex I, 1971.

U.N. Doc. A/CONF. 48/WG.i/CRP.io, 1972.

UN General Assembly, World Summit on Sustainable Development: Resolution adopted by the General Assembly, 21 February 2003, A/RES/57/253, available at https://www.refworld.org/docid/3f49ff934.html (last accessed on 12 August 2020).

UNGA Res 1831 (XVII) (18 December 1962), UN Doc A/Res/XVII/1831.

GEF documents

GEF/C.46/09, May 6, 2014, available at https://www.thegef.org/sites/default/files/council-meeting-documents/GEF.C.46.09_Co-Financing_Policy_May_6_2014_2.pdf (last accessed on March 27, 2021).

Global Environmental Facility (GEF), *About Us*, available at www.thegef.org/gef/whatisgef (last accessed on July 30, 2020).

Global Environmental Facility (GEF), *Accessing Resources Under the Least Developed Countries Fund*, May 2, 2011, 7.

Global Environmental Facility (GEF), *Climate Change Adaptation*, available at www.thegef.org/gef/adaptation (last accessed on August 9, 2020).

Global Environmental Facility (GEF), *GEF Agencies*, available at www.thegef.org/gef/gef_agencies (last accessed on July 3, 2020).

Global Environmental Facility (GEF), *Funding*, https://www.thegef.org/about/funding (last accessed on August 20, 2020).

Global Environmental Facility (GEF), *Instrument for the Establishment of the Restructured Global Environmental Facility*, Washington, October, 2011, available at https://www.thegef.org/sites/default/files/publications/GEF_Instrument_Oct2011_final_0_1.pdf (last accessed on September 30, 2015).

Global Environmental Facility (GEF), *Operational Guidelines for Expedited Funding for the Preparation of National Adaptation Programs of Action by Least Developed Countries*, April 2002, available at https://unfccc.int/sites/default/files/gefsecnapaguideeng.pdf (last accessed on August 9, 2020).

Global Environmental Facility (GEF), *Operational Guidelines for the Application of the Incremental Cost Principle*, GEF/C.31/12May 14, 2007, available at https://www.thegef.org/ sites/default/files/ documents/C.31.12 _Operational _Guidelines_ for_Incremental_Costs-2007_0.pdf (last accessed on July 30, 2020).

Global Environmental Facility (GEF), *Poznan Strategic Program*, https://www.thegef.org/content/poznan-strategic-program (last accessed on August 5, 2020).

Global Environmental Facility (GEF), *Review of the Global Environment Facility Earth Fund August 2011*, Evaluation Report No. 62, August 2011.

Global Environmental Facility (GEF), *The GEF Assembly*, available at https://assembly.thegef.org/assembly/overview (last accessed on August 14, 2020).

Global Environmental Facility (GEF), *The GEF Resource Allocation Framework*, GEF/C.27/Inf.8/Rev.1, October 17, 2005, available at https://www.thegef.org/sites/default/files/council-meeting-documents/C.27.Inf_.8.Rev_.1_RAF_1.pdf (last accessed on August 14, 2020).

WTO documents

World Trade Organization (WTO), *Declaration on the TRIPS Agreement and Public Health*, WT/MIN(01)/DEC/2, 20 Nov. 2001, Para 5(a), available at https://www.wto.org/english/thewto_e/minist_e/min01_e/mindecl_trips_e.htm (last accessed on August 10, 2020).

World Trade Organization (WTO), *Doha WTO Ministerial 2001: TRIPS*, WT/MIN (01)/DEC/2, 20 November 2001.

World Trade Organization (WTO), *Working Group on Trade and Transfer of Technology*, available at https://www.wto.org/english/tratop_e/devel_e/dev_wkgp_trade_transfer_technology_e.htm (last accessed on May 31, 2020).

Online materials

Adaptation Fund, available at https://www.adaptation-fund.org/about/governance/board/ (last accessed on August 10, 2020)

Adaptation Fund, *Direct Access*, available at https://www.adaptation-fund.org/about/direct-access/ (last accessed on September 3, 2019).

Adaptation Fund Board (AFB), *Operational Policies and Guidelines for Parties to Access Resources from the Adaptation Fund* (amended in October, 2017), available at https://www.adaptation-fund.org/wp-content/uploads/2017/08/OPG-amended-in-October-2017-1.pdfhttps://www.adaptation-fund.org/about/governance/board (last accessed on August 10, 2020).

Capacity Building in the Development and Transfer of Technologies, Technical Paper, FCCC/TP/2003/1 November 26, 2003, available at http://unfccc.int/resource/docs/tp/tp0301.pdf (last accessed on January 23, 2019)

Carbon Brief, 'In-depth Q&A: How "Article 6" Carbon Markets Could "Make or Break" the Paris Agreement', September 29, 2019, available at https://www.carbonbrief.org/in-depth-q-and-a-how-article-6-carbon-markets-could-make-or-break-the-paris-agreement (last accessed on July 29, 2020)

Center for Climate and Energy Solutions, *Market-Based Strategies*, available at https://www.c2es.org/content/market-based-strategies (last accessed on August 10, 2020).

Center for Climate and Energy Solutions, *What's Ahead for Carbon Markets after COP 21?*, available at https://www.c2es.org/document/whats-ahead-for-carbon-markets-after-cop-21/ (last accessed on August 6, 2020).

Congressional Research Service, *The Green Climate Fund (GCF)*, available at https://fas.org/sgp/crs/misc/IF10382.pdf (last accessed on July 30, 2020).

Dahlke, S., *Solar Home Systems for Rural Electrification in Developing Countries, An Industry Analysis and Social Venture Plan*, available at www. csbsju.edu/Documents/CSB%20Sustainability /Solar%20Paper. pdf (last accessed on September 30, 2015).

Draft Memorandum of Understanding between the Conference of the Parties and the Council of the Global Environment Facility: Annex on the Determination of Funding, Necessary and Available for the Implementation of the Convention, FCCC/CP/1996/9, 21 May 1996, available at http://unfccc.int/cop3/resource/docs/cop2/09.pdf (last accessed on July 30, 2020).

European Commission, 'Environment', available at http://ec.europa.eu/environment/eussd/ (last accessed on August 12, 2020).

Netherlands Development Finance Company, available at https://www.fmo.nl/k/n114/news/view/1129/179/Worlds-First-Clean-Compost-Plant-opened-in-Bangladesh.html (last accessed on September 30, 2019).

G-77 and China Proposal, *Financial Mechanism for Meeting Financial Commitments under the Convention*, available at http://unfccc.int/files/kyoto_protocol/application/pdf/g77_china_financing_1.pdf (last accessed on July 30, 2020).

Global Environmental Facility (GEF), *Types of Project*, available at https://www.thegef.org/about/funding/project-types (last accessed on September 3, 2019).

Grameen Bank, available at www.grameen.com/ (last accessed on September 30, 2015).

International Law Association (ILA), available at https://www.ila-hq.org/index.php/about-us/aboutus2 (last accessed on August 25, 2020).

Oxfam, *Climate 'Fiscal Cliff' Looms for Developing Countries if Leaders Come to Doha with No New Money*, available at https://www.oxfam.org/en/press-releases/climate-fiscal-cliff-looms-developing-countries-if-leaders-come-doha-no-new-money (last accessed on April 15, 2020).

Proposal by the President Informal Compilation of L-Documents, Version 15/12/2018, available at https://unfccc.int/sites/default/files/resource/Informal%20Compilation_proposal%20by%20the%20President_rev.pdf (last accessed on August 25, 2020).

Stern, T., The Shape of a New International Climate Agreement, speech given at the Delivering Concrete Climate Change Action: Towards 2015 Conference, October 22, 2013, available at https://www.files.ethz.ch/isn/171926/The%20Shape%20of%20a%20New%20International%20Climate%20Agreement.pdf (last accessed on April 5, 2020).

United Nations, *LDC Identification Criteria & Indicators*, available at https://www.un.org/development/ desa/dpad/least-developed-country-category/ldc-criteria.html (last accessed on June 14, 2020).

United Nations Environment Programme (UNEP), available at www. unep.org/ green economy /Default. aspx?tabid=29784 (last accessed on September 30, 2015).

UNEP-DTU, available at www.cdmpipeline.org/cdm-projects-type.htm#1 (last accessed on July 16, 2015).

United Nations Framework Convention on Climate Change (UNFCCC), *Fact Sheet: Financing Climate Change Action – Investment and Financial Flows for a Strengthened Response to Climate Change*, June, 2009, available at https://unfccc.int/files/press/backgrounders/application/pdf/fact_sheet_financing_climate_change.pdf (last accessed on August 12, 2020).

United Nations Framework Convention on Climate Change (UNFCCC), *Introduction to Climate Finance*, available at https://unfccc.int/topics/climate-finance/the-big-picture/introduction-to-climate-finance (last accessed on September 2, 2019).

United Nations Framework Convention on Climate Change (UNFCCC), *Introduction to Mitigation*, available at https://unfccc.int/topics/mitigation/the-big-picture/introduction-to-mitigation (last accessed on August 10, 2020).

United Nations Framework Convention on Climate Change (UNFCCC), *Investment and Financial Flows to Address Climate Change*, 2008, available at http://unfccc.int/resource/docs/publications/financial_flows.pdf (last accessed on August 10, 2020).

United Nations Framework Convention on Climate Change (UNFCCC), *Report on Activities and Performance of the Technology Executive Committee for 2012*, UN Doc. FCCC/SB/2012/2, 18 October, 2012, para 35(g), available at: https://unfccc.int/resource/docs/2012/sb/eng/02.pdf (last accessed on July 21, 2020).

United Nations Framework Convention on Climate Change (UNFCCC), Small-scale CDM Programme of Activities Design Document Form (CDM SSC-PoA-DD)) Version 03, *Improving Kiln Efficiency in the Brick Making Industry in Bangladesh*

(Reference No. 5125), Version 15, Date 18/04/2011, 4, https://cdm.unfccc.int/Projects/DB/DNV-CUK1313585039.34/view.

United Nations Framework Convention on Climate Change (UNFCCC), *Technology Framework*, available at https://unfccc.int/ttclear/tec/tech-transfer-framework.html (last accessed on August 31, 2020).

United Nations Framework Convention on Climate Change (UNFCCC), *Technology Mechanism*, available at https://unfccc.int/ttclear/support/technology-mechanism.html (last accessed on September 2, 2019).

United Nations Framework Convention on Climate Change (UNFCCC), *Technology Mechanism Enhancing Climate Technology Development and Transfer*, available at https://unfccc.int/ttclear/misc_/StaticFiles/gnwoerk_static/TEM/0e7cc25f3f9843ccb98399df4d47e219/174ad939936746b6bfad76e30a324e78.pdf (last accessed on August 15, 2015).

United Nations Framework Convention on Climate Change (UNFCCC), *Technology Transfer Framework*, available at http://unfccc.int/ttclear/templates/render_cms_page?TTF_home (last accessed on August 3, 2020).

United Nations Framework Convention on Climate Change (UNFCCC), What Do Adaptation to Climate Change and Climate Resilience Mean?, available at https://unfccc.int/topics/adaptation-and-resilience/the-big-picture/what-do-adaptation-to-climate-change-and-climate-resilience-mean (last accessed on August 10, 2020).

United Nations Framework Convention on Climate Change (UNFCCC), *Warsaw Outcomes*, available at https://unfccc.int/process/conferences/the-big-picture/milestones/outcomes-of-the-warsaw-conference (last accessed on August 21, 2020).

United Nations Conference on Environment and Development, available at https://www.britannica.com/event/United-Nations-Conference-on-Environment-and-Development (last accessed on August 25, 2020).

WWR Bio Fertilizer Ltd., *Fact Sheet*, available at www.wasteconcern.org/latestNews/leaflet%20 final.pdf (last accessed on September 30, 2019).

Other documents

ILA Resolution 3/2002, in *ILA Report of the Seventieth Conference*, 2002, Principle 2.

Project Design Document Form (CDM-PDD), *Composting of Organic Waste in Dhaka*, Version 17, 9 December 2005.

Project Design Document Form (CDM-SSC-PDD) Version 03, *Improving Kiln Efficiency in the Brick Making Industry in Bangladesh*, (Registration No. 5125), Version 15, Date 18/04/2011.

Programme Design Document Form for Small-scale CDM Programme of Activities (F-CDM-SSC-PoA-DD) Version 02.0, *Energy Efficiency Program in Rural Bangladesh*, Version 01, Date: 14/08/2012.

Small-scale CDM Programme of Activities Design Document Form (CDM SSC-PoA-DD) – Version 01, *Improved Cooking Stoves in Bangladesh*, Version 07.1, 28/06/2011.

Small-scale CDM Programme of Activities Design Document Form (CDM-SSC-CPA-DD), *Installation of Solar Home Systems in Bangladesh (30Wp and 40Wp)*, Version 02, November 6, 2007.

Small-scale CDM Programme of Activities Design Document Form (CDM SSC-PoA-DD) - Version 01, *Efficient Lighting Initiative of Bangladesh (ELIB), Version* 07, Date: 22/04/2011.

Index

For Product Safety Concerns and Information please contact our EU representative GPSR@taylorandfrancis.com
Taylor & Francis Verlag GmbH, Kaufingerstraße 24, 80331 München, Germany

www.ingramcontent.com/pod-product-compliance
Ingram Content Group UK Ltd.
Pitfield, Milton Keynes, MK11 3LW, UK
UKHW022133190926
475702UK00013B/1777
* 9 7 8 1 0 3 2 0 2 2 8 9 5 *